Visualizing Data in R 4

Graphics Using the base, graphics, stats, and ggplot2 Packages

Margot Tollefson

Apress®

Visualizing Data in R 4: Graphics Using the base, graphics, stats, and ggplot2 Packages

Margot Tollefson
Stratford, IA, USA

ISBN-13 (pbk): 978-1-4842-6830-8
https://doi.org/10.1007/978-1-4842-6831-5

ISBN-13 (electronic): 978-1-4842-6831-5

Managing Director, Apress Media LLC: Welmoed Spahr
Acquisitions Editor: Steve Anglin
Development Editor: Matthew Moodie
Coordinating Editor: Mark Powers

Cover designed by eStudioCalamar

Cover image designed by Freepik (www.freepik.com)

Distributed to the book trade worldwide by Apress Media, LLC, 1 New York Plaza, New York, NY 10004, U.S.A. Phone 1-800-SPRINGER, fax (201) 348-4505, e-mail orders-ny@springer-sbm.com, or visit www. springeronline.com. Apress Media, LLC is a California LLC and the sole member (owner) is Springer Science + Business Media Finance Inc (SSBM Finance Inc). SSBM Finance Inc is a **Delaware** corporation.

For information on translations, please e-mail booktranslations@springernature.com; for reprint, paperback, or audio rights, please e-mail bookpermissions@springernature.com.

Apress titles may be purchased in bulk for academic, corporate, or promotional use. eBook versions and licenses are also available for most titles. For more information, reference our Print and eBook Bulk Sales web page at http://www.apress.com/bulk-sales.

Any source code or other supplementary material referenced by the author in this book is available to readers on GitHub via the book's product page, located at www.apress.com/9781484268308. For more detailed information, please visit http://www.apress.com/source-code.

Printed on acid-free paper

For Clay.

Table of Contents

About the Author

Margot Tollefson, PhD, is a semiretired freelance statistician, with her own consulting business, Vanward Statistics. She received her PhD in statistics from Iowa State University and has many years of experience applying R to statistical research problems. Dr. Tollefson has chosen to write this book because she often creates graphics using R and would like to share her knowledge and experience. Her professional blog is on WordPress at vanwardstat. She has social media accounts on LinkedIn, Facebook, and Twitter. Her social media name is @vanstat on Twitter.

About the Technical Reviewer

Tom Barker is an engineer and technology leader, a professor, and an author. He has authored several books on web development, data visualization, and technical leadership, including *High Performance Responsive Design, Intelligent Caching, Pro JavaScript Performance: Monitoring and Visualization,* and *Pro Data Visualization Using R and JavaScript.*

Acknowledgments

I would like to acknowledge the Comprehensive R Archive Network (CRAN). Without the R documentation, for which the Comprehensive R Archive Network is responsible, this book could not have been written. Also, my husband, Clay, for bearing with me while I wrote.

PART I

An Overview of plot()

CHAPTER 1

Introduction: plot( ), qplot( ), and ggplot( ), Plus Some

R provides many ways to visualize data. Graphics in the R language are generated by functions. Some functions create useful visualizations almost instantly. Other functions combine together to create highly coded sophisticated images. This book shows you how to generate both types of objects.

In the first part of this book, we look in detail at the plot() function – the most basic and versatile of the plotting functions. The functions par(), layout(), and split.screen(), which set global plotting parameters and layout options, are also described, as well as graphics devices.

The second part covers the functions in the ggplot2 package, starting with qplot() and ggplot(). The functions qplot() and ggplot() are simpler to use in many ways than the earlier R functions. Truthfully, the syntax used in the ggplot2 package requires long strings of names and arguments – but the autocomplete function in RStudio makes code entry quite easy.

The third part of the book includes six appendixes containing the canned plotting functions in the graphics and stats packages. The appendixes are sorted by the type of object to be displayed.

1.1 plot( ), par( ), layout( ), and split.screen( )

The function plot() takes an object or objects and creates an image based on the class of the object(s). There are many arguments to plot() that affect the appearance of the image. The arguments can be given values within the call to plot(), or many can be assigned globally using the function par(). After the initial call to plot(), there are several ancillary functions that can be used to add to the image. If having more than one plot on a page is the goal of the user, the functions par(), layout(), or split.screen() can be used to set up the format for multiple plots.

© Margot Tollefson 2021
M. Tollefson, *Visualizing Data in R 4*, https://doi.org/10.1007/978-1-4842-6831-5_1

In Chapter 2, we describe the basics of the plot() function. In Chapter 3, the various arguments to plot() are categorized. The ancillary functions for plot() are introduced in Chapter 4. In Chapter 5, the methods (types of plots) for which plot() is defined are presented. In Chapter 6, the possible arguments to the function par() are described, and a way to set up multiple plots using par(), layout() or split.screen() is given. Also, graphics devices are covered.

1.2 qplot() and ggplot()

The functions qplot() and ggplot() in the ggplot2 package provide alternatives to plot(). Default plots generated by qplot() and ggplot() tend to look nicer than default plots generated by plot(). For simple plots, qplot() is sufficient to give an elegant-looking graphic. The function ggplot() provides for more plotting options than qplot(). Some of the syntax used in the ggplot2 package is not used in standard R.

In ggplot2, a theme for a graphic can be defined using theme() or by a canned theme function beginning with "theme_". The objects to be plotted are "mappings" and are assigned in the function aes(). The type of image to be displayed is a geometry or statistic and is assigned by functions beginning with "geom_" or "stat_". The appearance of the graphic can be changed by using aes(), "aes_" functions, "geom_" functions, "stat_" functions, and/or other formatting functions. More than one aesthetic, geometry, and statistic can be used to create an image. The appearance of the image can be changed by running a formatting function from within another function or by running a formatting function separately.

In Chapter 7, we look at qplot(), ggplot(), and the syntax of the ggplot2 package. Chapter 8 introduces the theme(), "theme_", and "element_" functions, as well as the aes() and "aes_" functions. In Chapter 9, geometry, statistic, annotate, and the borders() functions are described. Chapter 10 goes over various functions in the ggplot2 package that also change the appearance of the image.

1.3 The Appendixes

Other than plot(), qplot(), and ggplot(), which are in the base and ggplot2 packages, there are many plotting functions in the graphics and stats packages. The functions are useful for data cleaning, data exploration, and/or model fitting. For many of the functions, the graphical arguments used by plot() can be assigned. The specialized plotting functions are given in the appendixes at the end of this book, along with brief descriptions of what the functions do and how to use them.

Appendix A lists functions used with contingency tables. Appendix B gives functions for continuous variables. Appendix C lists functions that generate multiple plots. Appendix D gives functions that smooth data. Appendix E gives plotting functions used in time series analysis. Appendix F lists the plotting functions that are in the stats and graphics packages and not covered in the first five appendixes.

1.4 Software Versions and Hardware Used in This Book

The versions of R used in this book are R 4.0.1 and R 4.0.3; the versions of RStudio are 1.3.595 and 1.3.1093. Since R and RStudio are constantly changing, the Comprehensive R Archive Network (CRAN) provides news on changes to R. The news for R 4.0.1 and R 4.0.0 can be found at `https://cran.r-project.org/doc/manuals/r-release/NEWS.pdf`. The beginning of that news pdf is shown in Figure 1-1.

NEWS for R version 4.0.1 (2020-06-06)

NEWS   *R News*

CHANGES IN R 4.0.1

NEW FEATURES:

- `paste()` and `paste0()` gain a new optional argument `recycle0`. When set to true, zero-length arguments are recycled leading to `character(0)` after the sep-concatenation, i.e., to the empty string `""` if collapse is a string and to the zero-length value `character(0)` when collapse = NULL.
  A package whose code uses this should depend on 'R (>= 4.0.1)'.

- The `summary(<warnings>)` method now maps the counts correctly to the warning messages.

BUG FIXES:

- `aov(frml,...)` now also works where the `formula` deparses to more than 500 characters, thanks to a report and patch proposal by Jan Hauffa.

- Fix a dozen places (code, examples) as `Sys.setlocale()` returns the new rather than the previous setting.

- Fix for adding two complex **grid** units via `sum()`. Thanks to Gu Zuguang for the report and Thomas Lin Pedersen for the patch.

- Fix `parallel::mclapply(...,mc.preschedule=FALSE)` to handle raw vector results correctly. PR#17779

- Computing the `base` value, i.e., 2, "everywhere", now uses `FLT_RADIX`, as the original 'machar' code looped indefinitely on the ppc64 architecture for the `longdouble` case.

- In R 4.0.0, `sort.list(x)` when `is.object(x)` was true, e.g., for x <-I(letters), was accidentally using `method = "radix"`. Consequently, e.g., `merge(<data.frame>)` was much slower than previously; reported in PR#17794.

- `plot(y ~ x,ylab = quote(y[i]))` now works, as e.g., for `xlab`; related to PR#10525.

- `parallel::detect.cores(all.tests = TRUE)` tries a matching OS name before the other tests (which were intended only for unknown OSes).

Figure 1-1. *R NEWS screenshot*

The computer used for the examples is a MacBook Air running macOS Catalina version 10.15.5.

1.5 Graphics Devices

R opens graphics objects in a graphics device. By default, R opens the graphics object on the computer screen, but the object can be written to a file using one of several image formats. Section 6.1 covers graphics devices.

R and RStudio provide ways to save graphics objects to image files by selecting links in the menus of the two programs. R automatically opens and closes the relevant devices when a link is used.

To work with graphics devices through code, see Section 6.1 or the R help pages for "device" and dev.cur(). Both Section 6.1.1 and the help page for "device" have a list of the functions on your device that open a graphics device to create a specific type of image file. Section 6.1.2 and the help page for dev.cur() give a list of the functions that manage graphics devices.

CHAPTER 2

The plot( ) Function

The plot() function in R creates a graphic from objects of specific R classes. A figure resulting from a call to plot() can contain text, lines, points, and/or images, and the areas of the graphic can be filled by colors or patterns. The kind of graphic displayed depends on the class of the object(s) to be displayed. For example, a single time series (an object of class ts) gives a line plot that is plotted over time.

2.1 Arguments and Default Values

By default, a graphic usually has black lines and text – with preset line, point, and text sizes and weights. Arguments that change the graphical properties of the graphic can be set in plot(). Some of the arguments are used to make changes to line, point, or text color; to line width or style; to point or text size; to the plotting character; to the style and font weight of text; and to fill colors or patterns.

Other arguments set alternative text for the axis labels or give a main title and a subtitle to the figure. The orientation, style, and weight of the text in the titles or labels can be changed.

Axes can be included or not included in the graphic created by plot(). If axes are initially included, the axis color and the color of tick marks can be changed by arguments within plot(). Axis line width, tick mark length, and tick mark spacing can be changed.

Axis tick labels can be assigned in the call to plot(). The color, size, and orientation of the axis tick labels can be changed. If necessary, a blank graphics object can be generated with plot(). In Chapter 3, we look closely at the arguments that are available to plot().

© Margot Tollefson 2021
M. Tollefson, *Visualizing Data in R 4*, https://doi.org/10.1007/978-1-4842-6831-5_2

2.2 Ancillary Functions

After the initial call to plot(), graphical information can be added to the original graphic by using ancillary functions. These functions are used to overlay other plots over the original plot and to add annotation to a plot. For example, a regression line can be added to a scatterplot, or a legend can be included in a plot.

There are several ancillary functions. Titles and axis labels can be added by using the ancillary function title() – instead of including titles and axis labels in the original call to plot(). Axes can be added with the function axis() if axes are suppressed in a call to plot(). Regression lines can be added to a graphic (in a few ways).

Most of the ancillary functions are eponymous, such as text(), points(), lines(), segments(), and arrows(). Others are not, such as polypath() or clip(). In Chapter 4, we list the ancillary functions in the graphics and stats packages and show how each function is used.

2.3 Methods

The methods of a function are those classes of objects for which a function is defined. In the graphics and stats packages, there are 29 methods defined for plot().

In Chapters 3 and 4, we usually use the version of plot() that takes an x, and possibly a y, as the object(s) to be plotted and which plots a scatterplot of x against index values or of y against x. The actual name of the function is plot.default().

However, since R automatically determines the method to use when running plot(), the ".default" extension is not necessary in the call to plot(). For plot.default(), the x and y would need to be equal-length vectors that can be coerced to numeric. The methods for plot() are given in Chapter 5, along with what each method creates.

2.4 The Graphics Devices and the Functions par(), layout(), and split.screen()

R plots are created in graphics devices. A graphics device can be opened on the screen of a computer or in a file external to R. (Some graphics devices are specific to a given operating system.) The arguments used by the plotting functions that are covered in Part 1 can be assigned in the plot() function and in the ancillary functions. When assigned in a plotting function, the arguments are used in the specific function in which the arguments are assigned. To globally assign arguments, the arguments can be assigned in the par() function.

The par() function contains the default values that many of the arguments to plot() and the ancillary functions use. The default arguments of par() can be changed – for a given R session or within a function call – by a call to par(). Most of the arguments in par() are the same as those arguments in plot() that affect the appearance of the graphic. Some arguments in par() can only be set in par().

R allows multiple plots to be put in one graphic. A grid for multiple plots can be created using one of two arguments of par(). The grid created by par() has the same number of columns in each row. Alternatively, the function layout() can be used to create a more flexible design, with differing numbers of columns in each row. The split.screen() function allows for placing plots at different locations on a graphics device.

In Chapter 6, the types of graphics devices are listed, as well as ways to work with graphics devices. More on par(), layout(), and split.screen() is also found in Chapter 6.

2.5 An Example

In Figure 2-1, an example is given of a plot of the sunspot.year time series (from the datasets package) using default arguments and the same plot done with some arguments set. The two plots are plotted in one figure.

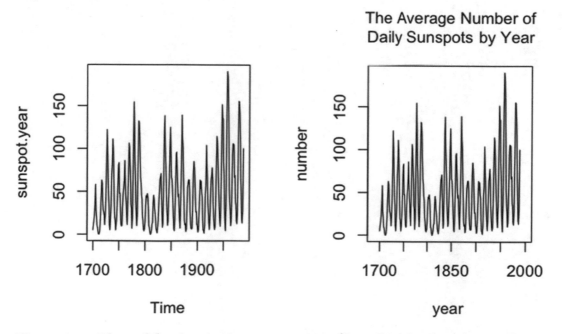

Figure 2-1. *Plots of the time series sunspot.year (found in the datasets package in R). The first plot uses the default argument settings in plot(). In the second plot, some of the arguments are set.*

The class of sunspot.year is ts, so the values in the time series are plotted against time. The default axis labels are Time on the x axis and the name of the object that is plotted on the y axis. By default, no title or subtitle is plotted.

For the preceding figure, the function par() is used to put two plots in a row into one figure. After plot() is run twice, the number of plots per figure is changed back to one by running par() again. Changes to par() remain in effect throughout an R session, unless changed.

CHAPTER 3

The Arguments of plot( )

Many arguments can be used in plot(). In this chapter, we go over the arguments. The arguments are grouped by categories – arguments that affect overall appearance, the appearance of lines and points, and details. We look at the effects on the appearance of graphics by using examples, with data from an R dataset. In this chapter, the function plot.default(), which plots scatterplots, is used for the examples. While most of the arguments in this chapter can be used in all or most versions of plot(), a few are specific to plot.default().

3.1 The Dataset

In this section, we work with the LifeCycleSavings dataset from the datasets package. Since the datasets package is loaded by default in RStudio, for most users the dataset is available to access. To bring the dataset into the workspace in order to look at the contents, enter the following at the R prompt:

```
data( "LifeCycleSavings" )
```

To look at the dataset in RStudio, double-click "LifeCycleSavings" (in the Data section of the Environment window in the upper-right pane). The Console (lower-left window) will display

```
> force(LifeCycleSavings)
             sr pop15 pop75     dpi  ddpi
Australia 11.43 29.35  2.87 2329.68  2.87
Austria   12.07 23.32  4.41 1507.99  3.93
```

(Here, only the first two observations are displayed.) The dataset will also appear in the Source (upper-left) window.

© Margot Tollefson 2021
M. Tollefson, *Visualizing Data in R 4*, https://doi.org/10.1007/978-1-4842-6831-5_3

A description of the dataset from the R documentation follows:

Intercountry Life-Cycle Savings Data

Description

Data on the savings ratio 1960–1970.

Usage

LifeCycleSavings

Format

A data frame with 50 observations on 5 variables.

[,1]	*sr*	*numeric*	*aggregate personal savings*
[,2]	*pop15*	*numeric*	*% of population under 15*
[,3]	*pop75*	*numeric*	*% of population over 75*
[,4]	*dpi*	*numeric*	*real per-capita disposable income*
[,5]	*ddpi*	*numeric*	*% growth rate of dpi*

Details

Under the life-cycle savings hypothesis as developed by Franco Modigliani, the savings ratio (aggregate personal saving divided by disposable income) is explained by per-capita disposable income, the percentage rate of change in per-capita disposable income, and two demographic variables: the percentage of population less than 15 years old and the percentage of the population over 75 years old. The data are averaged over the decade 1960–1970 to remove the business cycle or other short-term fluctuations.

Source

The data were obtained from Belsley, Kuh and Welsch (1980). They in turn obtained the data from Sterling (1977).

References

Sterling, Arnie (1977) Unpublished BS Thesis. Massachusetts Institute of Technology.

Belsley, D. A., Kuh. E. and Welsch, R. E. (1980) Regression Diagnostics. New York: Wiley.

—R documentation for the datasets package

The five variables in the dataset are aggregate personal savings (sr), the percentage of the population under 15 years of age (pop15), the percentage of the population over 75 years of age (pop75), real per-capita disposable income (dpi), and the percentage growth rate of real per-capita disposable income (ddpi). The values of the variables are averages taken over the years 1960–1970, and the averages were found for 50 countries.

3.2 Changing the Overall Appearance in plot()

The first argument to plot() is always x – an R object of an appropriate class. If x (or x and y) is a vector object of the numeric class, plot() plots a scatterplot. (For scatterplots, a numeric vector y of the same length as x can be included but is not necessary.) The first example is a scatterplot using the default values of the arguments of plot().

In Listing 3-1, code that plots a default scatterplot is given. The scatterplot is a plot of the percentage of the population under 15 (y) against the percentage of the population over 75 (x), both from the LifeCycleSavings dataset.

For data frames, a variable in the data frame can be accessed by the data frame name followed by a dollar sign followed by the variable name. For example, LifeCycleSavings$pop75 accesses the pop75 variable in the LifeCycleSavings data frame.

Listing 3-1. The code for a default scatterplot

```
plot(
  LifeCycleSavings$pop75,
  LifeCycleSavings$pop15
)
```

The plot is in Figure 3-1.

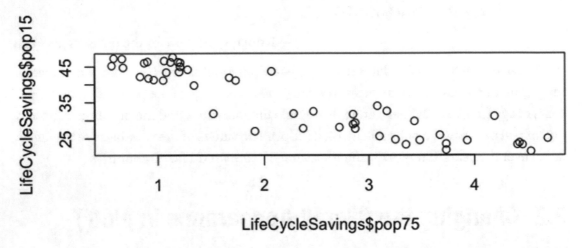

Figure 3-1. *Default scatterplot of two variables from the LifeCycleSavings dataset*

Note that the first argument is on the x axis (horizontal axis) and the second on the y axis (vertical axis). Also, the graphic does not contain a title or subtitle, and the axis labels contain the names of the variables in the dataset. The points are scattered so that the most extreme points are close to the axes. In this chapter, we will show how to change the appearance of, mainly, this plot by setting arguments.

3.2.1 Labels and Axis Limits

A title and subtitle can be added to the plot, and the axis labels can be changed. To add a title, we use the argument main. The title will display above the plot. To add a subtitle, we use the argument sub. The subtitle will display below the x axis label. To specify the x and y axis labels, we use the arguments xlab and ylab. Setting either to "" will suppress the label. For all of the four arguments, the value is a character vector that is usually one element long.

Line breaks can be added to a character string by including "\n" in the character string at the location of the line break. Or a character vector with more than one element puts each element on a separate line (except with the argument sub).

The axis limits are the values from which the axis starts and at which the axis ends. Having the start value greater than the end value is an accepted option. To set the x axis and y axis limits of the plot, we use the arguments xlim and ylim. The format for the two arguments is a numeric vector of length two, where the first number is the beginning limit and the second number is the ending limit. By default, points outside the limits do not plot.

An example of setting the labels and axis arguments is seen in Listing 3-2.

Listing 3-2. Code to plot a scatterplot where the title, subtitle, x axis label, y axis label, x limits, and y limits have been set

```
plot(
  LifeCycleSavings$pop75,
  LifeCycleSavings$pop15,
  main="Percentage under 15 versus Percentage over 75\nfor 50 Countries",
  sub="More Under 15 Means Less Over 75 on Average",
  xlab="Percentage over 75",
  ylab="Percentage under 15",
  xlim=c( 0, 5.25 ),
  ylim=c( 18, 52 )
)
```

In Figure 3-2, the code has been run.

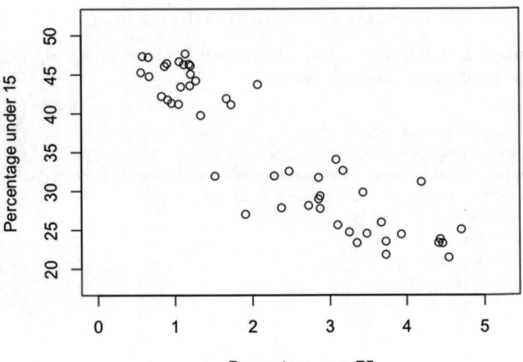

Figure 3-2. Scatterplot plotted using the arguments main, sub, xlab, ylab, xlim, and ylim

3.2.2 Box Type, Aspect Ratio, Annotation, and Expanded Plotting

Whether to include a border, the type of border to include, and the aspect ratio of a plot can be changed. Also, annotation can be shut off, and points can be plotted outside the limits of the plot. The relevant arguments are frame.plot for including a border, bty for the box type, asp for the aspect ratio, ann for annotation, and xpd for expanded plotting.

The argument frame.plot is a logical single-value argument that tells R whether to put a frame around the plot. If the argument is a vector of length greater than one, only the first value is used, and a warning is given. The default value is TRUE.

If frame.plot is TRUE, the argument bty describes the type of box. The argument takes character values and can take on the values "o", "l", "7", "c", "u", "]", and "n". The value "o" is the default and indicates a four-sided box. The first six values (the capital letter for the letters) look like the shape of the box that the value creates.

The value "l" plots the left and bottom axes; the value "7" plots the right and top axes; the value "c" plots the top, left, and bottom axes; the value "u" plots the left, bottom, and right axes; and the value "]" plots the bottom, right, and top axes. The value "n" indicates to not draw a box. Figure 3-3 shows the six options other than the default, "o".

The following code created the six plots in Figure 3-3.

Listing 3-3. Plotting with bty set to six different values

```
plot( LifeCycleSavings$pop75, LifeCycleSavings$pop15, bty="l", main="bty = l" )
plot( LifeCycleSavings$pop75, LifeCycleSavings$pop15, bty="7", main="bty = 7" )
plot( LifeCycleSavings$pop75, LifeCycleSavings$pop15, bty="c", main="bty = c" )
plot( LifeCycleSavings$pop75, LifeCycleSavings$pop15, bty="u", main="bty = u" )
plot( LifeCycleSavings$pop75, LifeCycleSavings$pop15, bty="]", main="bty = ]" )
plot( LifeCycleSavings$pop75, LifeCycleSavings$pop15, bty="n", main="bty = n" )
```

In Figure 3-3 are the plots generated by the code in Listing 3-3.

Examples of Changing bty

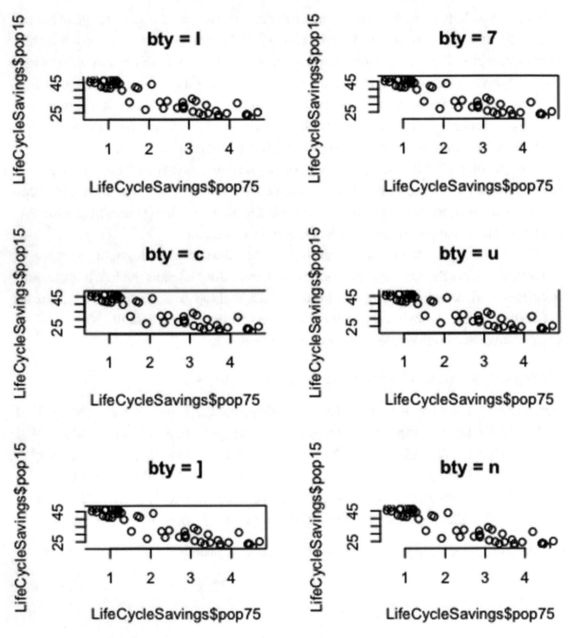

Figure 3-3. *Box style examples for bty equal to "l", "7", "c", "u", "]", and "n"*

To change the aspect ratio of a plot, we set asp to the desired ratio of units of width to units of height for the size of the plot as displayed on the device.

R takes the length of a unit of the y axis on the plot and multiplies the unit by the aspect ratio to get the length of a unit of the x axis on the plot. The ratio of the plot dimensions is taken into account.

The ratio of height to width of the plot can be adjusted in RStudio by changing the size of the window in which the graphic plots. The easiest way to change the size of the window is to point and drag the edges of the plot window (the lower-right window in RStudio) – using the handles at the center of each window edge. The View in the RStudio menu also gives options for working with the windowpane. When an image is saved to a file or the clipboard, RStudio gives the option of changing the dimensions of the plot – by adjusting the dimensions of the x and y axes independently.

Working with a graphic directly is an option. In RStudio a plot can be zoomed and then adjusted by pointing at the handles at the centers or corners of the edges of the plot and dragging. In R, a plot opens in a Quartz window that can be adjusted by pointing and dragging.

The example in Figure 3-4 shows the effect of adjusting the aspect ratio of Figure 3-1. In Figure 3-1, the units on the x axis go from 0.5 to 5, and the units on the y axis go from 20 to 50. The x axis is 4.5 times as wide as the y axis is high. The argument asp is not set but is – from the dimensions – the 4.5 units on the x axis divided by the 30 units on the y axis and that quantity divided by 4.5 (the physical length of the x axis divided by the physical length of the y axis), or 0.033.

The plots in Figure 3-4 show two examples of setting asp. The code to create the plots in the figure follows (Listing 3-4).

Listing 3-4. The code to demonstrate setting asp in plot()

```
plot(
  LifeCycleSavings$pop75, LifeCycleSavings$pop15,
  asp=0.1,
  main="asp = 1/10"
)
plot(
  LifeCycleSavings$pop75, LifeCycleSavings$pop15,
  asp=0.01,
  main="asp = 1/100"
)
```

The result from running the code is in Figure 3-4.

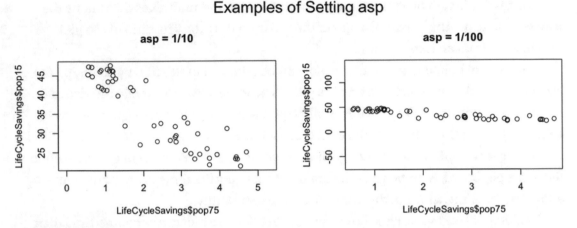

Figure 3-4. *Two examples of setting asp; asp equals 0.1 and asp equals 0.01*

In the first plot, asp is set to 0.1. From Figure 3-4, for the first plot, the y axis goes from 20 to 48.4 and the x axis goes from -0.18 to 5.50. For both axes, the plots are centered on the x and y means. The ratio of the dimensions of the plot is 1:2 (the width is two times as wide as the height is high.) Multiplying the range of the y axis, 28.4, by 0.1 gives 2.84; and 2.84 times 2 equals 5.68, the range of the x axis. There are 10 units of y for every unit of x.

For the second plot, asp equals 0.01. The ratio of the plot dimensions is still 1:2. The y axis goes from -80 to 146, while the x axis goes from 0.5 to 5.02. Multiplying the range of the y axis, 226, by 0.01 gives 2.26; and 2.26 times 2 is 4.52, the range of the x axis. There are 100 y units for every unit of x.

The argument ann tells R whether to include axis labels (or a title or subtitle). The default value is TRUE. Setting ann equal to FALSE suppresses the labels – as can be seen in Figure 3-5.

The code for Figure 3-5 follows (Listing 3-5).

Listing 3-5. The code for plotting with ann set to FALSE

```
plot(
  LifeCycleSavings$pop75, LifeCycleSavings$pop15,
  ann=FALSE
)
```

The plot resulting from the code is in Figure 3-5.

Example of ann = FALSE

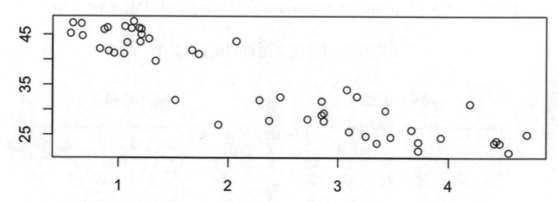

Figure 3-5. *A plot with ann set to FALSE*

Points (and lines) can be plotted outside of the plotting limits by using the argument xpd. The default value for xpd is FALSE – points outside of the plotting limits are not plotted. Setting xpd to TRUE plots any points outside of the plotting limits but inside the region for the plot. Setting xpd to NA plots any points outside of the plotting limits and inside the display region of the graphic. Figure 3-6 shows the three options, with the x limits on the plot set to 2 and 3.

The code for the plots in Figure 3-6 follows (Listing 3-6).

Listing 3-6. Code for the examples of the argument xpd in Figure 3-6

```
plot(
  LifeCycleSavings$pop75, LifeCycleSavings$pop15, xlim=c( 2, 3 ),
  xpd=FALSE,
  main="xpd = FALSE"
)

plot(
  LifeCycleSavings$pop75, LifeCycleSavings$pop15, xlim=c( 2, 3 ),
  xpd=TRUE,
  main="xpd = TRUE"
)
```

```
plot(
  LifeCycleSavings$pop75, LifeCycleSavings$pop15, xlim=c( 2, 3 ),
  xpd=NA,
  main="xpd = NA"
)
```

See the plots resulting from running the code in Listing 3-6 in Figure 3-6 below.

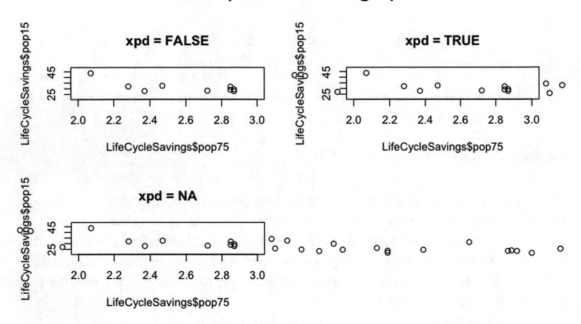

Figure 3-6. *Examples of setting xpd*

3.3 Points and Lines

R plots are made up of points and lines in most cases – although text and images can be added or can be part of the default plot for certain classes of objects. Points are plotted using a plotting character. Any string with one character can be used as a plotting character for a point, as can be a number of symbols on most devices.

Lines can be plotted as a solid line or as one of a number of dashed patterns. In this section, we look at some of the options for points and lines.

3.3.1 Types of Plots

The function plot() allows nine types of plots, set by the argument type. From the R help page for plot(), the argument type can take on the values "p" for points, "l" for lines, "b" for both, "c" for the lines part of "b", "o" for both points and lines where the lines plot over the points, "h" for vertical lines (at the height of the data points), "s" for step functions with steps that go from horizontal to vertical, "S" for step functions with steps that go from vertical to horizontal, and "n" for no plotting.

Examples of type set to "l", "b", "c", and "o" are given in Figure 3-7. The code in Listing 3-7 produced the plots. (The same data points we have been plotting are used, but the pop75 data are first sorted and the sort is used to order the pop15 data points. That way, the lines are in a good order.)

Since the character strings used to give titles to the plots in Figure 3-7 contain values that are character strings, the escape character "\" allows the quotation marks to be displayed within the titles.

Listing 3-7. Code to create ordered points and to create plots for type set equal to "l", "b", "o", and "c"

```
ord = order(
  LifeCycleSavings$pop75
)
pop75.ordered = LifeCycleSavings$pop75[ ord ]
pop15.ordered = LifeCycleSavings$pop15[ ord ]

plot(
  pop75.ordered, pop15.ordered,
  type="l",
  main="type = \"l\""
)
```

```
plot(
  pop75.ordered, pop15.ordered,
  type="b",
  main="type = \"b\""
)
plot(
  pop75.ordered, pop15.ordered,
  type="o",
  main="type = \"o\""
)
plot(
  pop75.ordered, pop15.ordered,
  type="c",
  main="type = \"c\""
)
```

Figure 3-7 follows.

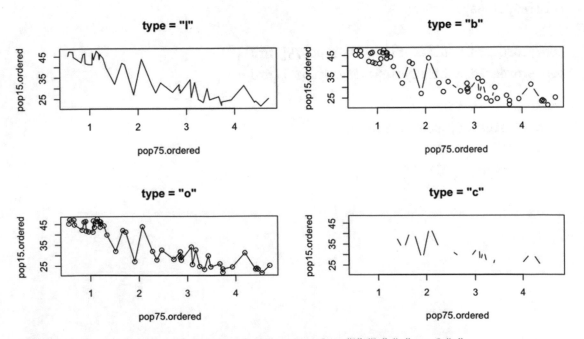

Figure 3-7. *Examples of plots with type equal to "l", "b", "o", and "c"*

In Figure 3-8, examples of the options for types "h", "s", "S", and "n" are given. The code is given first (Listing 3-8).

Listing 3-8. Code for plots in Figure 3-8

```
plot(
  pop75.ordered, pop15.ordered,
  type="h",
  main="type = \"h\""
)
plot(
  pop75.ordered, pop15.ordered,
  type="s",
  main="type = \"s\""
)
plot(
  pop75.ordered,   pop15.ordered,
  type="S",
  main="type = \"S\""
)
plot(
  pop75.ordered, pop15.ordered,
  type="n",
  main="type = \"n\""
)
```

Figure 3-8 follows.

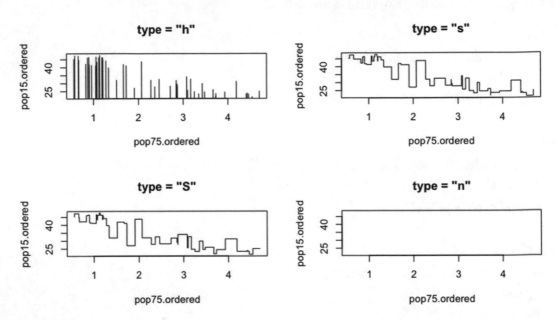

Figure 3-8. *Examples of plots with type set to "h", "s", "S", and "n"*

3.3.2 The Arguments pch and lty

To set the plotting character, we use the argument pch. The argument pch can be set to any one-character value, or collection of one-character values, available to R on the device of the user (see Section 3.4). Also, the integers 0–25 can be used to plot symbols available in R. If pch is set equal to a collection of values, R cycles through the values as the points are plotted. In Listing 3-9 and Figure 3-9, the 26 symbols are plotted for some of the points in Figure 3-1.

Listing 3-9. Code for the example of pch using the R symbols

```
plot(
  pop75.ordered[18:43],
  pop15.ordered[18:43],
  main="pch = 0:25",
  pch=0:25
)
```

Example of Setting pch to 0 through 25

pch = 0:25

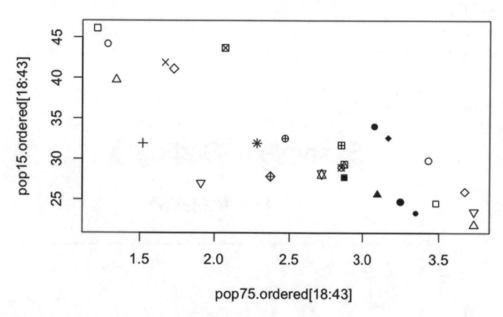

Figure 3-9. *Example of using the R symbols for the plotting characters*

Lines come in solid lines or lines of dots and/or dashes. The type of line is specified with the argument lty. From the R help page for par(), the argument can take on the numeric values of 0 for no line, 1 for a solid line, 2 for a dashed line, 3 for a dotted line, 4 for a dotted and dashed line, 5 for a line with a long dash, and 6 for two dashes. The argument can also take on the character strings "blank", "solid", "dashed", "dotted", "dotdash", "longdash", and "twodash" – which give the same results as the numbers.

One can create a custom pattern made up of a character string of 2, 4, 6, or 8 hexadecimal digits. The first digit is the number of unit lengths for the first section of the line, the second digit is how many unit lengths to leave blank, and so on. For most devices, a unit length is 1/96 inch. For example, setting lty equal to "626565" spells out "mi mi mi ..." in Morse code. See Listing 3-10 and Figure 3-10 for the line with lty equal to "626565".

Listing 3-10. Case of setting a custom line style

```
plot(
  pop75.ordered, pop15.ordered,
  type="l",
  lty="626565",
  main="lty = \"626565\""
)
```

Figure 3-10 follows.

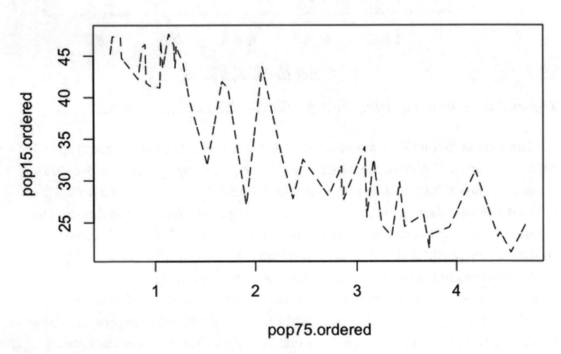

Figure 3-10. *Example of a custom line style*

3.4 Details

This section covers the myriad small details that can be changed in plot(). The sections cover colors, character font styles and weights, character sizes, qualities of lines, axis styling, and working with log scales.

3.4.1 Colors

Anything generated in plot() can be assigned a color. There are seven arguments associated with colors: col, col.main, col.sub, col.lab, col.axis, bg, and fg. The argument col sets the color of what is plotted. The arguments col.main, col.sub, col.lab, and col.axis set the color of the title, subtitle, labels, and axes, respectively. In plot(), fg sets the color of the box around the plot, and bg sets the fill color for pch's 21–25 and otherwise has no effect.

The values of col.main, col.sub, col.lab, col.axis, and fg must be a one-element color designator. The values of col and bg can be a multielement vector of color designators. For points in the plot types "p", "b", "c", and "h", the colors will cycle through the points. For the lines in the plot types "l", "b", "c", "s", and "S", the line takes on the color of the first value in col.

3.4.1.1 Assigning Colors with Character Strings

Colors in R can be assigned with a character string, a positive integer, or a function. There are 657 defined colors in R, each with a name – such as "lightblue". The collection of names is listed by running the function colors(). The color "transparent" can be used for fill colors.

Colors can also be assigned by character strings containing hex codes for colors. The hex codes have the form "#RRGGBBAA" where RR, GG, and BB are two-digit hexadecimal numbers giving the hues of red, green, and blue in the color and AA – which is optional – is a two-digit hexadecimal number giving the transparency of the color.

For the colors, the value of 00 is the darkest hue, and the value of FF is the lightest hue. For the transparency, the value 00 indicates the plotting character is totally transparent, and the value of FF indicates the plotting character is opaque. If AA is not included, the transparency level is set to FF.

The value "#000000" plots black, and the value "#FFFFFF" plots white. A gray scale can be created by changing the transparency of "#000000". However, those elements, of the collection generated by running colors(), that have index values of 152–253 and 260–361 are the colors "gray", "gray0", … "gray100" and "grey", "grey0", … "grey100".

The grey and gray colors are different names for the same colors – called aliases. The colors "gray" and "grey" are a light shade of gray, while "gray0"/"grey0" to "gray100"/"grey100" are a gray scale from darker shades to lighter shades of gray. A gray scale can also be created with the function gray()/grey() or gray.colors()/grey.colors().

3.4.1.2 Assigning Colors with Integers

Colors can be assigned using integers. For a given number, the color associated with the number is assigned by the function palette(). Running palette() with no arguments gives the colors in the current palette – which are associated sequentially with the integers starting with 1. Running palette() with an argument resets the palette. The colors in a palette cycle, so any positive integer value for col will return a color.

Only one argument can be set in palette(). The argument is either a one-element character vector containing the name of a built-in palette or a multielement character vector of the color names and/or hex codes to be included in the palette.

To see the names of the built-in palettes, run palette.pals(). Once a palette is selected, the palette remains in effect until another palette is selected. To return to the default palette, run palette("default"). Currently, the default palette is "R4".

Most palettes have a small number of colors, but up to 1024 colors can be assigned. For example, to create a palette with the 657 colors in colors(), one can run palette(colors()).

To select a subset of a palette, use the function palette.colors(). The function palette.colors() takes four arguments. The first argument is n, which is a positive integer that tells R to select the first n colors of the palette. If set to NULL – the default value – all of the colors are used. The second argument is a character string containing the name of the palette.

The third argument is alpha, which sets the opacity of the palette and can take on a value between zero and one. The argument alpha is not supported on all devices. Zero gives total transparency and one gives total opacity. The fourth argument is recycle, which tells R to recycle colors if n is larger than the number of colors in the palette. The default value for recycle is FALSE. If recycle is FALSE and n is greater than the number of colors, then all of the colors are returned and a warning is given.

3.4.1.3 Assigning Colors with Functions

There are functions that generate color codes. The functions hsv(), hcl(), hcl.colors(), rgb(), rainbow(), heat.colors(), terrain.colors(), topo.colors(), cm.colors(), gray(), and gray.colors() generate hex codes to assign colors.

The function hsv() generates codes based on the hue, saturation, and value of a color. The function takes three arguments, h, s, and v – for hue, saturation, and value. The three arguments take vectors of numeric values between zero and one inclusive. The vectors do not need to be of the same length, and the vectors cycle.

Instead of entering three separate vectors in hsv(), a single matrix with three columns can be entered, where the first column gives the values for h, the second for s, and the third for v.

The argument h gives the hue of the color, with 0 associated with red and 1 associated with purple-red, and the shading going from red to orange to yellow to green to blue to violet to purple to purple-red. The argument s gives the depth of the color, with 0 being no color (black if v equals 0 and blank if v equals 1) and 1 associated with the strongest color. The argument v gives the amount of black in the color, with 0 being black and 1 being a color with no black.

The function hcl() creates hex color codes based on the hue, chroma, and luminance of the color. The function takes five arguments: h for hue, which is 0 by default; c for chroma, which is 32 by default; l for luminance, which is 85 by default; alpha, which has no default; and fixup, which is TRUE by default. The argument alpha is not supported on all devices.

The argument h can take on numeric values from 0 to 360. Zero is red, 120 is green, and 240 is blue. The hue shades between the numbers – in a circle. The argument c is equivalent to the saturation in the hsv() function but can take on any nonnegative value. However, if the value is larger than 360, the hue changes.

The argument l operates like the value argument in the hsv() function but takes on numeric value between 0 and 100. The argument alpha sets the transparency level of the color, with 0 having total transparency and 1 having no transparency. The argument fixup, if set to TRUE, will change color codes that are illegal to codes that are legal.

The function hcl.colors() generates hex codes for a given hcl palette. The collection of hcl palettes are listed by running hcl.pals(). The function hcl.pals() takes one argument – type. By default, type equals NULL – for which all of the hcl palettes are listed. The other options for type are "qualitative", "sequential", "diverging", and "divergingx". See the help page for hcl.pals() for a discussion of where to use the four types.

The arguments to hcl.colors() are n, for the number of colors to choose; palette, for the hcl palette name; alpha, for the level of transparency; rev, to reverse the order of the colors; and fixup, for fixing illegal color specifications. The argument n is a positive integer; palette is an hcl palette name and defaults to "Viridis"; alpha is as described in the description of hsv() and defaults to NULL; rev is a one-element logical vector with a default value of FALSE; and fixup is a one-element logical vector with a default value of TRUE.

The function rgb() generates hex color codes based on red, green, and blue levels in the colors. The function takes on six arguments: red, green, blue, and alpha, not supported on all devices; names, by default NULL; and maxColorValue, by default 1. The value of maxColorValue is the maximum value that red, green, blue, and alpha can take. According to the help page on rgb(), if the maxColorValue is set equal to 255, red, green, blue, and alpha are coerced to integer values between 0 and 255 and the algorithm is most efficient. However, any positive number can be used as maxColorValue. The argument names assigns names to the colors, but has no other effect.

The function rainbow() creates a spectrum of hex color codes. The function takes the arguments n, for the number of codes to generate; s, for the saturation level; v, for the value level; start, for the beginning hue; end, for the ending hue; alpha, for the transparency (not supported on all devices); and rev, to reverse the colors.

The arguments s, v, start, end, and alpha are single-element numeric vectors that must be between 0 and 1, inclusive. For s and v, the default value is 1. For start, the default value is 0. For end, the default value is max(1, n-1)/n. As the hue goes from 0 to 1, the colors go from red to orange to yellow to green to blue to violet to purple to purple-red. The argument rev is a logical variable with default value FALSE.

The functions heat.colors(), terrain.colors(), topo.colors(), and cm.colors() all take the same three arguments – n, alpha, and rev, with the same definitions as in rainbow(). (The cm in cm.colors() stands for cyan magenta.)

The function gray()/grey() creates hex color codes for a gray gradient. The arguments of the function are level and alpha. The argument level is a numeric vector that takes on values between 0 and 1 inclusive and that gives the hues on the gray scale of the colors – 0 gives black and 1 gives white. The argument alpha is the transparency and also takes on values from 0 to 1 inclusive – 0 is transparent and 1 is opaque. The arguments level and alpha do not have default values.

In Listing 3-11 and Figure 3-11, hex color codes are generated and plotted.

Listing 3-11. Code to demonstrate generating and plotting hex color codes on the gray scale

```
> gray(
+      ( 11:60 )/100,
+      1
+ )[1:7]
[1] "#1C1C1CFF" "#1F1F1FFF" "#212121FF" "#242424FF" "#262626FF"
[6] "#292929FF" "#2B2B2BFF"

> plot(
+      pop75.ordered, pop15.ordered,
+      main="col=gray( ( 11:60 )/100, 1 )",
+      col=gray( ( 11:60 )/100, 1 )
+ )
```

Figure 3-11 follows.

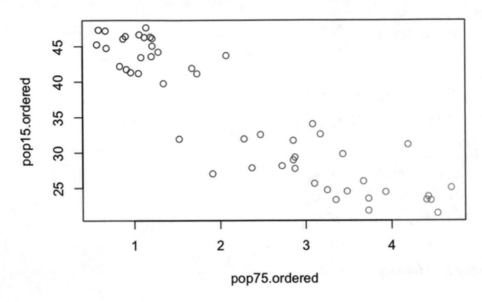

Figure 3-11. *Example of assigning a gray scale to col using gray()*

The function gray.colors()/grey.colors() is easier to use and more flexible than gray()/grey(). The function takes on six arguments. The first three are n for the number of colors; start for the beginning level of gray, by default 0.3; and end for the ending level of gray, by default 0.9. The arguments start and end must be between 0 and 1 inclusive, and n must be a positive integer.

The fourth argument is gamma – for a nonlinear gradient. The argument gamma is the exponent on start and end. Smaller values, which can be negative, give less gradient. Setting gamma to 1 gives a linear gradient. The argument must be a numeric vector of a length that divides evenly into n. The argument cycles and has a default value of 2.2.

The last two arguments are alpha for transparency – 0 is transparent and 1 is opaque (not supported on all devices) – and rev which tells R to reverse the order of the colors if set to TRUE and which is FALSE by default. The argument alpha must be between 0 and 1 inclusive.

There are two functions that convert between rgb, character string, and hsv specifications. The function col2rgb() converts character string color specifications to rgb codes. The function takes two arguments, col – any object that can be used as a value of the argument to col in plot() – and alpha, a logical variable which indicates whether to return the level of alpha and which is by default FALSE. In Listing 3-12 is an example of the function.

Listing 3-12. Example of the function col2rgb()

```
> col2rgb(
+     list( "#ffffff", "gray", 1, 3 ),
+     alpha=TRUE
+ )
      [,1] [,2] [,3] [,4]
red    255  190    0   97
green  255  190    0  208
blue   255  190    0   79
alpha  255  255  255  255
```

The function rgb2hsv() converts red, green, and blue levels to hue, saturation, and value levels. The function takes four arguments – r, g, b, and maxColorValue – which are as described under the description of rgb().

In Listing 3-13, two examples are given of rgb2hsv().

Listing 3-13. Two examples of rgb2hsv()

```
> rgb2hsv(
+     200,
+     200,
+     0,
+     maxColorValue = 255
+ )
        [,1]
h 0.1666667
s 1.0000000
v 0.7843137
```

```
> rgb2hsv(
+       1,
+       1,
+       0,
+       maxColorValue = 1.275
+ )
        [,1]
h 0.1666667
s 1.0000000
v 0.7843137
```

Note, both calls to rgb2hsv() give the same result.

According to the help pages in R, different operating systems use different color bases. See the help pages for colorConvert() and colorConverter() for more information on converting between the bases. Also, to create a color space, see the help page for make.rgb().

3.4.2 Fonts and Font Families

Fonts are the style of the text displayed in a graphic. Fonts have families and weights. The family gives the design of the font. The weight gives the depth and inclination of the font. The font families available to R mostly depend on the device on which the graphic is displayed, although the Hershey vector fonts are built in in R. For most families, the weight can be plain, bold, italic, or bold italic.

3.4.2.1 Font Families and Assigning the Font Family in plot()

In plot(), the font family for displayed text is assigned by the argument family. The argument takes a one-element character vector containing the name of the font. The value of family affects the title, subtitle, axis labels, axis tick labels, and plotting character.

From the help page for par(), the argument must be at most 200 bytes. Any font family available on the device on which the graphic is to be displayed can be used, as well as the Hershey vector fonts. The name of the family must be exactly as listed.

The default value for family is " ", which tells R to use the default font of the device – which on my device is "Arial Unicode" (looking in Finder ➤ Go ➤ Computer ➤ Macintosh HD ➤ Library ➤ Fonts.) The families available on the device of a manufacturer can be found by accessing the help pages of a manufacturer – or, for desktops and laptops, by opening a program such as Pages or Word and looking at the available fonts.

In R, the Hershey vector font families are built in. The fonts were developed for use in plotting and maintain shape when rotated and resized because the fonts are made up of vectors (straight lines). From the help page for Hershey in R, there are eight Hershey font families available for use in plot(): "HersheySerif", "HersheySans", "HersheyScript", "HersheyGothicEnglish", "HersheyGothicGerman", "HersheyGothicItalian", "HersheySymbol", and "HersheySansSymbol".

To see the available nonstandard characters for the Hershey families, run demo(Hershey) in R or RStudio. In what is given in the following, escape signatures are codes that tell R to plot a given nonstandard character. The demo lists the following:

1. The available family styles and weights (the Cyrillic and EUC families are not available through plot())

2. The escape signatures for the symbol families

3. The escape signatures for the non-ASCII Latin-1 characters – which can be used with all of the Hershey families except the symbol families

4. The special escape signatures – which are mainly for astrological symbols, but there are a few others, and which can be used with any Hershey family that can be used with plot()

5. The Cyrillic octal codes – not available through plot()

6. Two pages of raw escape signatures – which can be used with any of the families that can be assigned in plot()

For the raw and special codes, the family does not affect the plotted character.

To use a font family in plot(), set family to the name of the font family. Escape signatures can be used directly in a character string. R will interpret the escape signature correctly.

In Listing 3-14, the code to set "HersheySerif" as the font family and to use the escape signature for a flower pot in the title is given.

Listing 3-14. Code to set the HersheySerif family as the font family in plot() and to use the escape signature for a flower pot in the title

```
plot(
    pop75.ordered, pop15.ordered,
    family="HersheySerif",
    main="The Young    \\#H0864    The Old"
)
```

In Figure 3-12, the plot is generated.

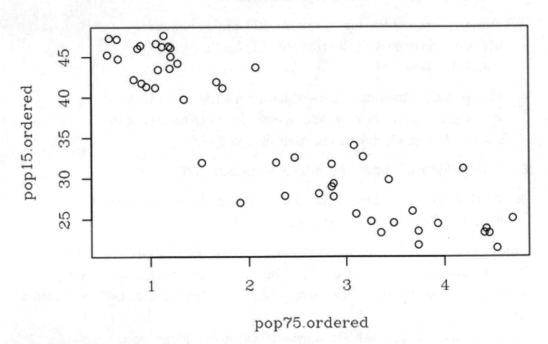

Figure 3-12. *Example of the HersheySerif font family, with the escape signature for a flower pot in the title*

3.4.2.2 Font Weights in plot()

Font weights are set with the arguments font, font.main, font.sub, font.lab, and font.axis – for the plotting character, title, subtitle, axis labels, and axis tick labels, respectively. The arguments take on integer values 1–4. Some font families allow larger integers – for example, 5, 6, and 7 in "HersheySerif". Usually, setting font to 1 gives plain text; setting font to 2 gives bold text; setting font to 3 gives italic text; and setting font equal to 4 gives bold and italic text. However, the effect given does not always hold.

In Listing 3-15, the code for setting font weights is shown, where the font arguments are set equal to 1–7.

Listing 3-15. Code for an example of font arguments set equal to 1–7

```
plot(
  pop75.ordered, pop15.ordered,
  main="font.main = 4, font = 2, font.axis = 1",
  sub="font.sub = 3",
  xlab="font.lab = 2",
  ylab=" font.lab = 2",
  pch="2",
  font=2,
  font.main=4,
  font.sub=3,
  font.lab=2,
  font.axis=1
)

plot(
  pop75.ordered, pop15.ordered,
  main="font.main = 5, font.axis = 2",
  sub="font.sub = 6",
  xlab="font.lab = 7",
  ylab=" font.lab = 7",
  pch="1",
  font.main=5,
```

```
font.sub=6,
font.lab=7,
font.axis=2
)
```

The result of running the code in Listing 3-15 is in Figure 3-13.

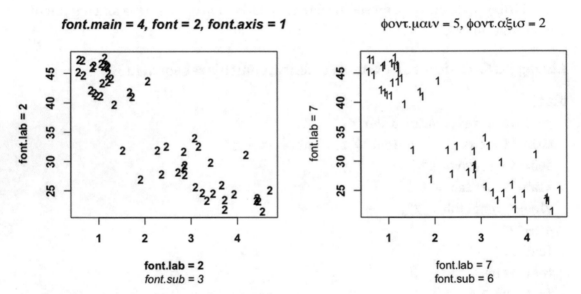

Figure 3-13. *Example of changing the weight arguments: In the first plot, font=2, font.main=4, font.sub=3, font.lab=2, and font.axis=1. In the second plot, font is not set, font.main=5, font.sub=6, font.lab=7, and font.axis=2*

Note that the labels on the axis ticks are the weight of the argument of font if font is given.

3.4.3 Character Size in plot()

The default character sizes are set by R. To determine the default character size for a plotting character, there are four read-only (cannot be set but can be read) variables that give character size: cin, cra, csi, and cxy.

The argument cin is the width and height of a character in inches; cra is the width and height of a character in pixels if pixels make sense for the device (otherwise, usually about 1/72 of an inch); csi is the height of characters in inches; and cxy should be the two elements of cin divided by the two elements of the argument pin – which is a settable argument and is the dimensions of the plotting region in inches.

The arguments cin, cra, csi, and cxy can be read by using the function par() – see the code in Listing 3-16.

Listing 3-16. The read-only character size arguments, cin, cra, csi, and cxy, and the settable variable pin

```
> par( "cin", "cra", "csi", "cxy", "pin" )
$cin
[1] 0.15 0.20

$cra
[1] 10.8 14.4

$csi
[1] 0.2

$cxy
[1] 0.1621959 4.0434891

$pin
[1] 4.135000 1.399583
```

For cxy, if the plotting region has not been adjusted, then the elements are equal to what is expected. However, if the plotting region is changed, then the values of cxy do not equal what the values should. See Listings 3-17 and 3-18.

Listing 3-17. The values of pin, cin/pin, and cxy when the plotting region has not been adjusted

```
> par( "pin" )
[1] 4.135000 1.399583

> par( "cin" )/par( "pin" )
[1] 0.0362757 0.1428997

> par( "cxy" )
[1] 0.0362757 0.1428997
```

Listing 3-18. Setting the value of pin and the values of cin, cxy, pin, and cin/pin after the change

```
> par( pin = c( 3, 1.5 )  )
> par( "cin", "cxy", "pin" )
$cin
[1] 0.15 0.20

$cxy
[1] 0.22356 3.77280

$pin
[1] 3.0 1.5

> par( "cin" )/par( "pin" )
[1] 0.0500000 0.1333333
```

See the help page for par() for more information.

Character sizes in a plot are set by the arguments cex, cex.main, cex.sub, cex.lab, and cex.axis – which change the size of the plotting character and the characters in the title, subtitle, axis labels, and axis tick labels, respectively. For all the arguments, the default character sizes are relative to the value of cex. However, changing cex in plot() does not affect the sizes of the other graphical elements. (The argument cex can be changed in par() – which does affect the other graphical elements.)

The cex argument has a value of 1 by default – which means the size of a character is given by the value of cin. The default value of cex.main is 1.2. The default values of cex.sub, cex.lab, and cex.axis are all 1. Setting the value of any of the cex arguments multiplies the default character size by the value of the argument.

See Listing 3-19 and Figure 3-14 for an example of using cex, cex.main, cex.sub, cex. lab, and cex.axis.

Listing 3-19. Code of the example of using the five cex arguments

```
plot(
  pop75.ordered, pop15.ordered,
  main="cex.main = 1.5, cex=0.4, cex.axis = 0.7",
  sub="cex.sub = 1.5",
  xlab="cex.lab = 1.2",
```

```
ylab="cex.lab = 1.2",
cex=.4,
cex.main=1.5,
cex.sub=1.5,
cex.lab=1.2,
cex.axis=0.7
)
```

The result of running the code in Listing 3-19 is in Figure 3-14.

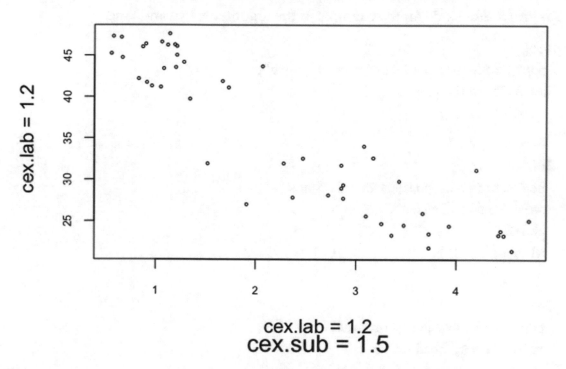

Figure 3-14. *Example of changing cex, cex.main, cex.sub, cex.lab, and cex.axis*

3.4.4 Line Details: lwd, lend, ljoin, and lmitre

Lines generated by plot can be styled. The line width can be set; and, for the style of line ends and line joints, there are a few options. The four arguments that affect lines are lwd, lend, ljoin, and lmitre.

The argument lwd affects the width of lines. The argument can be set to any positive number and has a default value of 1. From the help page for par(), the graphical interpretation of lwd depends on the device on which the graphic is plotted, so the effect may not be consistent between devices.

The argument lend describes the style of the end of a line. The argument can take on the integer value 0, 1, or 2 or the character value "round", "butt", or "square". The default value is 0 or "round".

In Listing 3-20 and Figure 3-15, examples of lwd and lend are given.

Listing 3-20. Code for the example of the arguments lwd and lend

```
plot(
  pop75.ordered, pop15.ordered, type="b",
  main="default plot",
  xlim=c( 2, 3 )
)

plot(
  pop75.ordered, pop15.ordered, type="b",
  main="lwd=2, lend=0",
  lwd=2,
  xlim=c( 2, 3 )
)

plot(
  pop75.ordered, pop15.ordered, type="b",
  main="lwd=3, lend=1",
  lwd=3,
  lend=1,
  xlim=c( 2, 3 )
)
```

```
plot(
  pop75.ordered, pop15.ordered, type="b",
  main="lwd=4, lend=2",
  lwd=4,
  lend=2,
  xlim=c( 2, 3 )
)
```

Figure 3-15 follows.

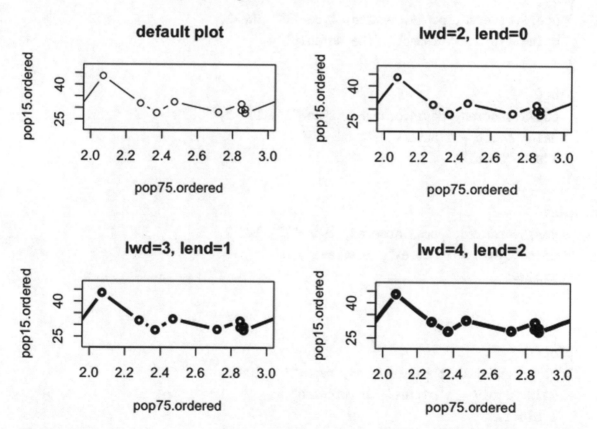

Figure 3-15. *An example of changing lwd and lend – with a default plot (lwd=1 and lend=0) and plots with lwd=2, 3, and 4 and with lend=0, 1, and 2, respectively*

The argument ljoin affects how lines connect. There are three possibilities for ljoin, which can also be a number or a character string: 0 or "round", 1 or "mitre", and 2 or "bevel". If 1 or "mitre" is chosen, then the argument lmitre can be set to control where mitering turns into beveling. (From the help page of par(), some devices are not affected by mitering.) The default value of ljoin is 0 or "round"; the default value of lmitre is 10; and lmitre must be greater than or equal to 1.

See Figure 3-16 for examples of mitering, as well as rounded and beveled joins. In Listing 3-21, the code for four plots demonstrating ljoin and lmitre is given.

Listing 3-21. Code for the plots showing the effect of ljoin and lmitre

```
plot(
  pop75.ordered, pop15.ordered, type="l", lwd=2,
  main="ljoin = \"round\" (the default)"
)

plot(
  pop75.ordered, pop15.ordered, type="l", lwd=2,
  main="ljoin = \"bevel\"",
  ljoin="bevel"
)

plot(
  pop75.ordered, pop15.ordered, type="l", lwd=2,
  main="ljoin = \"mitre\", lmitre=2",
  ljoin=1,
  lmitre=2
)

plot(
  pop75.ordered, pop15.ordered, type="l", lwd=2,
  main="ljoin = \"mitre\", lmitre=100",
  ljoin=1,
  lmitre=100
)
```

In Figure 3-16, the plots resulting from running the code are given.

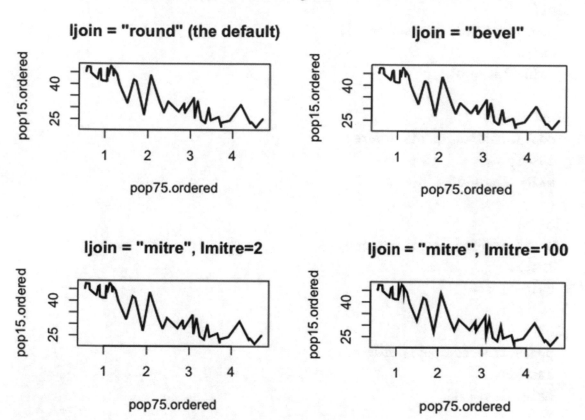

Figure 3-16. *Examples of setting ljoin and lmitre*

3.4.5 Making Changes to the Axes

There are a number of ways to make changes to axis ticks and axis tick labels within the call to plot(). The orientation of axis tick labels with respect to the axis can be changed. Ticks can be set to start at the edge of a plot or a short distance within the plot. The plotting of axis ticks and axis tick labels can be turned off. With care, the values and spacing of ticks can be controlled. The length and direction of the ticks can be set.

The orientation of the axis tick labels is set by the argument las – which can take on the values 0, for parallel to the axis; 1, for always horizontal; 2, for perpendicular to the axis; and 3, for always vertical. The default value is 0.

In Listing 3-22, code is given for four plots that illustrate the four axis tick label styles.

Listing 3-22. Code for the example of las set to 0, 1, 2, and 3

```
plot(
  pop75.ordered, pop15.ordered,
  las=0,
  main="las = 0"
)
plot(
  pop75.ordered, pop15.ordered,
  las=1,
  main="las = 1"
)
plot(
  pop75.ordered, pop15.ordered,
  las=2,
  main="las = 2"
)
plot(
  pop75.ordered, pop15.ordered,
  las=3,
  main="las = 3"
)
```

In Figure 3-17, the plots are generated.

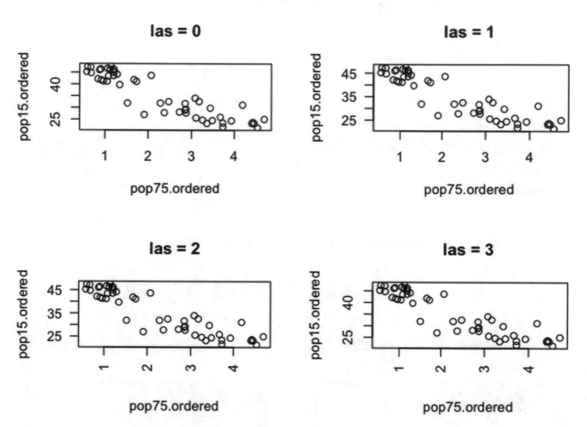

Figure 3-17. *Example of setting the axis tick label orientation argument, las, to 0, 1, 2, and 3*

The arguments xaxs and yaxs determine whether to put a space of 4% of the axis range on both ends of the x and/or y axis. The possible arguments are "r" and "i". The value "r" is the default and indicates to use the 4% space. The value "i" indicates no space.

In Listing 3-23, the code for the example of using xaxs and yaxs is given.

Listing 3-23. Code for setting the edge space in a plot

```
plot(
  pop75.ordered, pop15.ordered,
  main="xaxs = \"r\", yaxs = \"r\"",
  xaxs="r",
  yaxs="r"
)

plot(
  pop75.ordered, pop15.ordered,
  main="xaxs = \"i\", yaxs = \"i\"",
  xaxs="i",
  yaxs="i"
)
```

In Figure 3-18, the plots from Listing 3-23 are shown.

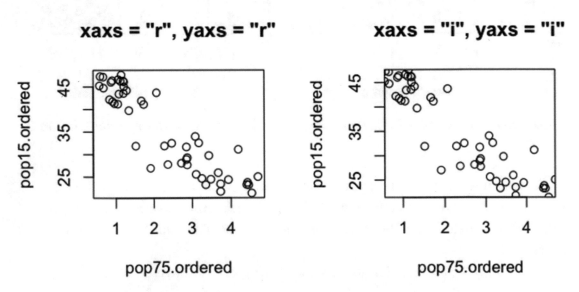

Figure 3-18. *An example of setting up a plot with and without a space on the edges*

The choice of not to annotate a plot with axis ticks and axis tick labels is made with the arguments axes, xaxt, and yaxt. The argument axes is a logical argument of length one that tells R whether to include axes. The default value is TRUE – to include axes.

The arguments xaxt and yaxt do the same for the individual axes but are character vectors of length one. Setting xaxt and/or yaxt to "s", "l", or "t" plots a standard axis on the x and/or y axis. Setting xaxt and/or yaxt to "n" suppresses the axis tick and axis tick label annotation.

Listing 3-24 gives the code for a plot showing the effect of xaxt and yaxt.

Listing 3-24. Code for the example of setting xaxt and yaxt

```
plot(
  pop75.ordered, pop15.ordered,
  main="xaxt = \"n\", yaxt = \"s\"",
  xaxt="n",
  yaxt="s"
)
```

In Figure 3-19, the plot showing the influence of setting xaxt and yaxt is given.

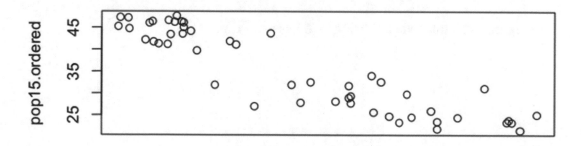

Figure 3-19. *An example of using xaxt to suppress axis ticks and axis tick labels on the x axis*

Controlling tick mark spacing is a bit tricky. The arguments to set spacing are lab to set spacing for both axes and xaxp and/or yaxp to set spacing for axes individually. However, R uses the spacing given by las, xasp, and/or yasp as a guide, but chooses "pretty" intervals that may or may not follow the guide. Setting xlim and/or ylim, along with lab, xaxp, and/or yaxp, can help.

The argument lab takes a three-element integer vector. The first element sets the number of ticks on the x axis, the second sets the number of ticks on the y axis, and the third is not used. The default value is c(5, 5, 7). In Listing 3-25, the code for two example plots using las is given.

Listing 3-25. Examples of setting las with and without xlim and ylim

```
plot(
  pop75.ordered, pop15.ordered,
  main="lab = c( 10, 7, 7 )",
  lab=c( 10, 7, 7 )
)

plot(
  pop75.ordered, pop15.ordered,
  main="lab = c( 10, 7, 7 )\nxlim=c( 0.5, 5 ), ylim=c( 20, 50 )",
  lab=c( 10, 7, 7 ),
  xlim=c( 0.5, 5),
  ylim=c( 20, 50 )
)
```

In Figure 3-20, the code in Listing 3-25 has been run.

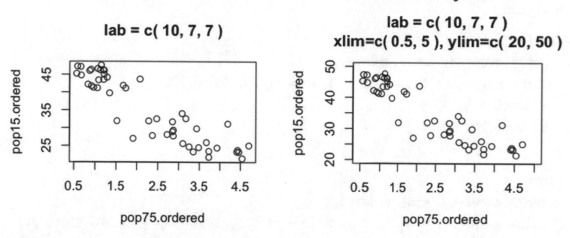

Figure 3-20. *Examples of using las for tick spacing with and without setting xlim and ylim*

Note that in the first plot, there are nine ticks on the x axis and five ticks on the y axis, even though las requested ten on the x axis and seven on the y axis. In the second plot, there are ten ticks on the x axis and seven on the y axis – as set by las.

To put the ticks where the ticks should be, subtract the left (bottom) axis limit from the right (top) axis limit and divide the difference by the tick mark interval and then add one to the result. Use the resulting value for the number of ticks. In Figure 3-20, for example, (5.0 – 0.5)/0.5 + 1 = 10 and (50 – 20)/5 + 1 = 7, so las is set equal to c(10, 7, 7), where the third number can be any nonnegative number.

The arguments xaxp and yaxp can be used to set spacing for each axis independently. Both arguments take a three-element numeric vector. The first element is the lower limit of the axis, the second element is the upper limit of the axis, and the third number is the number of tick spacing intervals. Once again, the argument is a guide, but R will choose a "pretty" spacing.

In Listing 3-26, the code for an example of using xaxp and yaxp is given.

Listing 3-26. Code to demonstrate xaxp and yaxp with and without setting xlim and ylim

```
plot(
  pop75.ordered, pop15.ordered,
  main="xaxp = c( 0.5, 5, 9 )\nyaxp = c( 20, 50, 6 )",
  xaxp=c( 0.5, 5, 9 ),
  yaxp=c( 20, 50, 6 )
)

plot(
  pop75.ordered, pop15.ordered,
  main="xaxp = c( 0.5, 5, 9 ), xlim = c( 0.5, 5 )\nyaxp = c( 20, 50, 6 ),
  ylim = c( 20, 50 )",
  xaxp=c( 0.5, 5, 9 ),
  yaxp=c( 20, 50, 6 ),
  xlim=c( 0.5, 5),
  ylim=c( 20, 50 )
)
```

In Figure 3-21, the plots are generated.

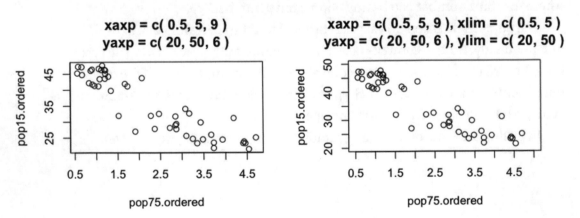

Figure 3-21. *Example of setting xaxp and yaxp with and without using xlim and ylim*

Once again, the spaces in the first plot are not those of xaxp and yaxp; the spaces are those of xaxp and yaxp in the second plot. Note that the number of spaces is one less than the number of ticks.

The length and direction of ticks are set by the arguments tck and tcl. Both arguments take a numeric vector of length one.

The argument tck, if tcl is not set, gives the length and direction of the tick marks. If the value is positive, the tick marks are plotted into the plot; if negative, the tick marks are plotted away from the plot. If tck is set to 1, grid lines are drawn.

If the absolute value of tck is greater than 0.5 and less than or equal to 1, the length plotted on both axes is the absolute value of tck times the length of the axis that is perpendicular to the tick mark axis. If tck is between -0.5 and 0.5, the length on both axes is the absolute value of tck times the length of the shorter axis. The value of tck can also be greater than 1, where the grid lines extend beyond the edge of the plot. The default value for tck is NA.

If tcl is set, then R ignores tck. The length of a tick is then tcl times the line height for characters. As with tck, negative values point away from the plot, and positive values point into the plot. The default value of tcl is -0.5. From the help page for par(), if tcl is set to NA, then tck is set to -0.01.

In Listing 3-27, code for two examples of setting tck and tcl is given.

Listing 3-27. Code to generate two plots with tck and tcl set

```
plot(
  pop75.ordered, pop15.ordered,
  main="tck = 1",
  tck=1
)

plot(
  pop75.ordered, pop15.ordered,
  main="tck = NA, tcl=0.5",
  tck=NA,
  tcl=0.5
)
```

In Figure 3-22, the code for the two plots in Listing 3-27 is run.

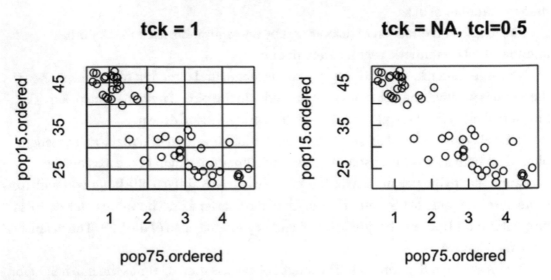

Figure 3-22. *An example of setting tck and tcl*

3.4.6 Working with Log Scales

Sometimes plots are clearer if a log scale is used on one or both axes. A log scale is a scale for which the spacing of the axis tick marks is linear in the base 10 log of the x or y values rather than linear in the values. However, the labels for the tick marks are in the units of the x or y values. To set up a log scale, the argument log is used. To annotate the scale, xaxp and yaxp can be used. As with linear scales, xaxp and yaxp are just guides. R will create "pretty" axis notation.

The argument log takes a character vector of length one for a value. The possible values are "x", for a log scale on the x axis; "y", for a log scale on the y axis; and "xy" or "yx", for a log scale on both axes. For the arguments xaxp and yaxp, the notation on the axis that uses a log scale is controlled by the third value of xaxp and/or yaxp.

Three values can be used: 1, 2, or 3. According to the help page for par(), the lower and upper limits of xaxp and/or yaxp must be powers of ten. In that case, with the third value of xaxp and/or yaxp set to 1, only the powers of ten are annotated. For 2, one and five times the powers of ten are annotated. For 3, one, two, and five times the powers of ten are annotated. However, in my example, the y limits of the first plot are not equal to powers of ten; and, on my device, R handles the limits well.

The variable dpi (real per-capita disposable income), from the LifeCycleSavings dataset, is appropriate for a demonstration of log scales and is used in Listing 3-28 and Figure 3-23. See Listing 3-28 for the code used to create the plots in Figure 3-23.

Listing 3-28. Code to create the variable dpi.ordered and plot the example plots for log, xaxp, and yaxp

```
dpi.ordered = LifeCycleSavings$dpi[ ord ]

plot(
  pop75.ordered, dpi.ordered,
  main="log = \"y\"\nyaxp = c( 50, 6000, 2 ), ylim=c( 50, 6000 )",
  log="y",
  yaxp=c( 50, 6000, 2 ),
  ylim=c( 50, 6000 )
)

plot(
  pop75.ordered, dpi.ordered,
  main="log = \"xy\", xaxp = c( 0.1, 10, 3 ), xlim= c( 0.1, 10)\nyaxp =
  c( 10, 10000, 2 ), ylim = c( 10, 10000 )",
  log="xy",
  xaxp=c( 0.1, 10, 3 ),
  yaxp=c( 10, 10000, 2 ),
  xlim=c( 0.1, 10 ),
  ylim=c( 10, 10000 )
)
```

In Figure 3-23, the plots in the example are given.

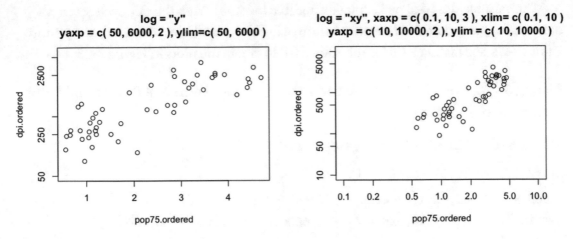

Figure 3-23. *Example of using log, xaxp, and yaxp to create log scales*

CHAPTER 4

Ancillary Functions for plot()

There are functions in R that can be used to add to a plot once plot() has been run (or when plot() is run). Such functions can do things like add a regression line to a scatterplot or put text next to a point. In this chapter, those ancillary functions found in the graphics and stats packages are covered. The chapter is broken into four sections: the overall appearance, the functions assigning objects to locations, the functions that plot lines or line-like objects, and specialized functions.

There are a few arguments to plot.default() that were not covered in Chapter 3 – including panel.first and panel.last. Setting panel.first or panel.last to an ancillary function runs the function before or after y is plotted against x in plot(), respectively. Also, many of the arguments that can be set in plot() can also be set in ancillary functions after plot() is run.

4.1 Functions That Affect Overall Appearance

There are seven functions that affect the overall appearance of a plot: title(), for titles and axis labels; axis(), to set up individual axes; axTicks(), to generate axis tick mark locations; box(), to put a border around a plot; grid(), to set up a grid in a plot; clip(), to set where to clip the output from the ancillary function; and rug(), to put a "rug" (univariate data plot) on a side of a plot.

When run after a call to plot(), the ancillary functions will plot over anything plotted in the call to plot(). For axis labels, the second set of labels plot over the first. Both are visible and the result is usually unreadable. Running plot() with ann set equal to FALSE gives a plot with title and axis label annotation removed.

© Margot Tollefson 2021
M. Tollefson, *Visualizing Data in R 4*, https://doi.org/10.1007/978-1-4842-6831-5_4

The axes and axis tick annotation also can be excluded in the call to plot(). Running plot() with axes equal to FALSE gives a plot with the axes and axis tick annotation removed.

4.1.1 The title() Function

The title() function can be used to put titles, subtitles, and x and y axis labels on a plot. The function takes six specified arguments, plus many of the arguments in par(). The specified arguments are main, for the title of the plot; sub, for the subtitle of the plot; xlab, for the label on the x axis; ylab, for the label on the y axis; line, for the line on which to plot the text in main, sub, xlab, and/or ylab; and outer, for whether to plot the text in an outer margin.

The main, sub, xlab, and ylab arguments, as used in plot(), can also be used the same way in title(). By another method, for each of main, sub, xlab, and ylab, the argument can be set equal to a list of up to four elements. The first element in the list is the text to be plotted. The other arguments are font, col, and/or cex.

The font.*, col.*, and cex.* arguments used in plot() can also be used in title(). The font family can be changed in title() too, by setting the argument family to the font family name. For all of these, the arguments take the same kinds of values as in plot().

To adjust where on the side of the plot the text prints, the argument adj can be used. (The argument adj also works in plot().) The argument is a single-element numeric vector with a value between 0 and 1, inclusive. If adj equals 0, the title, subtitle, and x axis label plot at the start of the x axis; and the y axis label plots at the lower start of the y axis. If adj equals 1, the title, subtitle, and x axis label plot at the right end of the x axis; and the y axis label plots at the top end of the y axis. If adj is between 0 and 1, the elements plot proportionately between the two extremes. The default value is 0.5.

Two arguments can be used to control on which line the titles and axis labels plot: line and mgp. In R, lines are ordered from the edge of the plot out, starting with zero. By default – on my device – the title and axis labels plot at 1.7 lines, and the subtitle plots at 2.7 lines.

The argument line tells title() on which line to plot the title, subtitle, xlab, and/or ylab. The value of line can be any nonnegative numeric vector, but only the first element is used. If line is set in title() and a subtitle and x axis label are being used, there is a problem since the x axis label and the subtitle will overlie.

Here are a few ways to deal with this problem. If the default placement of the title is acceptable, then the argument mgp can be used to place the axis labels and subtitle. The argument mgp is an argument of par() and is a three-element numeric vector with nonnegative elements. Only the first element is used in title(). (The other two are used in axis().) The value gives the line on which the axis labels plot. The subtitle then plots at one line more extreme with respect to the axis. The default value for mgp is c(3, 1, 0).

Another way is to run title() twice, once to plot the title – using line – and once to plot the labels and subtitle, using mgp. Or run title() three or four times setting line each time and plotting one or two elements each time.

Using par(), an outer margin can be set (see Section 6.2.1.1). (By default, the outer margin is zero lines deep on all sides.) If an outer margin has been set, title() has an argument outer – for putting the titles and/or axis labels in the margin. The argument outer is a one-element logical vector and equals FALSE by default.

Sometimes mathematical expressions are included in a title or label. The function expression() can be used to generate a large number of mathematical expressions. (The function expression() can be used in plot() too.) To see the list of expressions, go to the help page for plotmath.

To include a mathematical expression in a title or axis label, paste together the character string inside expression(). For example: main = expression(paste("An Integral: ", integral(sin(x)*dx, -pi , pi))).

In Listing 4-1, code is given for an example of using title().

Listing 4-1. Code for an example of setting main, sub, xlab, ylab in repeated calls to title()

```
plot(
  pop75.ordered, pop15.ordered,
  ann=F
)

title(
  main=expression(
    paste(
      "Example of expression():",
      integral( sin(x)*dx, -pi, pi )
    )
  ),
```

```
  cex.main=1.5,
  font.main=4,
  col.main=gray( 0.3 ),
  line=2,
  adj=0
)

title(
  xlab=list(
    "population over 75",
    cex=1.2,
    font=4,
    col=gray( 0.7 )
  ),
  line=2.5,
  adj=0.5,
  family="serif"
)

title(
  ylab="population under 15"
)

title(
  sub=list(
    "bottom left",
    cex=1.3,
    font=1,
    col=gray( 0.5 )
  ),
  line=2.5,
  adj=0,
  family="mono"
)
```

```
title(
  sub=list(
    "bottom right",
    cex=1.3,
    font=1,
    col=gray( 0.5 )
  ),
  line=2.5,
  adj=1,
  family="sans"
)
```

In Figure 4-1, the result from running the code in Listing 4-1 is shown.

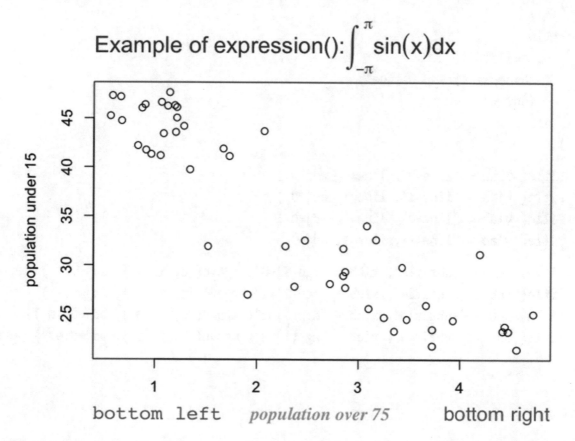

Figure 4-1. *Example of setting a title, x axis label, y axis label, and two subtitles using repeated calls to title()*

Note that two subtitles have been plotted, both on the same line as the x axis label, but offset – left and right – by setting adj. The font weights are different for some of the calls; and, in the call to plot the title, the font weight is ignored because the argument is an expression. The font families vary on the x axis, from left to right – the families are mono, serif, and sans.

In Listing 4-2, code is given for an example of using line and mgp.

Listing 4-2. Code demonstrating line spacing using line and mgp

```
plot(
  pop75.ordered, pop15.ordered,
  ann=F,
  col.axis=gray( 0.7 )
)

title(
  main=list(
    "Example of mgp & line",
    font=4
  )
)

title( ylab = "line=0", line=0, adj=0 )
title( ylab = "line=1", line=1, adj=0 )
title( ylab = "line=2", line=2, adj=0 )
title( ylab = "line=3", line=3, adj=0 )

title( sub = "subtitle", xlab = "mgp[1]=0", mgp=c( 0, 1, 0 ), adj=.22 )
title( sub = "subtitle", xlab = "mgp[1]=1", mgp=c( 1, 1, 0 ), adj=0.5 )
title( sub = "subtitle", xlab = "mgp[1]=2", mgp=c( 2, 1, 0 ), adj=0.78 )
title( sub = "subtitle", xlab = "mgp[1]=3", mgp=c( 3, 1, 0 ), adj=0.97 )
```

In Figure 4-2, the code has been run.

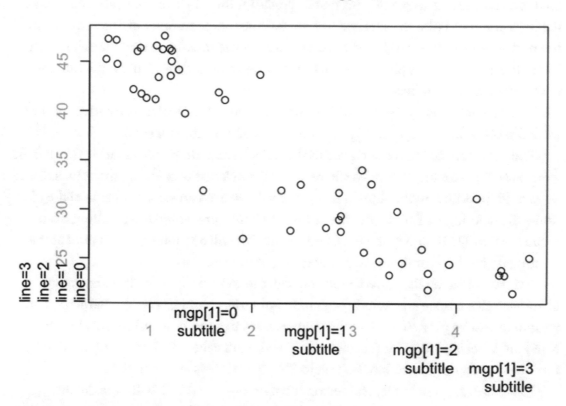

Figure 4-2. *Line placement using line and mgp[1]*

Note that the lines are as expected – out from the plot. Also, the subtitle plots below the x axis label.

4.1.2 The axis() and axTicks() Functions

Axes can be put onto a plot individually by running plot() with axes set to FALSE and using the functions axis() and optionally axTicks() to create the axes. From the help page for axis(), the function takes 16 specified arguments as well as additional arguments from par().

4.1.2.1 The axis() Function

The first eight arguments to axis() are side for the side on which to put the axis, at for the locations on the axis to put the tick marks, labels for the labels to put by the tick marks, tick for whether to plot the axis and tick marks, line for the number of lines away from the plot to put the axis, pos for where on the axis perpendicular to the axis being plotted to put the axis, outer for plotting the axis in an outer margin, and font for the font weight of the axis tick mark labels.

The side argument takes one of four integer values: 1, 2, 3, or 4. The corresponding sides are bottom, left, top, and right. There is no default value for side.

The at argument is a numeric vector that tells R where to put tick marks. The default value is NULL – that is, R decides where to put the tick marks based on the values of xaxp or yaxp (depending on the side) in par(). The values of at can extend outside of the plot limits. By default, R will only plot the tick marks if they are within the plot limits. But, if xpd is set to TRUE or NA, the full extent of the axis will be plotted, with a limit at the plotting region edge or device region edge, respectively.

If the value of labels is not of mode logical, the value must be of the same length as at and a vector whose elements are of mode numeric, complex, raw, or character. The argument can be a list. If an element of labels is set to a nonfinite value (NA, Inf, -Inf, or NaN), no label is plotted for that element. The default value of labels is TRUE – that is, R creates "pretty" numeric labels. If set to FALSE, no labels are plotted.

The tick argument is a logical vector of length one. If set to TRUE – the default value – the axis and ticks are plotted. If set to FALSE, the axis and ticks are not plotted.

The line, mgp[3], and pos arguments each tell R where to put the axis. If pos is set, line and mgp[3] are ignored. If pos is NA and line is set, mgp[3] is ignored. If both line and pos are NA and the value of mgp[3] is the default value of 0, then the axes plot at line 0. The default value for pos is NA, the default value for line is NA, and the default value for mgp[3] is the value in par() – by default, 0.

The argument line or mgp[3] (the argument mgp[2] gives the line where the axis tick mark labels are plotted) is a one-valued numeric vector and is measured in lines away from the plot. The argument can be negative. The argument pos is also a one-valued numeric vector and, for sides 1 and 3 (the horizontal sides), gives the y coordinate where the axis is to be plotted. For sides 2 and 4 (the vertical sides), pos gives the x coordinate where the axis is to be plotted.

The argument outer tells whether to put the axis in the outer margin. The argument is a logical vector of length one and is FALSE by default.

The argument font is the font weight of the axis tick mark labels. Font can take on those values of font that the font family in use allows. The default value is NA, which uses the value of font in par() – which is 1 by default on my device.

See Listing 4-3 for the code for an example of side, at, labels, and pos.

Listing 4-3. Code for the example of side, at, labels, and pos – using xpd

```
plot(
  pop75.ordered, pop15.ordered,
  axes=FALSE
)

title(
  main="Example of side, at, labels, pos, & xpd",
  font.main=1,
  line=3
)

axis(
  1,
  at=c( .25, 1, 2, 3, 4, 5 ),
  labels=c(NA, 1:4, NA),
  pos=20,
  xpd=TRUE
)

axis(
 2,
  at=c( 20, 30, 40, 50 ),
  labels=c( NA, 30, 40, NA ),
  pos=0.25,
  xpd=TRUE
)

axis(
  3,
  at=c( 0.25, 1, 2, 3, 4, 5 ),
  labels=FALSE,
```

```
  pos=50,
  xpd=TRUE
)

axis(
  4,
  at=c( 20, 30, 40, 50 ),
  labels=FALSE,
  pos=5,
  xpd=TRUE
)
```

In Figure 4-3, the code in Listing 4-3 is run.

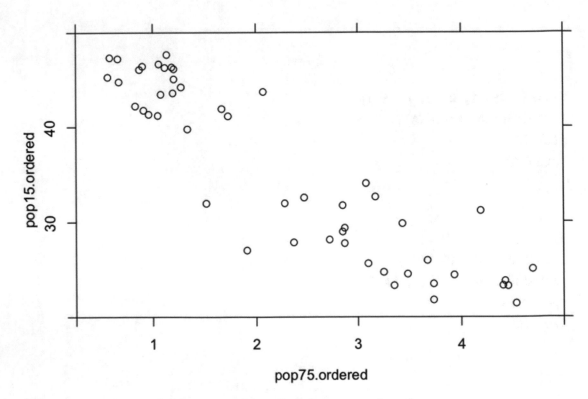

Figure 4-3. *Example of using side, at, labels, pos, and xpd*

Note that the axes are manually created. The axis tick label names are assigned manually, as well as where the axes start and stop. Tick marks are set at specific locations, and the axes are allowed to plot outside the plotting region.

The second eight arguments are lty for the line type of the axis and axis tick marks, lwd for the line width of the axis, lwd.ticks for the line width of the axis tick marks, col for the color of the axis, col.ticks for the color of the axis tick marks, hadj to adjust the axis tick label position in the direction parallel to the reading direction of the labels, padj to adjust the axis tick label position in the direction perpendicular to the reading direction of the labels, and gap.axis to stop plotting when a tick mark label gets too close to the next tick mark label.

The argument lty takes the same values as when used in plot(). The default value is "solid".

The arguments lwd and lwd.ticks take on the same values as lwd when used in plot(). Setting lwd and/or lwd.ticks to a value less than or equal to 0 will suppress the line and/or the ticks. The default value for lwd is 1 and for lwd.ticks is the value of lwd.

The arguments col and col.ticks take the same kinds of values as col when col is used in plot(). The default values of col and col.ticks are NULL, which tell R to use the color associated with the value of fg in par() – which on my device is black by default.

The argument hadj is a single-valued numeric vector that takes on values from 0 to 1 inclusive or takes on a value that is nonfinite (NA, Inf, -Inf, or NaN). For a value of 0, hadj puts the axis tick label to the right – in the direction of reading. The value of 1 puts the label to the left in the direction of reading. The default value of hadj is NA. The value of NA or any nonfinite value centers the label on the tick marks if the reading direction is parallel to the axis. If the reading direction is perpendicular to the axis, the axis tick mark labels are justified to the side adjacent to the axis.

The argument padj is a numeric vector that can be of any length greater than or equal to one. The argument takes on values between 0 and 1, inclusive, or nonfinite values and cycles if the vector is shorter that the number of labels. If the argument padj is 0, R puts the axis tick label as far up as the label can go – looking in the direction of reading. The value of 1 puts the label as far down as the label can go – looking in the direction of reading. The default value of padj is NA – which means padj takes on the default value of the argument las in par() (0 on my device) – as padj does for any nonfinite value.

The last argument, gap.axis, takes a single-value numeric vector and can be negative. According to the help page for axis(), the character size of an "m" is multiplied by gap. axis to determine the smallest acceptable gap between the labels. If negative, the labels are allowed to overlap up to the size of "m" times the negative of the value of gap.axis. The default value is NA, which multiplies the size of "m" by 1 for axis tick mark labels that are parallel to the axis and by 0.25 for those perpendicular to the axis.

The information on this page is from the help page for axis() in R. See Listing 4-4 for the code for an example of setting lty, lwd, lwd.ticks, col, col.ticks, side, and font.

Listing 4-4. Code for the example of lty, lwd, lwd.ticks, col, col.ticks, side, and font in axis()

```
plot(
  pop75.ordered, pop15.ordered,
  axes=FALSE,
  xlab=""
)

title(
  "Example of lty, lwd, lwd.ticks, col, col.ticks, & font",
  font.main=1
)

axis(
  1,
  at=c( .25, 1, 2, 3, 4, 5 ),
  labels=c(
    rep(
      "mmmmmmmmmm",
      6
    )
  ),
  hadj=0.3,
  padj=( 1:6 )/7,
  gap.axis=-1,
  line=3
)
```

```
axis(
  1,
  at=c( .25, 1, 2, 3, 4, 5 ),
  labels=c(
    rep(
      "mmmmmmmmmmm",
      6
    )
  ),
  hadj=0.3,
  padj=( 1:6 )/7,
  gap.axis=-2
)

axis(
  2,
  at=c( 20, 30, 40, 50 ),
  labels=c( 20, 30, 40, 50 ),
  lty="dashed",
  lwd=3,
  lwd.ticks=4,
  col=gray( 0.8 ),
  col.ticks=gray( 0.6 ),
  col.axis=gray( 0.6 ),
  font=2
)
```

In Figure 4-4, the code in Listing 4-4 is run.

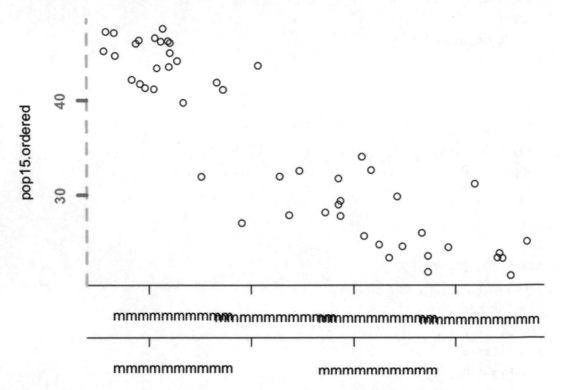

Figure 4-4. *Example of using lty, lwd, lwd.ticks, col, col.ticks, and font in axis()*

Note that in the first call to axis (on side 1, line 3), gap.axis equals -1, so an overlap of one "m" is allowed and only two labels were plotted. In the second call (on side 1, line 0), gap.axis equals -2, so an overlap of two "m's" is allowed and all four labels plot. The value of padj increases from left to right too.

In the third call to axis (on side 2), the line type of the axis has been changed. Also, the line widths and colors of the axis and axis tick marks have been changed. The argument col.axis was used to change the axis tick mark label color. Similarly, cex.axis could have been set.

4.1.2.2 The axTicks() Function

The axTicks() function generates axis ticks and can be used as an argument for at in axis(). For log scales, a call to plot() that includes a side with a log scale must have occurred to set up the ticks.

The function takes five arguments: side for the side on which to plot the axis, axp for a guide for axTicks() of where to set the axis extremes and for the number of intervals between axis tick marks, usr for axis limits in the units of user coordinates, log to use a log scale, and nintLog for a lower limit on the number of axis tick mark intervals for the log scale if a log scale is used – which is just a guide for R. This information is from the help page for axTicks().

The argument side is a one-element integer vector and is the same as in axis(). The argument has no default value.

The argument axp is a three-element numeric vector that, for side equal to 1 or 3, behaves like xaxp in plot() and, for sides 2 and 4, behaves like yaxp in plot(). The three values of axp give a lower limit and an upper limit for the locations of the tick marks and the number of intervals between the tick marks (and is just a guide for axTicks()).

The default value of axp is NULL – for which the value used by axTicks() is the value of xaxp or yaxp in par(), depending on the side.

The argument usr is a two-element numeric vector that gives the locations of the limits of the axis. If log is TRUE, then the units of usr are in powers of ten. The argument axp and the argument usr do strange things when used together, so one or the other should be used. The default value of usr is NULL, and in this case usr is set equal to the value in par() of usr[1:2] for an x axis or usr[3:4] for a y axis.

The argument log is a one-element logical vector that indicates a log scale for the axis. The argument should only be set to TRUE if a log scale has been set up in plot() for the given side of the plot. The default value is NULL in which case log is set equal to the value of xlog or ylog in par(), depending on which side is plotted.

The argument nintLog is the minimum number of intervals for the log scale and, according to the help page of axTicks(), only has an effect if log is TRUE. The default value is NULL, for which value the argument takes on the value of the first or second element of lab in par() – depending on if the side is 1 or 3 or 2 or 4. The argument does not appear to have an effect.

In Listing 4-5, some examples of running axTicks() are given.

Listing 4-5. Examples of using axp, usr, log, and nintLog in axTicks()

```
>  #open an empty plotting window (with no x and(or) y).

> plot.new()

> axTicks(
2,
axp=c( 20, 50, 6 )
)
[1] 20 25 30 35 40 45 50

> axTicks(
2,
usr=c( 20, 50 )
)
[1] 0.0 0.2 0.4 0.6 0.8 1.0

> axTicks(
2,
axp=c( 20, 50, 6 ),
usr=c( 20, 50 )
)
[1] 20 25 30 35 40 45 50

> axTicks(
2,
axp=c( 20, 5000, 3 ),
log=TRUE,
nintLog=8
)
[1]   4 10

> axTicks(
2,
usr=c( 0.6, 3.8 ),
log=TRUE,
nintLog=8
)
```

```
Error in axTicks(2, usr = c(0.6, 3.8), log = TRUE, nintLog = 8) :
  invalid positive 'axp[3]'

> axTicks(
2,
axp=c( 20, 5000, 3 ),
usr=c( 0.6, 3.8 ),
log=TRUE,
nintLog=8
)
 [1]    4   10   20   40  100  200  400 1000 2000 4000

> # open a plotting window with a log scale on the y axis

> plot(
pop75.ordered, dpi.ordered,
axes=FALSE,
log="y"
)

> # the y axis

> 10^c( 0.6, 3.8 )
[1]    3.981072 6309.573445

> axTicks(
2
)
[1]  100  200  500 1000 2000

> axTicks(
2,
axp=c( 20, 5000, 3 ),
log=TRUE,
nintLog=8
)
[1]    20   40  100  200  400 1000 2000 4000
```

```
> axTicks(
2,
usr=c( 0.6, 3.8 ),
log=TRUE,
nintLog=8
)
[1]   20   50  100  200  500 1000 2000 5000

> axTicks(
2,
axp=c( 20, 5000, 3 ),
usr=c( 0.6, 3.8 ),
log=TRUE,
nintLog=8
)
 [1]    4   10   20   40  100  200  400 1000 2000 4000

> # the x axis

> axTicks(
1
)
[1] 1 2 3 4

> axTicks(
1,
axp=c( 0, 5, 5 )
)
[1] 0 1 2 3 4 5

> axTicks(
1,
usr=c( 0, 5 )
)
[1] 1 2 3 4

> axTicks(
1,
```

```
axp=c( 0, 5, 5 ),
usr=c( 0, 5 )
)
[1] 0 1 2 3 4 5
```

Note that if a plot has not been run, axp gives the correct values, but usr assumes a unit length axis. Also, using log equal to TRUE gives erratic results if a log scale has not been plotted.

4.1.3 The box(), grid(), clip(), and rug() Functions

The box(), grid(), clip(), and rug() functions affect the overall appearance of a plot. Flexibility with regard to color, line style, and line width can make for a graphic easier to read.

4.1.3.1 The box() Function

The box() function puts a box around a plot. The function takes two arguments, as well as some of the arguments to par().

The first argument is which. The argument takes four possible values: "plot", "figure", "inner", and "outer". The value "plot" puts a box around the plot. For a single plot with no outer margin, "figure", "inner", and "outer" all give the same result – to put a box around the outside of the figure.

For more than one plot in the graphic and no outer margin, using "figure" puts a box around the figure that was last plotted. The values "inner" and "outer" both put a box around the entire graphic. If there is an outer margin, "inner" puts a box around the group of figures and inside the outer margin, and "outer" frames the outer margin. The default value of which is "plot".

The second argument is lty for line type. The argument takes the same values as the argument lty in plot(). The default value of lty is "solid".

According to the help page for box(), the color of the box is set by col if col is not NA. If col is NA and fg is not NA, then the color is given by the value of fg. If both col and fg are NA, the color of the box is given by the value of col in par() – "black" by default on my device.

In Listing 4-6 is the code for an example of using box().

Listing 4-6. Code demonstrating which, lty, col, and lwd in box()

```
plot(
  pop75.ordered, dpi.ordered,
  axes=FALSE,
  log="y"
)

title(
  main="Example of which, lty, col, & lwd in box()",
  font.main=1
)

box(
  which="plot",
   lty="dashed",
  col=gray( 0.8 ),
  lwd=2
)

box(
  which="figure",
  lty="longdash",
  col=gray( 0.2 ),
  lwd=2
)
```

In Figure 4-5, the code in Listing 4-6 is run.

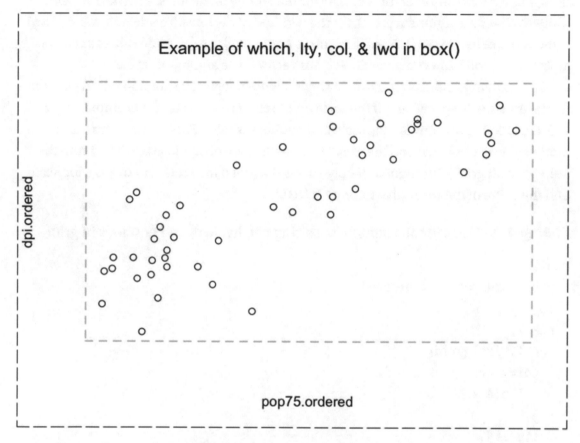

Figure 4-5. *Example of using which, lty, col, and lwd in box()*

Note that the outer box is dark gray, while the inner box is light gray. Also, the outer box uses long dashes, while the inner box uses dashes. The outer box is around the figure. The inner box is around the plot. For both boxes, the line width is 2.

4.1.3.2 The grid() Function

The grid() function takes six arguments – with no option for using the arguments in par(). The first two arguments are nx and ny, for the number of cells in the horizontal and vertical dimensions. The default value of nx is NULL, and the default value of ny is the value of nx. If nx or ny is set equal to NULL, R plots grid lines for the x or y dimension where the tick marks would be if the default values from axTicks() were used. If set to NA, the grid for the x or y axis is not plotted.

The third argument is col for the color(s) of the grid, with the default value equal to "lightgray"; the fourth argument is lty for the type(s) of the lines, with default value "dotted". The fifth argument is lwd, for the width(s) of the lines. The default value of lwd is the value of lwd in par(). All of these three arguments use the same values as can be assigned in plot() and can be multielement vectors. The arguments cycle.

The sixth argument is equilogs – a single-element logical vector that tells R whether to plot an equally spaced grid if the scale on the axis is a log scale, for example, at 1, 10, 100, and 1000. If nx or ny is a log scale and equilogs is set to FALSE, then a grid line is plotted at every tick mark on the axis. The default value of equilogs is TRUE. From the help page on grid(), the argument only affects the plot if the scale on x or y is a log scale and the value of the respective nx or ny is NULL.

Listing 4-7. Code for an example of setting col, lty, lwd, and equilogs in grid()

```
plot(
  pop75.ordered, dpi.ordered,
  log="y",
  cex=2,
  panel.first=grid(
    col=gray(
      ( 0:4 )/5
    ),
    lty=1:5,
    lwd=( 2:6 ),
    equilogs=FALSE
  )
)

title(
  main="Example of col, lty, lwd, and equilogs in grid()"
)
```

The plot generated by Listing 4-7 is shown in Figure 4-6.

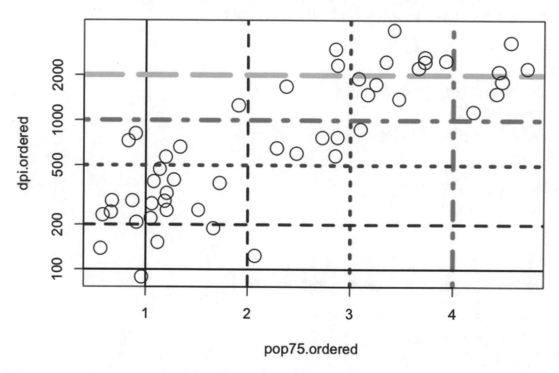

Figure 4-6. *Example of using col, lty, lwd, and equilogs in grid()*

Note that grid() was run using panel.first in plot(), so the grid was plotted before the points. As a result, the points overlie the grid. If the points were plotted first, the grid would overlie the points. Also, the line style, line width, and line color change as the values of x and y increase.

4.1.3.3 The clip() Function

The clip() function sets the clipping region – the region inside of which the ancillary functions plot. The function takes four arguments, x1, x2, y1, and y2, for the corners of the clipping region. The arguments are measured in the units on the x and y axes.

According to the help page for clip(), lines, rectangles, and polygons are handled internally, but the handling of text is done by the device on which the graphic is displayed, so may not behave as expected. The clipping region is reset when a new plot is done or when the argument xpd is changed.

In Listing 4-8, code for an example of using clip() is given.

Listing 4-8. Code for the example of using clip()

```
red = seq( 1, 50, 4.3 )[ -5 ]
plot(
  pop75.ordered, pop15.ordered,
  type="n",
  main="Example of using clip()"
)

clip(
  -0.5, 6, 19, 52
)

text(
  pop75.ordered[ red ], pop15.ordered[ red ],

  row.names(
    LifeCycleSavings
  )[ ord ] [ red ],
  cex=.7
)
```

In Figure 4-7, the code in Listing 4-8 is run.

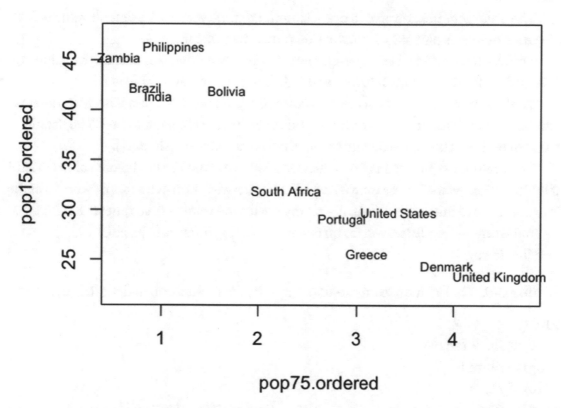

Figure 4-7. *Example of using clip()*

Note that the text has been allowed to print outside of the plotting region. Clipping can also be used inside the plotting region to set differing colors (see the example given on the help page for clip()).

4.1.3.4 The rug() Function

The rug() function plots a one-dimensional plot along a side of a plot. Lines are plotted – perpendicular to the side – where points occur, and all of the lines are the same height.

The arguments of rug() are x, for the data vector to be plotted; ticksize, for the length of the lines; side, for the side on which to plot the rug; lwd, for the width of the lines; col, for the color of the lines; quiet, for telling R whether to print warnings when data fall outside the range of the axis; and some of the arguments of axis() – for example, line and pos. This information is from the help page for rug().

The argument x takes a numeric vector of arbitrary length. There is no default value for x.

The argument ticksize takes a one-element numeric vector. The default value is 0.03. Negative tick sizes plot away from the side rather than into the plot.

The argument side takes a one-element integer vector that can take on the values 1, 2, 3, and 4 – for the bottom, left, top, and right sides. The default value is 1.

The arguments lwd and col are the standard arguments from par(). Both arguments can take multielement vectors as values, but only the first element is used. The default value of lwd equals 0.5; the default value of col is the value of fg in par().

The argument quiet can take on the value TRUE or FALSE. The default value is TRUE if the R option "warn" is less than 0 and FALSE otherwise. Run getOption("warn") at the R prompt to see the value of "warn" – on my device the value is 0, so quiet is FALSE.

In Listing 4-9, code is given for an example of using ticksize, side, col, lwd, and line in rug().

Listing 4-9. Code for an example of using x, ticksize, side, col, lwd, and line in rug()

```
plot(
  pop75.ordered,
  dpi.ordered,
  log="y",
  main="Example of x, ticksize, side, lwd, and col in rug()"
)

rug(
  pop75.ordered,
  ticksize = 0.03,
  side = 1,
  lwd=1,
  line=2.5,
  col=gray( 0.4 )
)

rug(
  dpi.ordered,
  ticksize = -0.04,
  side = 4,
```

```
    lwd=1,
    col=gray( 0.2 )
)
```

In Figure 4-8, the code in Listing 4-9 is run.

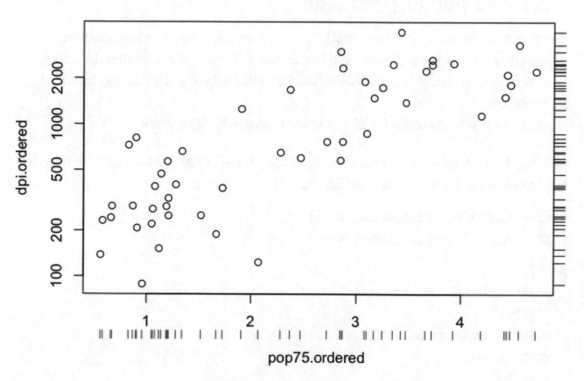

Example of x, ticksize, side, lwd, and col in rug()

Figure 4-8. *Example of x, ticksize, side, col, lwd, and line in rug()*

Note that the rug on side 1 is between the axis label and the axis tick mark labels. The argument line was set to 2.5, and the argument ticksize was positive. For side 4, ticksize was negative and line was not set.

4.2 Functions Defined at Points

In this section, we cover those ancillary functions in the stats and graphics packages that plot objects by point locations. The points(), text(), symbols(), image(), and rasterImage() functions are described.

4.2.1 The points() Function

The first function we look at is points(). The function takes the same arguments as the plotting arguments of plot.default() in Section 3.3. Some of the arguments are x, y, type, pch, col, bg, cex, and lwd. See Section 3.3 or the help page for points() for more information.

In Listing 4-10, the code for an example of using points() is given.

Listing 4-10. Code for an example of using points() to annotate the data with the income tercile: low, middle, and high terciles of income

```
tri1 = quantile( dpi.ordered, 0.33)
tri2 = quantile( dpi.ordered, 0.67)

plot(
  pop75.ordered, dpi.ordered,
  log="xy",
  main="Example of points()",
  font.main=1,
  type="n"
)

points(
  pop75.ordered, dpi.ordered,
  pch=ifelse(
    dpi.ordered<=tri2,
    ifelse(
      dpi.ordered<=tri1,
      "L",
      "M"
    ),
```

```
    "H"
  ),
  cex=0.7
)
```

In Figure 4-9, the code in Listing 4-10 is run.

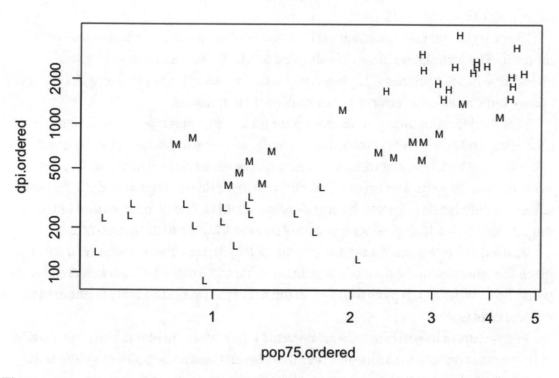

Figure 4-9. *An example of using points to annotate points in a plot with a letter indicating the tercile in which the y variable falls*

Note that using the values of L, M, and H allows the user to see the spread of values of the percentage of the population over 75 years of age by income tercile. The R function quantile() is used to find the terciles.

4.2.2 The text() Function

The text() function is similar to points() in that the function puts a character string at locations, but the character string can have more than one character in the string. The arguments to text() are x and y, for the locations of points; labels, for the strings to print at the points; adj, for adjusting the location of the labels in a circle around the point; pos, to place the labels at four locations around the point; offset, for the amount of offset to use with pos; vfont, for using the Hershey font families and weights for the labels; and the standard cex, col, and font.

The x argument has no default and is a vector of values that can be coerced to numeric. The y argument has a default value of NULL – that is, x becomes y and an index variable becomes x. If y is given, y is not necessarily the same length as x – y will cycle – but y must be a vector that can be coerced to numeric.

The labels argument is a character vector (or a vector that can be coerced to character) and contains the labels that are assigned to the index and x (or the x and y) locations. The labels argument is not necessarily the same length as x and cycles. According to the help page on text(), if labels is longer than x, then x (and y if y is used) will cycle until labels comes to the last element of labels. The default value of labels is seq_along(x$x), which gives a sequence of numbers from 1 to the length of x.

The adj argument takes a numeric vector of length one or two. A value of 0 tells R to place the label just to the right of the point. A value of 0.5 plots the label centered on the point. For a value of 1, R plots the label to the left of the point. The label is centered in the vertical direction.

For vectors of length two, the second value tells R where to plot the character string in the vertical direction; a value of 1 tells R to plot just below the point, 0.5 plots at the level of the point, and 0 plots just above the point.

For most devices, any values for adj will do, but not all devices will be able to plot text for values that fall outside of the interval zero to one. Negative values can be used on most devices.

For adj, the distance between the string and the point depends on the size of the string. The default value of adj is NULL – which centers the text in over the point in both the horizontal and the vertical directions.

The pos argument also positions the labels. The argument can take on the values 1, 2, 3, and 4 – for below, to the left, above, and to the right of the point. The offset argument is used with pos and gives the distance from the point that the label is plotted.

The default values of pos and offset are NULL and 0.5. If pos is set, the value of adj is ignored.

An argument in par() that affects string printing in text() (and text() only) is srt, for rotating the string. The argument takes a one-element numeric vector and rotates the string by the value of the argument, where the value is in degrees of rotation starting at 0 (parallel to the x axis). The default value of str is the value of string in par() – which, on my device, is 0.

Another argument in par() – that affects line height – is lheight. The argument increases or decreases the space between lines in strings with more than one line. According to the help page for par(), the value of lheight multiplies the value of cex to give a new line height. The default value of lheight is 1. The argument is only used in text() and the function strheight().

In Listing 4-11, code is given for an example of using adj, pos, offset, and srt.

Listing 4-11. The code for the example of using adj, pos, offset, and srt in text()

```
plot(
  pop75.ordered, pop15.ordered,
  main="Example of adj, pos, offset, srt in text()",
  font.main=1,
   xlim=c( 1, 1.8 ),
  ylim=c( 39, 45.5 ),
  col=grey( 0.4 )
)

# adj

text(
  pop75.ordered[16], pop15.ordered[16],
  labels="(1,0)",
  adj=c( 1, 0 ),
  cex=0.7
)
text(
  pop75.ordered[16], pop15.ordered[16],
  labels="(0,0)",
  adj=c( 0, 0 ),
```

```
  cex=0.7
)
text(
  pop75.ordered[16], pop15.ordered[16],
  labels="(0,1)",
  adj=c( 0, 1 ),
  cex=0.7
)
text(
  pop75.ordered[16], pop15.ordered[16],
  labels="(1,1)",
  adj=c( 1, 1 ),
  cex=0.7
)
text(
  pop75.ordered[17], pop15.ordered[17],
  labels="(1.5,-0.5)",
  adj=c( 1.5, -0.5 ),
  cex=0.7
)
text(
  pop75.ordered[17], pop15.ordered[17],
  labels="(-0.5,-0.5)",
  adj=c( -0.5, -0.5 ),
  cex=0.7
)
text(
  pop75.ordered[17], pop15.ordered[17],
  labels="(-0.5,1.5)",
  adj=c( -0.5, 1.5 ),
  cex=0.7
)
text(
  pop75.ordered[17], pop15.ordered[17],
  labels="(1.5,1.5)",
```

```
  adj=c( 1.5, 1.5 ),
  cex=0.7
)

# pos

text(
  pop75.ordered[22], pop15.ordered[22],
  labels="pos=1",
  pos=1,
  cex=0.7
)
text(
  pop75.ordered[22], pop15.ordered[22],
  labels="pos=2",
  pos=2,
  cex=0.7
)
text(
  pop75.ordered[22], pop15.ordered[22],
  labels="pos=3",
  pos=3,
  cex=0.7
)
text(
  pop75.ordered[22], pop15.ordered[22],
  labels="pos=4",
  pos=4,
  cex=0.7
)

# pos and offset

text(
  pop75.ordered[20], pop15.ordered[20],
  labels="pos=1 offset=1",
  pos=1,
```

```
  offset=1,
  cex=0.7
)
text(
  pop75.ordered[20], pop15.ordered[20],
  labels="pos=2 offset=1",
  pos=2,
  offset=1,
  cex=0.7
)
text(
  pop75.ordered[20], pop15.ordered[20],
  labels="pos=3 offset=1",
  pos=3,
  offset=1,
  cex=0.7
)
text(
  pop75.ordered[20], pop15.ordered[20],
  labels="pos=4 offset=1",
  pos=4,
  offset=1,
  cex=0.7
)

#  str

text(
  pop75.ordered[10], pop15.ordered[10],
  labels="srt=45",
  srt=45,
  cex=0.7
)
```

In Figure 4-10, the code in Listing 4-11 is run.

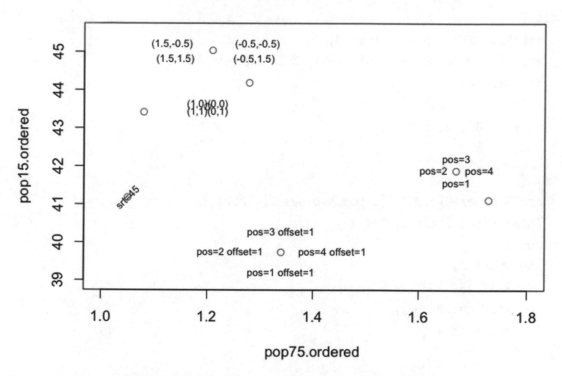

Figure 4-10. *Example of setting adj, pos, offset, and srt in text()*

The vfont argument allows text() to use the Hershey font families and weights. The argument takes a two-element character vector or the value NULL. The first element is the family of the font, and the second element is the weight of the font – for example, vfont=c("serif", "plain"). (The names of the font families and weights are listed on the first pdf of the pdf's generated by running demo("Hershey").) If vfont is not set, the font family and weight are those in par() if family and font are not specified in text(). The default value of vfont is NULL.

The argument cex sets the size of the characters and takes a positive numeric vector. In text(), R multiplies the value of cex in par() by the value of cex in text() to give the multiplier for the device default character size. The default value of cex in text() is 1.

The arguments col and font (and also family) take the same values as in plot() and, by default, take their values from par(). All of cex, col, and font can have multiple elements, and the values cycle.

In Listing 4-12, code is given for an example of using cex, col, font, and lheight in text().

Listing 4-12. The code to demonstrate using cex, col, font, and lheight in text()

```
plot(
  pop75.ordered, pop15.ordered,
  main="Example of cex, col, font, & lheight in text()",
  font.main=1,
  xlim=c( 1, 1.8 ),
  ylim=c( 39, 45.5 )
)

text(
  pop75.ordered[ 10:23 ], pop15.ordered[ 10:23 ],
  labels="pos=2\nlheight=1.2",
  pos=2,
  lheight=1.2,
  cex=3:17/15,
  col=grey( 6:19/25 ),
  font=c( 1, 3 )
)
```

In Figure 4-11, the code in Listing 4-12 is run.

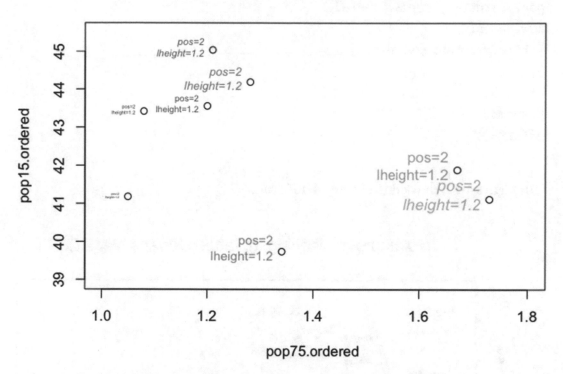

Figure 4-11. *An example of using cex, col, font, and lheight in text()*

In Listing 4-13, code is given for using pos to carefully place labels on points so that the labels do not overlic.

Listing 4-13. An example of carefully using pos to move text so that labels do not overlie

```
nms =c( 4, 3, 1, 4, 4, 1, 3, 4, 2, 1, 3, 1, 1, 4, 3, rep( 4, 35 ) )
plot(
  pop75.ordered, pop15.ordered,
  main="Example of cleaning up label overlaps in text()",
  font.main=1,
  cex=0.3,
  xlim=c( 0.5, 2.2 ),
  ylim=c( 39, 48.5 )
)
```

```
text(
  pop75.ordered, pop15.ordered,
  row.names(
    LifeCycleSavings[ ord, ]
  ),
  cex=0.6,
  pos=nms,
  offset=0.3
)
```

In Figure 4-12, the code in Listing 4-13 is run.

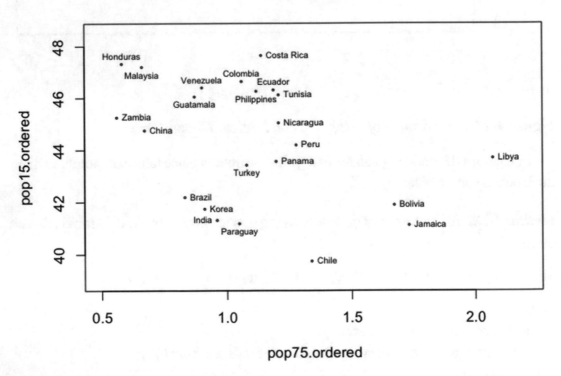

Figure 4-12. *Example of cleaning up labels that overlie using pos in text()*

Note that the vector nms contains 50 elements, each of which assigns a value to each of the 50 labels. Note, also, that not all of the data points are within the x and y limits of the plot and those not within the limits are not plotted.

4.2.3 The symbols() Function

The symbols() function plots shapes at specific points on a plot. The shapes that can be plotted are circles, squares, rectangles, stars, thermometers, and boxplots. Unlike text() and points(), the function symbols() is both a standalone function and a function that can be used as an ancillary function to plot(). In this chapter, we look at symbols() as an ancillary function.

The arguments to symbols() are x and y, for the locations of the points; circles, to plot circles; squares, to plot squares; rectangles, to plot rectangles; stars, to plot stars; thermometers, to plot one-level or two-level thermometers; boxplots, to plot boxplots; inches, for the size of the shape; add, to determine if the plot is standalone; fg, for colors like the outline of the shape; bg, for colors that fill in the background of a shape; and, if symbols is used as a standalone function, many of the same arguments used in plot(). The arguments x and y are either two numeric vectors that are the same length or x set equal to a numeric vector and y set equal to NULL. There is no default value for x, and the default value for y is NULL.

The circles argument takes a numeric vector of length equal to the length of x. The radii of the plotted circles are then scaled by the values of the argument. The actual size depends on the value of the argument inches.

The squares argument also takes a numeric vector of length equal to the length of x. The lengths of the sides of the squares that are plotted are scaled by the values of the argument. Again, the actual sizes depend on the value of the argument inches.

The rectangles argument takes a numeric matrix with the number of rows equal to the length of x and with two columns. The first column gives the widths of the rectangles, and the second column gives the heights of the rectangles – where the actual sizes depend on the value of inches.

The stars argument takes a numeric matrix with the number of rows equal to the length of x and with at least three columns. The plot of a star connects locations – with one location for each column in the matrix. The locations are at distances – from the x-y point. The actual distance depends on the value of inches. For values set to NA, the distance from the point is set to zero – which can be used to plot spikes at various distances.

The thermometers argument takes a numeric matrix with the number of rows equal to the length of x and with three or four columns. The first column gives the widths of the thermometers. The second column gives the heights. The third (and fourth if used) column(s) should have values between 0 and 1, inclusive. The function puts a line (or two lines if a fourth column is used) proportionally up the thermometer based on the proportions in the third (and fourth) column(s). The actual sizes of the thermometers depend on the value of inches.

The boxplots argument takes a numeric matrix with the number of rows equal to the length of x and with five columns. The first column gives the width of the box. The second column gives the height of the box. The third and fourth columns give the lengths of the lower and upper whiskers, respectively. The fifth column gives the proportional distance up the box that the median is plotted and should be between 0 and 1, inclusive. The actual sizes of the boxplots depend on the value of inches.

The circles, squares, rectangles, stars, thermometers, and boxplots arguments do not have default values. If an element of one of the arguments is NA, then the point is not plotted – except for stars, where the point value is set to zero.

The inches argument is either a logical vector or a numeric vector – both of arbitrary length. Only the first value is used. If set equal to TRUE or numeric, the reference size is one inch.

If set equal to FALSE, the reference size is one unit on one or both of the axes. According to the help page for symbols(), for circles, squares, and stars, a unit on the x axis is used. For rectangles, the width uses a unit of the x axis, and the height uses a unit of the y axis. For thermometers, a unit of the y axis is used. For boxplots, the width uses a unit of the x axis, and the height and whiskers use a unit of the y axis. The default value is TRUE.

The size of the plotted shape is proportional to the reference size. For circles, the reference size times the values in the third column of the argument gives the lengths of the radii of the circles. For squares, rectangles, and stars, the size is referenced to the largest dimension of the shape.

The add argument can be a logical vector of arbitrary length, but if longer than one element, a warning is given. Only the first element is used. The argument, if set equal to FALSE, tells symbols() to plot a new plot. If set equal to TRUE, symbols() adds to the existing plot. The default value is FALSE. Here, we only consider the case where add equals TRUE.

The last two arguments of interest are fg and bg. The arguments fg and bg set colors and can take any argument that the argument col in par() can take (see Section 3.4.1). For circles, squares, rectangles, and stars, the fg argument sets the outline color for the shape, and bg sets the fill color.

For thermometers, if there are three columns in the argument, then the color of fg fills in the area below the level line in the thermometer and the outline of the shape, while the color of bg fills in the rest of the shape. The color of the two handles of the thermometers is set by the argument col. For thermometers with four columns, fg sets the color for the outline and the area between the two level lines, and bg sets the color for the rest of the area.

For boxplots, the color of the outline is set by fg and the color of the area inside the box is set by bg, while the color of the whiskers and median is set by col.

Both fg and bg can be multielement vectors and both cycle. The argument col can also be multielement, but only the first element is used. The default value for fg is the value of col in par() and for bg is NA – which gives a transparent background.

In Listing 4-14, code for an example of using symbol() is given.

Listing 4-14. Code for an example of using symbols() to plot circles, squares, rectangles, stars, thermometers, and boxplots

```
plot(
  pop75.ordered, pop15.ordered,
  main="Example of circles, squares, rectangles,\nstars,  thermometers, and
  boxplots in symbols()",
  type="n"
)

symbols(
  pop75.ordered[ 1:8 ], pop15.ordered[ 1:8 ],
  circles=1:8/8,
  inches=0.35,
  fg=grey( 1:8/20 ),
  bg=grey( 10:18/20 ),
  add=TRUE
)

symbols(
  pop75.ordered[ 9:16 ], pop15.ordered[ 9:16 ],
  squares=1:8/8,
  inches=0.35,
  fg=grey( 1:8/20 ),
```

```
  add=TRUE
)

symbols(
  pop75.ordered[ 17:24 ], pop15.ordered[ 17:24 ],
  rectangles=cbind( 1:8/8, 5:12/8 ),
  inches=0.35,
  fg=grey( 1:8/20 ),
  add=TRUE
)

symbols(
  pop75.ordered[ 25:32 ], pop15.ordered[ 25:32 ],
  stars=cbind( 1:8/8, 5:12/8, 1:8/8, 5:12/8 ),
  inches=0.35,
  fg=grey( 1:8/20 ),
  add=TRUE
)

symbols(
  pop75.ordered[ 33:40 ], pop15.ordered[ 33:40 ],
  thermometers=cbind( 1:8/8, 5:12/8, 1:8/20 ),
  inches=0.35,
  fg=grey( 0.5 ),
  add=TRUE
)

symbols(
  pop75.ordered[ 33:40 ], pop15.ordered[ 33:40 ],
  thermometers=cbind(
    1:8/8,
    5:12/8,
    1:8/20,
    1:8/20 + 8:1/20
  ),
  inches=0.35,
  fg=grey( 0.75 ),
```

```
    add=TRUE
)

symbols(
  pop75.ordered[ 41:50 ], pop15.ordered[ 41:50 ],
  boxplots=cbind(
    1:10/20,
    5:14/20,
    1:10/20,
    10:1/20,
    5:14/15
  ),
  inches=0.35,
  fg=grey( 0.75 ),
  add=TRUE
)
```

In Figure 4-13, the code in Listing 4-14 is run.

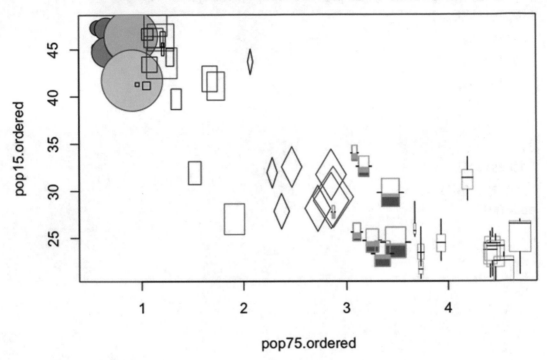

Figure 4-13. *Example of creating circles, squares, rectangles, stars, thermometers, and boxplots using symbols()*

Note that the circles are much larger than the squares, since the radius is one half of the diameter of a circle, while a square has same the length on all sides. Also, two calls to symbols were necessary to plot thermometers with two different colors below the levels.

4.2.4 The image() and rasterImage() Functions

The image() and rasterImage() functions plot a matrix of numbers in a grid, where each square in the grid takes on a color that depends on the value of the number. The function image() allows the user to set the coordinates of each row and column in the grid. The function rasterImage() sets the corner points and allows the image to be rotated.

4.2.4.1 The image() Function

The image() function takes 15 specified arguments and many of the arguments of par(). Like symbols(), image() can be run as a standalone function or as an ancillary function. Only 9 of the 15 arguments apply to image() as an ancillary function.

The first six arguments are x, for the x coordinates of the vertical grid lines; y, for the y coordinates of the horizontal grid lines; z (a matrix), for the grid points to plot; zlim, for upper and lower limits on the values of z that are to be plotted; and xlim and ylim, the standard arguments from plot() and used only if image() is run as a standalone function.

The x argument is either an ordered numeric vector or a list containing x, y, and optionally z. The length of x – or x[[1]] – is either the number of rows in z (for placing x at the x axis midpoint of the grid square) or the number of rows in z plus one (for placing x at the x axis boundary of the grid square.) Similarly, y – or x[[2]] – is an ordered numeric vector; and the length of y, or x[[2]], is the number of columns in z or the number of columns in z plus one. The x and y arguments do not have default values.

If x (or y) is on a logarithmic scale, the number of rows (or columns) plus one is the correct choice, since putting the grid line at the midpoint of the square does not make sense for a logarithmic scale. Also, the grid squares are open on the left and bottom and closed on the right and top – except for the first row and first column, which are closed on both the left and right and both the bottom and top, respectively.

The z – or x[[3]] – argument is a numeric or logical matrix that contains values used to create a matrix of color strings, with one – not usually unique – color for each grid square. Values of NA are acceptable for z and plot as transparent if the image is being added to an existing plot. The z argument does not have a default value.

The zlim argument is a two-element numeric vector giving the minimum and maximum values of z for which the points in z are actually plotted. As with missing points, the points not plotted are transparent. The default values of zlim are the minimum and maximum values of z.

The last nine arguments are col, for the color scale to use; add, for whether to create a standalone plot; the standard xaxs, yaxs, xlab, and ylab from plot() and only used with a standalone plot; breaks, for break points for the values of z, used for the color assignments; oldstyle, for the method of assigning break points; and useRaster, for the method of assigning color to the grid squares.

The col argument is a vector of standard color arguments (see Section 3.4.1) and sets the color gradient – each color in the vector will have a range of z values assigned to the color. Using a function to generate the color arguments, such as grey.colors(), makes the task of selecting colors easy. For example, assigning grey(4, rev=TRUE) to col gives a four-color gray scale that goes from light to dark as the value of z increases. The number of colors to include in the gradient depends on how fine the grid is and how much detail to include in the image. The default value of col is hcl.colors(12, "YlOrRd", rev = TRUE).

The add argument is a logical vector which can have more than one element, but only the first element is used and a warning is printed if the argument has more than one element. The default value of add is FALSE – to plot a standalone plot. In this chapter, we only cover the case of add equal to TRUE – to add to an existing plot.

The breaks argument is a numeric vector of length equal to the number of colors assigned by col plus one. The vector must be sorted in increasing order; or, according to the help page for image(), the vector is sorted by image() and a warning is given. The color of a grid square then depends on in which interval the z value falls. There is no default value for breaks. For axes that have a log scale, breaks must be set.

The oldstyle argument is a vector that can be coerced to logical and can have more than one element. If the argument has more than one element, only the first element is used, and a warning is given.

Let n be the number of colors assigned by col. If oldstyle is set to TRUE, the breaks are c(-0.5, 0.5, 1.5, ..., n+0.5)/n * (zlim[2] – zlim[1]) + zlim[1], which sets the middle of the first and last intervals to the z limits. If oldstyle is set to FALSE, the breaks are c (0, 1, 2, ..., n)/n * (zlim[2] – zlim[1]) + zlim[1], which sets the beginning of the first interval and the end of the last interval to the z limits.

If breaks is used, zlim is ignored. If breaks is not used, according to the help page for image(), the range of values within the zlim limits are divided into equidistant intervals. If the range is based on the midpoints of the intervals, colors at the edge of an interval can be outside the zlim limits and still be plotted.

The last argument of interest, useRaster, is a logical vector (or a vector that can be coerced to logical) that can be any length, but only the first element is used and a warning is given if there is more than one element. If set to TRUE, image() creates and plots a raster image. According to the help page for image(), the grid squares must be equally spaced if useRaster is to be set to TRUE. If set to FALSE, each grid square is plotted with a given color based on a polygon.

Raster images are more efficient in memory. From the help page for image(), if useRaster is FALSE, a raster image will still be plotted if getOption("preferRaster") is TRUE and dev.capablities("rasterImage") is "yes" or is "non-missing" when there are no NAs in z. On my device, the option preferRaster is NULL, and the device capability argument rasterImage is "yes" – so a raster image is not created when useRaster is FALSE. See the help page for image() for more information.

In Listing 4-15, code is given for an example of using zlim, col, add, oldstyle, and useRaster in image().

Listing 4-15. Code for the example of using zlim, col, add, oldstyle, and useRaster in image()

```
plot(
  pop75.ordered, pop15.ordered,
  main="Examples of col, add, zlim,\noldstlye, and useRaster in image()",
  xlim=c( 0.4, 5.1 ),
  type="n"
)

text(
  x=pop75.ordered[ c( 10, 25, 35, 47 ) ],
  y=34,
  labels=c(
    "oldstyle=FALSE\nzlim=c( 100, 170 )\ncolors=2\nmin( z )=94\nmax( z )=195",
    "oldstyle=TRUE\ncolors=2",
    "oldstyle=FALSE\nuseRaster=TRUE\ncolors=4",
    "oldstyle=TRUE\nuseRaster=TRUE\ncolors=4"
  ),
  cex=0.8
)

image(
  x=seq( -0.35, 0.35, length.out=87 ) +
    pop75.ordered[ 10 ],
  y=seq( -0.35, 0.35, length.out=61 ) * 9.64 * 61/87 +
    pop15.ordered[ 10 ],
  z=volcano,
  zlim=c( 100, 170 ),
  col=gray.colors( 2, rev=TRUE ),
  add=TRUE
)
```

```
image(
  x=seq( -0.35, 0.35, length.out=87 ) +
    pop75.ordered[ 25 ],
  y=seq( -0.35, 0.35, length.out=61 ) * 9.64 * 61/87 +
    pop15.ordered[ 25 ],
  z=volcano,
  col=gray.colors( 2, rev=TRUE ),
  useRaster=TRUE,
  add=TRUE
)

image(
  x=seq( -0.35, 0.35, length.out=87 ) +
    pop75.ordered[ 35 ],
  y=seq( -0.35, 0.35, length.out=61 ) * 9.64 * 61/87 +
    pop15.ordered[ 35 ],
  z=volcano,
  col=gray.colors( 4, rev=TRUE),
  add=TRUE
)

image(
  x=seq( -0.35, 0.35, length.out=87 ) +
    pop75.ordered[ 47 ],
  y=seq( -0.35, 0.35, length.out=61 ) * 9.64 * 61/87 +
    pop15.ordered[ 47 ],
  z=volcano,
  col=gray.colors( 4, rev=TRUE ),
  useRaster=TRUE,
  add=TRUE
)
```

Note that the dataset volcano is a dataset in the datasets package and so, for most users, is available by default. The dataset has 87 rows and 61 columns. According to the help page on volcano

Maunga Whau (Mt Eden) is one of about 50 volcanos in the Auckland vol-canic field. This data set gives topographic information for Maunga Whau on a 10m by 10m grid.

—Help page for volcano in R

And, from the help page, the dataset is

A matrix with 87 rows and 61 columns, rows corresponding to grid lines running east to west and columns to grid lines running south to north.

—Help page for volcano in R

Also note how the locations of the images are set up to give a uniform and scaled image. First, the image is set up with the same width and height and centered on zero in both the x and y directions.

However, the function image() scales the image to the units on the axes. So the y scale is multiplied by 9.64 – which is (par("cxy")[2]/par("cin")[2]))/(par("cxy") [1]/par("cin")[1])). The formula is the number of units of y in a character divided by the height of a character in inches with the result divided by the number units of x in a character divided by the width of a character in inches – that is, the number of units per inch on the y axis is divided by the number of units per inch on the x axis. Then 9.64 is multiplied by the number of rows in z divided by the number of columns in z, which gives the image the same scale as the matrix. Finally, the location for the image is added to the scaled image.

In Figure 4-14, the code in Listing 4-15 is run.

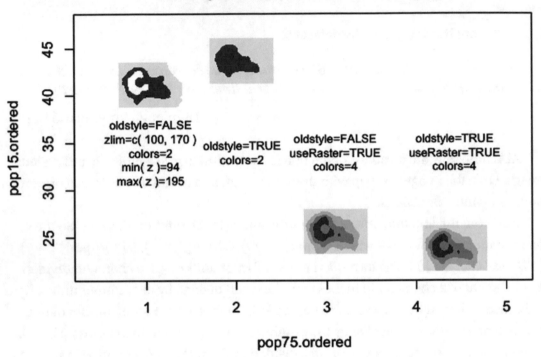

Figure 4-14. *An example of using zlim, col, add, oldstyle, and useRaster in image()*

Note, in the first image, high and low values of z are plotted as white (which is the default for transparent on my machine), since zlim is narrower than the range of z. In the first two images, only two colors are used. In the third and fourth images, four colors are used. Also, the old style images plot a little narrower for large values of z than the current style ones.

4.2.4.2 The rasterImage() Function

The rasterImage() function plots files of the raster class to create images. The function takes seven arguments plus many of the arguments in par(). The first argument of rasterImage is image, for an object that can be coerced to the raster class; the second, third, fourth, and fifth arguments are xleft, ybottom, xright, and ytop, for the location of the image; the sixth argument is angle, for the angle with which to rotate the image; and the seventh argument is interpolate, for whether to do linear interpolation on the image.

The argument image takes any object that can be coerced to class raster. The raster class is a class of objects that can be vectors, matrices, or arrays and that contain strings of color values. The function rasterImage() attempts to convert the value of image to an object of class raster by using as.raster() (which uses rgb() to do the conversion). For more information on converting to the raster class, go to the help page of as.raster().

The object must be a vector of class logical, numeric, character, or raw or of class matrix or array and of mode logical, numeric, character, or raw. If image is a vector, image() will plot horizontal lines at the color levels of the elements to fill out the dimensions of the image. There is no default value for image.

The arguments xleft and xright are the left and right coordinates on the x axis of the location for the image. The arguments ybottom and ytop are the lower and upper coordinates on the y axis of the location for the image. All four of the arguments can take a numeric vector of any length, and the elements cycle – for repeated plotting of the image. The values must be within the x and y limits of the plot. There are no default values for xleft, xright, ybottom, and ytop.

The argument angle tells image() to rotate the image around the bottom-left corner of the image. The angle of rotation is the angle specified by the argument – which is measured in degrees. The rotation is counterclockwise and starts parallel to the x axis. The default value is 0 – or parallel to the x axis.

The argument interpolate is a logical vector (or a vector that can be coerced to logical) of any length. If more than one copy of the image is plotted, the values of interpolate cycle. The default value of interpolate is TRUE.

According to the help page for rasterImage(), not all devices will plot raster images. Also, images may not scale if the plot is resized, depending on the device.

In Listing 4-16, code is given for an example of using rasterImage().

Listing 4-16. Code for the examples of using image, the location arguments, angle, and interpolate in rasterImage()

```
plot(
  pop75.ordered, pop15.ordered,
  main="Examples of image, the location arguments,\nangle, and interpolate
  in rasterImage()",
  type="n"
)
```

```
text(
  c( 0.75, 4.3, 1.4, 2.95, 4.35, 2.9 ),
  c( 46.5,  26,  24,    24,    30,  45 ),
  labels=c(
    "VECTORS",
    "MATRICES",
    "interpolate=FALSE\nangle=0",
    "interpolate=FALSE\nangle=0",
    "interpolate=TRUE\nangle=60",
    "interpolate=TRUE\nangle=0"
  ),
  cex=0.8
)

rasterImage(
  grey(
    1-( t( volcano )[ 61:1,]/max( volcano ) )
  ) ,
  xleft=-0.6 +
    pop75.ordered[ 20:22 ],
  ybottom=-0.6*10.94*61/87 +
    pop15.ordered[ 20:22 ],
  xright=0.6 +
    pop75.ordered[ 20:22 ],
  ytop=0.6*10.94*61/87 +
    pop15.ordered[ 20:22 ],
  interpolate=c( 0, 0, 1, 1 )
)

rasterImage(
  matrix(
    grey(
      1-( t( volcano )[ 61:1,]/max( volcano ) )
    ),
    nrow=61
  ) ,
```

```
xleft=-0.6 +
  pop75.ordered[ c( 30, 45 ) ],
ybottom=-0.6*10.94*61/87 +
  pop15.ordered[ c( 30, 45 ) ],
xright=0.6 +
  pop75.ordered[ c( 30, 45 ) ],
ytop=0.6*10.94*61/87 +
  pop15.ordered[ c( 30, 45 ) ],
angle =c( 0, 60),
interpolate=c( 0, 1, 1, 1 )
)
```

Note that volcano is transposed so that the columns become the rows and the rows become the columns. Also, rasterImage() starts plotting by putting the top row in the top position and so forth, so the rows of the transposed matrix are reversed.

The function grey() creates a vector, so in the second call to rasterImage(), a call to matrix() is done to recreate a matrix – of character color codes.

In Figure 4-15, the code in Listing 4-16 is run.

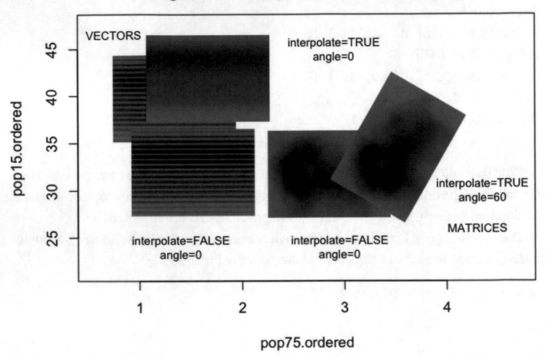

Figure 4-15. *Examples of setting image, the location arguments, angle, and interpolate in rasterImage()*

Note that, for the three plots of vectors, the image that used interpolation is much smoother than the images that did not. For the two plots of matrices, there is not a strong difference. Also, note that the elements of the argument to grey() are all between 0 and 1, inclusive, and are small for large values of volcano and large for small values of volcano. A lighter plot can be created by subtracting a constant less than 94 from volcano.

4.3 Functions That Use Lines

In this section, we cover ancillary functions that are based on lines. The functions are lines(), abline(), curve(), segments(), arrows(), rect(), polygon(), polypath(), and contour().

4.3.1 The lines() and abline() Functions

The lines() function is usually used to plot line plots. From the help page for lines(), the specified arguments are x, y, and type. Most arguments of par() that are not specified can be set too.

The arguments x and y are the standard arguments of plot.default(). If both are given, then both must be of the same length. There is no default value for x. The default value for y is NULL.

The argument type gives the type of line to be plotted. For a description of the types, see Section 3.3.1. The default value for type in lines() is "l" – that is, the points given by x and y are connected by lines in the order that the points appear in the vectors x and y.

The abline() function plots a straight line on a plot. The function takes seven specified arguments and some unspecified arguments of par(). Six of the arguments give the same information to abline() in different forms. The seventh argument is used with log scales.

The first two arguments are a and b, for the intercept and coefficient of the line. The arguments are one-element numeric vectors.

The third and fourth arguments are h and v, for plotting horizontal lines at the y values given by h and vertical lines at the x values given by v. The arguments are numeric vectors of arbitrary length.

The fifth argument, coef, is a two-element numeric vector containing the intercept and slope. (This vector can also be assigned to a with the same result as the assignation to coef.)

The sixth argument is reg. Any object that can be used as an argument to the function coef() can be assigned to reg. For example, lm(pop15.ordered ~ pop75. ordered) can be used as a value for reg. If the value of reg only contains one element (a regression with no intercept), then the intercept is set to zero, and the slope is set to the value of the element. If the value of reg contains more than two elements (a regression with multiple regressors), the intercept and first regression coefficient are used.

The arguments a, b, h, v, coef, and reg are NULL by default. The function detects the class of the first argument and can make a decision about whether the argument is a or coef, a without b, or reg and creates the line based on the decision. The arguments h and v must be specified by name or be in the correct place by order.

The argument untf takes a logical vector with one element. The argument is used when at least one of the scales on the axes is a log scale. The regression line must be fit on untransformed data, but if the ab line is plotted on a plot with log scales, then the line can be plotted to take the transformation into account by setting untf to TRUE. The default value is FALSE.

In Listing 4-17, the code for an example of lines() and abline() is given.

Listing 4-17. Code for an example of lines() and a, b, h, v, and untf in abline()

```
# the regression
reg.log = glm(
  dpi.ordered ~ pop75.ordered
)

coef( reg.log )
  (Intercept) pop75.ordered
    -278.5465        604.1452

# the plots
plot(
  pop75.ordered, dpi.ordered,
  type="n",
  main="Example of lines() and\na, b, h, and v in abline()"
)

lines(
  pop75.ordered, dpi.ordered,
  type="b",
  col=grey( 0.65 ),
  cex=0.4
)

abline(
  -279,
  604,
  h=c( 1000, 2000, 3000 ),
  v=c( 1, 2, 3, 4 )
)

plot(
  pop75.ordered, dpi.ordered,
  log="y",
  type="n",
```

```
  main="Example of untf in abline()"
)

lines(
  pop75.ordered, dpi.ordered,
  type="b",
  col=grey( 0.65 ),
  cex=0.4
)

abline(
  reg.log,
  h=c( 1000, 2000, 3000 ),
  v=c( 1, 2, 3, 4 ),
  untf=TRUE
)
```

In Figure 4-16, the code in Listing 4-17 is run.

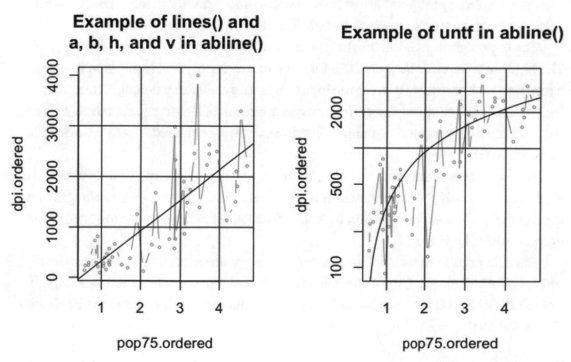

Figure 4-16. *Example of lines() and a, b, h, v, and untf in abline()*

Note that both plots are plots of the same data and the same line. The difference is that the second plot has a log scale on the y axis.

4.3.2 The curve() Function

The curve() function plots an object of class function or a mathematical expression – for example, sin() or x + 3 – against an input variable. The function curve() can be either a standalone function or an ancillary function. In this chapter, only the ancillary form of the function is covered.

The function curve() takes 11 specified arguments plus many unspecified arguments of par(). The first argument is expr, for the expression to be plotted. The second argument is from, for the first value of the variable to be input. The third argument is to, for the last value of the variable to be input. The fourth argument is n, for the number of points at which to evaluate the expression. The values of the input variable are evenly spaced between from and to.

The fifth argument is add, to indicate if the plot is standalone or ancillary. The sixth argument is type, for the type of line. The seventh argument is xname, for the name of the variable to be input. The eighth through tenth arguments are the standard xlab, ylab, and log from plot() and are only used when the plot is standalone. The eleventh argument is xlim, for the range of the variable to be input.

The expr argument is the function or mathematical expression to be plotted. The argument requires the name of a function or a mathematical expression that is a function of the variable used as the input – which is called x by default. The named function or mathematical expression must give a result of length equal to the length of the variable that is input. The named function can be user created. There is no default value for expr.

The next three arguments are from, to, and n – all of which take numeric vectors. In all three cases, only the first element is used. For n, a warning is given if the length of n is greater than 1. Not so for from and to. The default values of from and to are NULL. The default value of n is 101.

The add argument takes a logical vector of length one, which can take on a value of TRUE, FALSE, or NA. (Any other value for add, including multielement vectors, will default to FALSE.) Only the value of TRUE – for ancillary plot – is covered in this chapter. The default value is FALSE.

The type argument is the standard argument from plot() (see Section 3.3.1). The default value for type in curve() is "l" – for a line plot.

The xname argument takes a one-element character vector. The default value of xname is "x".

The xlim argument takes a two-element numeric vector. The two values give the range over which the input variable takes values. If add equals TRUE, the values of xlim are not necessarily equal to the limits of the x axis. By default, xlim equals NULL.

If from and to are specified, xlim defaults to c(from, to). If from and/or to is NULL, then from and/or to defaults to the respective element(s) of xlim – if xlim is not NULL. If from, to, and xlim are all NULL and add equals TRUE, the limits of the input variable are taken from the limits of the x axis.

In Listing 4-18, code for some examples of curve() is given.

Listing 4-18. Code for the examples of using expr, from, to, n, xname, xlim, add, and lty in curve()

```
plot(
  pop75.ordered, pop15.ordered,
  main="Examples of using expr,\nfrom, to, n, xname, xlim, add, & lty in
curve()"
)

curve(
  49.86 - 6.44*x,
  add=TRUE
)

curve(
  49.86 - 6.44*ex + 5*sin( ex/2.5*pi ),
  xname="ex",
  add=TRUE,
  lty="dotted"
)

curve(
  35*x/x,
  from=1.5,
  to=3.5, n=2,
```

```
  add=TRUE,
  lty="longdash"
)

curve(
  49.86 - 6.44*x + 5*cos( x/2.5*pi ),
  xlim=c( 1, 4 ),
  add=TRUE,
  lty="dashed"
)
```

In Figure 4-17, the code is run.

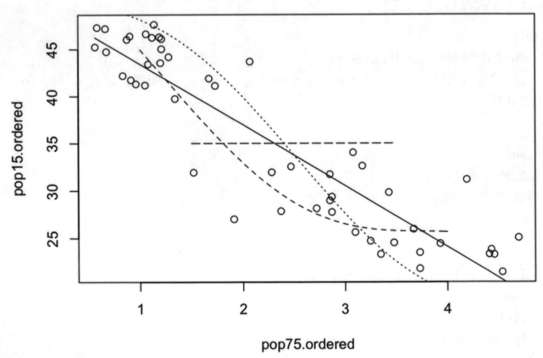

Figure 4-17. *Examples of using expr, from, to, n, xlim, xname, and add in curve()*

In the first (solid line) and second (dotted line) calls to curve() in Figure 4-17, the full range of x in the data is used for the plotted curve. In the third call (long dashed line), the arguments from and to are used to set the limits on x to 1.5 and 3.5. In the fourth call (dashed line), xlim is used to set the limits to 1 and 4. The third call shows one way to plot a horizontal line.

4.3.3 The segments() and arrows() Functions

The segments() function plots line segments, and the arrows() function plots line segments with arrowheads. Both are useful for annotating a plot. An example is given that applies both functions.

4.3.3.1 The segments() Function

The segments() function plots line segments. The function takes seven specified arguments and some unspecified arguments of par(). The first four arguments are x0, y0, x1, and y1, for the x and y endpoints of the segments. The last three specified arguments are the standard col, lty, and lwd from par() (see Sections 3.4.1, 3.3.2, and 3.4.4).

The x0, y0, x1, and y1 arguments take numeric vectors. The vectors are not necessarily the same length and cycle to fill out to the length of the vector with the longest length. The x0 and y0 arguments have no default values; the default values of x1 and y1 are x0 and y0, respectively.

The col, lty, and lwd arguments are vectors, are not necessarily the same length, and all cycle out to the length of the longest vector of x0, y0, x1, and y1. The default values of col, lty, and lwd are the values of the arguments in par().

4.3.3.2 The arrows() Function

The arrows() function is the same as segments, except that an arrowhead is drawn at one or both ends of the segment. The function also has arguments to style the arrowhead. The function takes ten specified arguments and some unspecified arguments of par().

The first four arguments are x0, y0, x1, and y1, which behave the same as with segments(). The fifth argument is length, for the length of the arms of the arrow. The sixth argument is angle, for the angle between the arms and the shaft of the arrow. The seventh argument is code, for where and how many arrowheads to plot. The eighth, ninth, and tenth arguments are col, lty, and lwd – which behave the same as in segments().

The length and angle arguments take numeric vectors of arbitrary lengths; but, for both, only the first element is used. The argument length is measured in inches, and the argument angle is measured in degrees. The default value of length is 0.25, and the default value of angle is 30.

The code argument takes an integer vector of arbitrary length, but only the first element is used. The values that the elements of the vector can take on are 1, 2, and 3. If code equals 1, the arrowhead is drawn at the end where the arrow starts; if 2, at the end where the arrow ends; if 3, at both ends. The default value is 2.

4.3.3.3 An Example of Using segments() and arrows()

In Listing 4-19, code is given for an example of using x0, y0, x1, y1, from, to, n, xname, add, and xlim in segments() and x0, y0, x1, y1, length, angle, and code in arrows().

Listing 4-19. Code for the example of using x0, y0, x1, and y1 in segments() and x0, y0, x1, y1, length, angle, and code in arrows()

```
plot(
  pop75.ordered, pop15.ordered,
  type="n",
  main="Example of segments() and arrows()"
)

text(
  pop75.ordered, pop15.ordered
)

text(
  c( 0.9, 1, 2.65, 4, 4.4 ),
  c( 31, 23, 47.3, 46, 36 ),
  paste( "segment", c(1:2, 4:6 ) ) )
)

segments(
  x0=pop75.ordered[ c( 1, 21, 24, 14, 25, 45 ) ],
  y0=pop15.ordered[ c( 1, 21, 24, 14, 25, 45 ) ] +
```

```
    rep( c( -2, 2 ), each=3 ),
  x1=pop75.ordered[ c( 21, 24, 42, 25, 45, 50 ) ],
  y1=pop15.ordered[ c( 21, 24, 42, 25, 45, 50) ] +
    rep( c( -2, 2 ), each=3 )
)

arrows(
  x0=c(  0.9,    4 ),
  y0=c( 33, 45 ),
  x1=c( 1.05, 3.2 ),
  y1=c( 36, 39 ),
  length=0.2,
  angle=20,
  code=2
)

arrows(
  x0=c( 2.15, 2 ),
  y0=c( 23.5, 46 ),
  x1=c( 1.4, 2.3 ),
  y1=c( 23, 47 ),
  length=0.1,
  angle=10,
  code=1
)

arrows(
  4.6,
  35,
  4.6,
  28.6,
  code=3
)
```

In Figure 4-18, the code in Listing 4-19 is run.

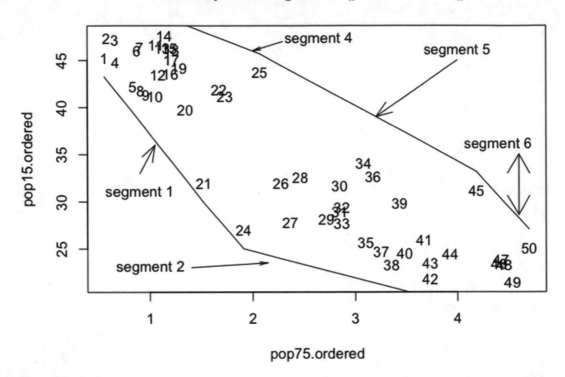

Figure 4-18. *Example of using x0, y0, x1, and y1 in segments() and x0, y0, x1, y1, length, angle, and code in arrows()*

Note that segment 3 is off the plot, so the segment was not included. Also, a call to text(), when just the coordinates of the locations are supplied, uses the index values of the x and y variables as the labels.

4.3.4 Functions That Plot Lines That Close on Themselves: rect(), polygon(), and polypath()

Lines that close on themselves are sometimes useful. This section covers the functions rect(), polypath(), and polygon(). The rect() function plots rectangles, and the polygon () and polypath() functions plot polygons. An example is given that applies the three functions.

4.3.4.1 The rect() Function

The rect() function plots rectangles based on the four corner points of the rectangle. The function takes ten specified arguments and some unspecified arguments of par(). The first four arguments are xleft, ybottom, xright, and ytop – for the locations of the four corners of the rectangles. The fifth and sixth arguments are density and angle – used for filling the rectangle with angled lines. Here, density is the number of lines per inch, and angle is the angle of the line from the horizontal.

The seventh argument is col – for the color of the angled lines or for a solid fill color, depending on the value of density. The eighth argument is border – for the color of the border if a border is plotted or to exclude a border. The ninth and tenth arguments are the standard lty and lwd from plot().

The first four arguments take numeric vectors of arbitrary length. The elements will cycle out to a length equal to the length of the longest of the vectors. If the length of a vector does not divide evenly into the length of the longest vector, then a warning is given, but the rectangles still plot. One rectangle is plotted for every element in the longest vector. However, if a value in a vector is NA, then the rectangle(s) associated with that element is not plotted. The NA values cycle like any of the other values. The location arguments do not have default values.

The density and angle arguments take numeric vectors of arbitrary length. The elements cycle out to the length of the longest of the location vectors. If an element of density is positive, then the number gives the number of lines per inch within the rectangle. Lines are plotted and, behind the plotted lines, the rectangle is transparent.

If density is 0, no lines are plotted, the rectangle is not filled with a color, and the rectangle is transparent. If NULL, the result depends on the value of col. For col set to a color, the color fills the rectangle; otherwise, the result is the same as setting density to 0. If density is negative or NA, the rectangle is filled with color. The default value of density is NULL.

The angle argument gives the angle from the horizontal at which the lines plot, in degrees. If angle equals NULL, no lines are plotted, and the rectangle is transparent. The default value of angle is 45.

The col argument is the standard argument from plot() (see Section 3.4.1 for the kinds of values that can be used). In rect(), col takes a vector of arbitrary length, which cycles out to the length of the longest vector of the location arguments.

If col takes a valid value other than NA or NULL and density equals a negative number, NA, or NULL, then the rectangle is filled with the color given by the value of col.

If col takes a valid value other than an NA or NULL and density takes a positive number, then col gives the color of the lines in the rectangle. If col equals NA or NULL, the rectangle is not filled with color; however, lines are plotted if density is a positive number (with the color set by the value of fg in par()). The default value of col is NA.

Colors in R can have levels of transparency from opaque to totally transparent (see Section 3.4.1). In rect(), if color does not equal NA or NULL, the fill color of a rectangle has the transparency given by the value of the col. With colors that are opaque and rectangles that overlap, the color of the last plotted rectangle covers any previous colors or lines.

The border argument takes a numeric, character, or logical vector of arbitrary length. The vector cycles to the length of the longest location vector. The argument sets the color of the border of the rectangle. The numeric and character vectors take the same kinds of values that col does. The logical vectors can take on the value TRUE or FALSE.

A value of NULL or TRUE tells rect() to use the color of the lines for the border if lines are drawn. Otherwise, the value of border is the value of fg in par(). A value of NA or FALSE omits the border from the plot. The default value of border is NULL.

The lty and lwd arguments are the standard arguments from par() (see Sections 3.3.2 and 3.4.4.). In rect(), lty and lwd affect both the lines and the border. The default value of lty is par("lty") and for lwd is par("lwd").

4.3.4.2 The polygon() Function

The polygon() function creates polygons and is slightly different from the polypath() function, which also plots polygons. Both functions automatically close the last values of x and y to the first values of x and y. The function polygon() takes eight specified arguments and some arguments of par() that are not specified (in the eighth place in the order of arguments).

The first two arguments, x and y (or x by itself, with y set to NULL), give the vertices of the polygon. The third through seventh arguments are density, angle, border, col, and lty, which behave mostly the same as with the function rect(). The eighth specified argument is fillOddEven. See the help page for polygon() for a description of what the argument does. On my device, the argument appears not to do anything.

If y is included, the arguments x and y are numeric vectors that must be of the same length. The vector y can be omitted – in which case x can be a two-column matrix containing, in the rows, the x and y values for the vertices. Alternatively, x is a vector for which the values plot in the vertical direction against a line where the line starts at 1 on the x axis and the first value of the vector on the y axis and ends at x equal to the length of the vector and y equal to the last value of the vector.

If NAs are placed at a given element of the vectors (or vector) or in a given row in the matrix, polygon() ends the polygon at the NAs and starts a new polygon with the numbers after the NAs.

See the description of rect() in the first part of this subsection for a description of density, angle, border, col, and lty. However, there is a small difference in how the arguments behave. In polygon, for col set equal to NULL, if density equals 0, the polygon is transparent, while if density equals NULL the polygon is not transparent. For rect(), both are transparent. The default values are the same between the functions.

The fillOddEven argument apparently can be set to any R object if density equals NA, NULL, a negative number, or 0. If density is a positive number, fillOddEven must be a vector that can be coerced to mode logical. If fillOddEven is longer than one element and density is larger than zero, then a warning is given, but not an error. The default value of fillOddEven is FALSE.

4.3.4.3 The polypath() Function

The polypath() function takes the same specified arguments as polygon(), except that density and angle are not included and lwd is not specifically included. The function only fills with colors, not with lines, so density and angle do not apply. Also, instead of fillOddEven, an argument, rule, has been included.

The border, col, and lty arguments all take the same values as with polygon(), but for multielement vectors, only the first element is used. If border equals NA, no border is plotted. If border equals NULL, the border takes on the color given by fg in par(). Otherwise, the border equals the color assigned to the argument.

In the case of col equal to NA or NULL, no color is plotted in the polygon, and the polygon is transparent. If col equals NA or NULL and border is not NA, the polygon is outlined in the color given by border. In all other cases, if col equals a color, the polygon is filled with the color given by col.

With multiple polygons plotted separately, for col equal to NA or NULL, the polygon is transparent. Solid colors are not transparent (the assigned colors can be). When multiple polygons are plotted from the same call to polypath(), the rule argument determines how the polygons behave when the polygons overlap.

When rule equals "winding", the direction that the polygon is drawn (clockwise or counterclockwise) affects how overlapping polygons behave. For nested or overlapping polygons, if the first two polygons plotted are both clockwise or both counterclockwise, then all of the polygons fill with the same color. If one is clockwise and one is not, then, where they overlap, the intersection is plotted white. For nested plots, the color and white alternate as the polygons get smaller.

With more than three overlapping plots, the rule gets more complex. The polygons appear to have the intersection of three polygons colored, the intersection of two polygons white if one is counterclockwise and one clockwise, and the intersection of two polygons colored if both have the same direction.

For the examples at which I looked, if rule equaled "evenodd", all of the plots plotted the same way. The first plot plotted colored, and the second plotted colored where the second plot did not overlap the first. Where the second plot overlapped the first, the second plotted white. Where the third plot did not overlap either of the first two plots, the third plotted colored. Where all three plots intersected, the plot plotted colored. Where only two intersected, the third plotted white if the underlying plot was colored or colored if the underlying plot was white.

4.3.4.4 An Example of rect(), polygon(), and polypath()

In Listing 4-20, code is given for examples of running rect(), polygon(), and polypath().

Listing 4-20. Code for the examples of rect(), polygon(), and polypath()

```
plot(
  pop75.ordered, pop15.ordered,
  type="n",
  xlab="",
  ylab="",
  main="Examples of rect(), polygon(), & polypath()"
)
text(
  c( 1.05, 2.42, 4 ),
  25,
  c( "rect()", "polygon()", "polypath()" )
)

rect(
  c(  0.85, 0.55, 1.05, 0.75 ),
```

```
  31,
  c( 1.35, 1.55 ),
  c( 42, 45 ),
  density=c( NA, 3 ),
  col=grey(
    c( 0.9, 0.7, 0.5, 0.3 )
  ),
  border=grey(
    c( 0.7, 0.3 )
  )
)

polygon(
  c( 2.8, 3.5, 2.1,  NA, 2.8, 3.3,   2.2, NA, 2.4,   3.2, 2.4 ) - 0.38,
  c( 42, 31,  31,  NA,  40,  32, 31.5, NA,  32, 32.5, 38 ),
  density=c( 3, 4, NA ),
  col=grey(
    c( 0.7, 0.45, 0.55 )
  ),
  fillOddEven=0,
  border=NULL
)

polypath(
  c( 2.8, 3.5, 2.1,  NA,  2.2,  3.3, 2.8,  NA, 2.4,   3.2, 2.4 ) + 1.2,
  c( 42,  31,  31,  NA, 31.5, 32,  40,  NA,  32, 32.5,  38 ),
  col="grey60",
  rule="winding",
  border=TRUE,
  lwd=2,
  lty="dashed"
)
```

In Figure 4-19, the code in Listing 4-20 is run.

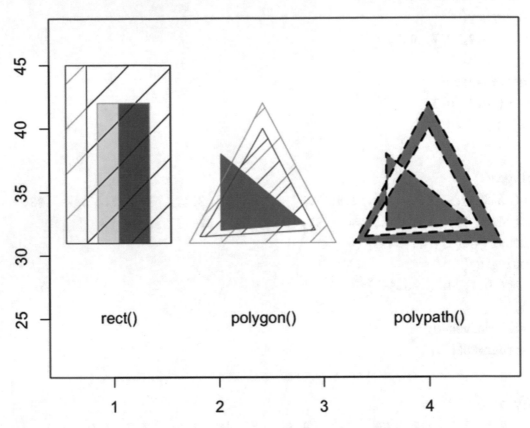

Figure 4-19. *Examples of using rect(), polygon(), and polypath()*

Note that, for the example of rect(), the light gray rectangle was plotted first, the rectangle with the light gray lines second, the dark gray rectangle third, and the rectangle with the dark gray lines last. The rectangle with the light gray lines extends from x equal to 0.55 to x equal to 1.55, but the rectangle with dark gray lines plots over the light gray lines from x equal to 0.75 to x equal to 1.55.

Similarly, the light gray rectangle extends from x equal to 0.85 to x equal to 1.35, but the dark gray rectangle plots over the light gray rectangle for x going from 1.05 to 1.35. Also, the dark gray lines are visible over the light and dark gray rectangles, since the rectangle with the dark gray lines was plotted last.

For the example of polygon(), three triangles are plotted. The outer triangle was plotted first, the middle triangle second, and the inner triangle last. All three triangles were plotted in one call to polygon by using NAs to separate each set of plotting instructions. Note that, although the lines are covered by the third triangle, the borders are visible on the third triangle. Plotting the third triangle in another call to polygon would fix the problem.

For the example of polypath(), the same three triangles are plotted as with the polygon() example. The first triangle is plotted clockwise, and the second and third triangles are plotted counterclockwise. The rule "winding" was used, so – since the first and second triangles are plotted in different directions – the second triangle is white and the first and third are dark gray. However, when the third triangle crosses the first triangle – since the two are plotted in different directions – the third triangle plots white over the gray of the first triangle. Note that the line type is "dashed" and the line width is 2 for the polypath() example.

4.3.5 The contour( ) Function

The contour() function plots contour plots. The function can be run as a standalone function or as an ancillary function. In this chapter, we only cover the function as an ancillary function. The dataset for the example is the volcano dataset from the datasets package. See Section 4.2.4.2 for a description of the dataset – or see the help page for volcano in R.

The contour() function takes 19 specified arguments as well as many unspecified arguments from par(). The first nine arguments are x, for the locations on the x axis where the rows of z are placed; y, for the locations on the y axis where the columns of z are placed; z, for the matrix of values for which the contours are calculated; nlevels, for the number of contour levels to use, only used if levels is not set; levels, for the levels to use for contours (takes precedence over nlevels); labels, for the labels on the contour lines; xlim and ylim, the standard arguments from plot(), only used with the standalone choice; and zlim, for the lower and upper levels of z to use.

The argument x can be a vector or a two- or three-element list – all of mode numeric. If x is a vector, the length of the vector is the number of rows in z. The vector must be in increasing order. Also, if x is a vector, y must be supplied as a separate vector. If x is a list, the list can contain x and y or x, y, and z as the two or three elements. The default value of x is seq(0, 1, length.out=nrow(z)) – which supplies the correct number of equally spaced values between 0 and 1, inclusive.

The argument y takes an increasing numeric vector of length equal to the number of columns in z. The default value of y is seq(0, 1, length.out=ncol(z)).

The argument z is a numeric matrix. The values in the rows are used to calculate contours in the vertical direction (above the x axis). The values in the columns are used to calculate contours in the horizontal direction (to the right of the y axis). Every value has an x and a y coordinate. The first row is associated with the first x value, and the row (which gives the values in the vertical direction that contour() uses) goes from the bottom of the plot to the top. There is no default value for z.

The fourth and fifth arguments are nlevels and levels. Either one or the other is assigned, but not both. The argument nlevels gives the number of contour levels to find. The argument levels gives values at which to create contours. A one-element integer vector is used for nlevels, and an arbitrarily long numeric vector is used for levels. The default value of nlevels is 10. The default value of levels is pretty(zlim, nlevels). (The function pretty() finds nice intervals within a set of limits, where a certain number of intervals are set. See the help page for pretty() for more information.)

The sixth argument is labels. The argument takes a character vector (or a vector that can be coerced to character) of arbitrary length. The elements cycle out to the number of levels. The default value of labels is NULL – that is, R creates the labels.

The seventh, eighth, and ninth arguments are xlim, ylim, and zlim. The arguments xlim and ylim only affect the plot if contour is run as a standalone function. The argument zlim gives the lower and upper limits for z within which the contours are formed. The argument takes a numeric vector of arbitrary length. The minimum and maximum of the values in the vector are used. The default values of xlim, ylim, and zlim are range(x, finite=TRUE), range(y, finite=TRUE), and range(z, finite=TRUE). (The function range() finds the range of a numeric object. The finite argument tells range() to ignore nonfinite values.)

The last ten arguments are labcex, for the character size in the labels; drawlabels, to tell contour whether to plot labels; method, for the method used to place the labels; vfont, to, optionally, use a Hershey font; the standard axes, frame.plot, col, lty, and lwd from plot() and par(); and add, for whether to run contour() as an ancillary plot or a standalone plot.

The labcex argument gives the character size of the labels. According to the help page for contour, the size is absolute, not relative to the value of cex in par(). The argument takes a numeric vector of arbitrary length, but only the first element is used. The default value is 0.6.

The drawlabels argument takes a logical vector (or a vector that can be coerced to logical) of arbitrary length, but only the first element is used. The default value is TRUE – that is, draw contour labels.

The method argument takes a character vector of arbitrary length, but only the first value is used. The possible character values for the first element are "simple", "edge", and "flattest". Any other value gives an error.

From the help page for contour(), the value of "simple" means labels are plotted at the edge of the plot and overlap the contour lines. The value of "edge" means labels are plotted at the edge of the plot and are embedded in the contour lines. The value of "flattest" means that labels are plotted at the flattest part of the contour and embedded in the contour. The default value of method is "flattest".

The vfont argument specifies a Hershey font family and font weight. The argument is a two-element character vector. To see the available fonts, run the Hershey demonstration, demo(Hershey), at the R prompt. To see an example of using a Hershey font, see Listing 4-20. There is no default value for vfont.

The axes and frame.plot arguments are only used when a standalone plot is created and are the standard arguments from plot(). The col, lty, and lwd arguments are the standard arguments in par(). The default value of col is the value of fg in par(). The default value of lty is the value of lty in par(). The default value of lwd is the value of lwd in par().

The add argument takes a logical vector (or a vector that can be coerced to logical) of arbitrary length, but, if longer than one element, only the first element is used and a warning is given.

In Listing 4-21 is code for an example of using contour(). The example plots contours for the dataset volcano. The package datasets is loaded by default in R, so for most users, the data can be accessed like any object in the workspace.

Listing 4-21. Code for an example of contour() using x, y, z, levels, labels, labcex, method, vfont, col, lty, lwd, and add

```
plot(
  pop75.ordered, pop15.ordered,
  type="n",
  xlab="x",
  ylab="y",
  xlim=c( 0, 5.5 ),
```

```
  ylim=c( 18, 52 ),
  main="Example of x, y, z, levels, labels, labcex,\nmethod, vfont, col,
lty, lwd, and add in contour()",
  sub="The volcano Dataset"
)

contour(
  x=0.5 + 4.5*seq( 0, 1, len=87 ),

  y= 20 +  30*seq( 0, 1, len=61 ),

  z=volcano,

  levels=c( 1:6*20+60 ),
  labels=paste( 1:6*20+60 ),
  labcex=0.8,
  method="flattest",
  vfont=c("serif", "bold"),
  col="grey10",
  lty="dotdash",
  lwd=2,
  add=TRUE
)
```

In Figure 4-20, the code in Listing 4-21 is run.

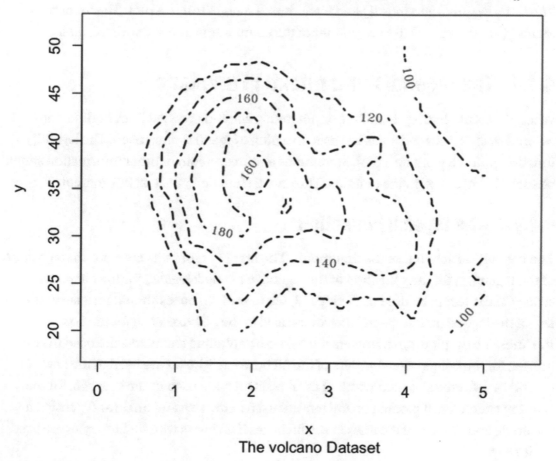

Figure 4-20. *Example of using x, y, z, levels, labels, labcex, method, vfont, col, lty, lwd, and add in contour()*

Note that six specific levels were chosen – 80, 100, 120, 140, 160, and 180. The minimum value for the volcano dataset is 94, so the contour at 80 is never used. Also, the Hershey font, serif bold, was used and the label size was set to 0.8. A line width of 2 and a dot-dashed line type were used. The color of the contours and labels was chosen to be a dark gray.

4.4 Functions to Provide Information About or to Interact with a Plot

This section covers the functions legend(), mtext(), indentify(), and locator(). The functions legend() and mtext() add legends and margin text to a plot. The functions identify() and locator() use the pointer of the computer to interact with the plot.

4.4.1 The legend() and mtext() Functions

When different plotting characters or differently colored or styled lines or differently colored or styled shaded areas are used in a plot, a legend is often used. The legend() function puts a legend on a plot. Sometimes a source, credit, or other information should be included in a plot, in the margins. The mtext() function puts text in a margin.

4.4.1.1 The legend() Function

The legend() function takes 39 arguments. The first 11 arguments are x, for the x position of the legend; y, for the y position of the legend, if needed; legend, for the character strings of the text to be used in the legend; fill, to say if fill boxes should be used in the key of the legend and to specify the colors used in the fill boxes; col, for the colors of the lines and/or plotting characters if lines and/or plotting characters are used in key; border, for the colors of the borders of the fill boxes if fill boxes are used in the key; lty and lwd, for the style and width of the lines if lines are used in the key; pch, for the plotting characters if plotting characters are used in the key; and angle and density, for the angle and density of the lines in the fill boxes if fill boxes with fill line styles are used in the key.

The x argument can take a one-element character string or numeric vector or a two-element numeric vector. The possible character strings are "topleft", "top", "topright", "left", "center", "right", "bottomleft", "bottom", and "bottomright" – although the strings can be shortened to unique identifiers, for example, "topl" for "topleft". The strings indicate the location of the legend.

If x is a one-element numeric vector and y equals NULL, by default legend() plots the legend with the top-left corner at 1 on the x axis and at the value of x on the y axis. If x is a two-element numeric vector and y equals NULL, legend() plots the legend between 1 and 2 on the x axis and between the two values of x on the y axis.

If x and y are one-element numeric vectors, by default the top-left corner of the legend is placed at x on the axis and y on the y axis. The function then finds good legend dimensions.

If x and y are two-element numeric vectors, the four values define the four corners of the legend box. If the box is too small for the legend, the legend plots outside the box.

The x argument has no default value, and y has a default value of NULL.

The legend argument gives the values for the legend. According to the help page for legend(), if the vector is not a character vector, legend() attempts to convert the vector to mode character using as.graphicsAnnot(). The vector is of arbitrary length, and the length gives the number of legend values. There is no default value for legend.

The fill argument takes a vector of color values (see Section 3.4.1 for the types of values that can be used) of arbitrary length. If fill is set to a value, boxes are plotted to the left of the legend text and filled with the color(s) set by fill or by fill lines of the color(s) given. Which happens depends on whether density is set. If an element of fill is set to 0, the respective box is transparent. The colors cycle out to the length of legend. The default value of col is NULL.

The col argument gives the colors of the lines or plotting characters used in the legend (instead of or besides fill boxes). Like fill, col is a vector of color values and is of arbitrary length. The argument elements cycle out to the length of legend. The value of 0 plots white. The default value of col is the value of col in par().

The border argument gives the color of the border around the fill boxes. The argument takes a vector of color values and is of arbitrary length and cycles. The value of 0 plots white. The default value of border is "black".

The lty, lwd, and pch arguments are the standard arguments from plot() (see Sections 3.3.2 and 3.4.4), although if an element of pch is a character string, the number of characters in the string can be greater than one. (Note, there is no internal connection between the legend and the colors, symbols, or lines used in the plot.) There are no default values for lty, lwd, and pch.

The density and angle arguments are those used for rect() and polygon() (see Section 4.3.4.) The arguments take numeric vectors of arbitrary length and cycle out to the length of legend. The density argument is measured in lines per inch, and angle is measured in degrees. The default value of density is NULL and of angle is 45.

The 12th through 16th arguments give values for the legend box and border. The arguments are bty, for the box type of the border; bg, for the background color of the legend box; box.lty, for the line type of the border; box.lwd, for the line width of the border; and box.col, for the color of the border.

The bty argument takes a vector of arbitrary length. Any value gives a four-sided box except "n" – for which a box is not plotted and a background color cannot be assigned. The default value of bty is "o".

The bg argument sets the background color and takes a vector of color values of arbitrary length. Only the first value is used. The default value of bg is the value of bg in par().

The box.lty, box.lwd, and box.col arguments take vectors of values of the types used by lty, lwd, and col in par(), respectively (see Sections 3.3.2 and 3.4.4). Only the first values of the vectors are used. The default values are the values of lty, lwd, and fg in par().

The 17th through 20th arguments affect characters and plotting characters. The arguments are pt.bg, for the background colors for when pch is set to 20, 21, 22, 23, 24 and/or 25 (see Section 3.3.2.); cex, for the size of the text in the legend; pt.cex, for the size of the plotting characters in the key; and pt.lwd, for the width of the lines forming the plotting characters.

The pt.bg argument takes a vector of the color values of arbitrary length and cycles out to the length of legend. The default value of pt.bg is NA – which means the background is transparent.

The cex argument takes numeric vectors of arbitrary length. If the length does not divide evenly into the length of legend, a warning is given, but the legend is plotted. If cex varies, the legend keys do not line up. The default value of cex is 1.

The pt.cex argument takes a numeric vector of arbitrary length. The value of pt.cex is the size of the plotting character. Even if pt.cex varies, if cex is a single value, the keys of the legend line up. The default value of pt.cex is cex. Both pt.cex and cex are relative to the size of cex in par().

The pt.lwd argument takes a numeric vector of arbitrary length. The values cycle out to the length of legend. The default value of pt.lwd is the value of lwd in par().

The 21st and 22nd arguments, xjust and yjust, give information about how the legend is justified with respect to the given x and y coordinates of the legend. The values of xjust and yjust only affect the position of the legend if the location is specified with numeric values and is not specified by two-element vectors.

The value of xjust moves the center of the legend to the left if the value is greater than 0.5 and to the right if the value is less than 0.5. The value of 0.5 gives a legend that is centered on the point in the horizontal direction. A value of xjust equal to 0 gives a legend whose center is one-half legend width to the right (0 – 0.5 = -0.5) of the x location. A value of -1.5 (-1.5 – 0.5 = -2) gives a legend whose center is two legend widths to the right of the x location. The default value of xjust is 0 – that is, the left side of the legend is located at the value of x.

For yjust, values greater than 0.5 move the legend down, and values less than 0.5 move the legend up. Once again, 0.5 centers the legend – this time on the y location. A value of 1 gives a legend whose center is one-half legend height below the y location (1 – 0.5 = 0.5) and so forth. The default value for yjust is 1 – that is, the location of the top of the legend is the value of y.

The 23rd through 28th arguments position the text and key within the legend box and format the text. The arguments are x.intersp, for the spacing between the legend keys and the legend values; y.intersp, for the spacing between the lines in the legend; adj, for justifying the legend text in the horizontal and vertical directions; text.width for the width of the text part of the legend box in the units of the x axis, which affects the right border of the box; text.col, for the color of the legend character strings; and text.font, for the font weights of the legend character strings.

The x.intersp argument takes a numeric vector of a length less than or equal to the length of legend. The argument cycles. If the length of x.intersp does not divide evenly into the length of legend, a warning is given, but the legend plots. If x.intersp is longer than legend, an error is given.

When x.intersp equals 0 and adj[1] equals the default value, the space between the center of a plotting character and the legend text is slightly more than zero. For fill boxes and lines, there is no space between the right of the fill box or the right end of the line and the legend text. A value of x.intersp equal to 1 puts the legend text about two character widths to the right of the fill box, line, or plotting character. A value of 2 gives about four character widths of space. Negative values move the legend text to the left. The default value of x.intersp equals 1.

The y.intersp argument takes a numeric vector that should be either one element long or the length of legend. Arguments longer than the length of legend give an error, and those that are both shorter than legend and longer than one element behave strangely.

The value 1 gives a space of about one-half line height between lines of legend text – if y.intersp takes on just one value and adj equals the default value. A value of 2 gives about two line heights. A value of 0 overlies the lines. A negative value reverses the order of the lines.

If a sequence of increasing or decreasing values are given for y.intersp, then the behavior of the line spacing changes. For example, if y.intersp equals 0:3/3, then there is about zero space between the first two lines, about one line spacing between the second and third lines, and about two lines of spacing between the third and fourth lines. Also, there is just a bit over zero space between the top border of the box and the first line and a space of about one line between the fourth line and the lower box border. The default value of y.intersp is 1.

The adj argument places the legend text with respect to the key on the lines of the legend. The argument takes a one- or two-element numeric vector. Other length vectors, and even matrices, can be assigned; but only the first two values of the vector or matrix are used.

The function adjusts the position of the legend text by using the value of adj. The adjustment is based on two numbers, the first for the horizontal position and the second for the vertical position. If adj takes a vector with a single element, then the second value is set to 0.5, and the value of the single element of adj becomes the first value.

If the first value of adj equals 0, the left end of the legend text is placed about one-and-one-half character widths to the right of the center of the fill boxes and/or plotting characters. For lines, the left end of the text is about one-and-one-half character widths to the right of the right end of the line.

A value of 0.5 places the left end of the legend text about one-third of the string width to the left of the center of the fill boxes and/or plotting characters. For lines, the left end of the text is about one-third of the string width from the right end of the line.

A value of 1 places the right end of the legend text about one-and-one-half character widths to the right of the center of fill boxes or plotting characters. For lines, the right end of the legend text is about one-and-one-half character widths to the right of the right end of the line. Values greater than 1 and less than 0 can be used.

The second value moves the text down if the value is more than 0.5 and up if less than 0.5. A value of 0.5 centers the text – with regard to the fill box, plotting symbol or line – in the vertical direction.

If the second value equals 1, then the top of the text (for capital letters) plots at the center of the fill box, plotting character, and/or line. If the second value equals 0, then the bottom of the text plots at the center of the fill box, plotting character, and/or line. Values greater than 1 and less than 0 can be used for the second value of adj.

In the next three paragraphs, we assume that x.intersp and y.intersp equal the default values. The default value for adj is c(0, 0.5).

The text.width argument takes a numeric vector of a length that is at most the length of legend. The value(s) must be nonnegative. The argument is ignored if the values of x and y are two-element vectors – in which case the width of the legend box is set by the values of x and y.

The width is measured in x axis units but is measured from the right of the first character in the legend text, not the left side of the legend box. The width affects the width of the legend box but has no effect on the legend – which will print outside the box if necessary.

If multiple values are given, legend() plots a legend for each one, but the legends are not transparent – so the legends will overlie each other. That is, the order of the values matters in the result. The default value is NULL – which indicates that R chooses the legend width.

The text.col and text.font arguments take vectors of arbitrary length, with the same types of values as col and font in plot(). The values cycle out to the length of legend. The default value of text.col is the default value of col in par() and of text.font is NULL – which indicates a plain weight on my device.

The 29th through 39th arguments give general arguments that affect the legend, including setting and formatting a title. The arguments are merge, for the placement of fill boxes and/or plotting characters if lines are also drawn; trace, for debugging the legend code; plot, for whether to plot the legend or return sizes; ncol, for the number of columns in the legend; horiz, for whether to plot a horizontal legend; title, to plot a legend title; inset, to inset the legend away from the plot border when the location of the legend box is specified by a character string; xpd, for whether to expand plotting outside the plot border; title.col, for the color of the title; title.adj, for adjusting the title left or right; and seg.len, for the length of key lines in character widths.

The merge argument takes a logical vector (or a vector that can be coerced to logical) of arbitrary length. However, if the length is greater than one, then a warning is given and only the first value is used.

If merge equals TRUE and lwd and/or lty is set to values and plotting characters are plotted, then the plotting characters plot at the middle of the line. If merge equals FALSE, the plotting characters plot at the right end of the line.

If lines and fill boxes are both plotted and merge equals TRUE, then the fill boxplots under the left end of the line. If merge equals FALSE, the fill boxes plot to the left of the lines – with a small overlap.

If all three of lines, fill boxes, and plotting characters are plotted and merge is set to TRUE, the fill boxes plot under the line on the left side of the line, and the plotting characters plot at the center of the line. If FALSE, the fill boxes plot to the left of the line and the plotting characters to the right.

Otherwise, merge has no effect. Note, the plotting characters and the lines are always the same color. The default value of merge is TRUE.

The trace argument takes a logical vector (or a vector that can be coerced to logical) of arbitrary length. If the length of trace is longer than one, a warning is given and only the first element is used. However, the legend plots. If trace is set to TRUE, some diagnostic information is printed at the R console. If FALSE, nothing is printed at the R console.

The plot argument takes a logical vector (or a vector that can be coerced to logical) of arbitrary length. However, if the length is longer than one, a warning is given and only the first element is used.

If plot equals TRUE, then the legend is plotted. If FALSE, the legend is not plotted. In both cases, setting the function call equal to an object assigns a list to the object containing the locations of the legend box and legend lines in the units of the x and y axes. The default value of plot is TRUE.

The ncol argument must be a one-element numeric vector with a value that is greater than or equal to one. The argument gives the number of columns in the legend. The legend expands out to make room for as many columns as are requested. For example, if there are four labels and three columns are requested, then the first two columns each contain two legend keys, and the third column contains none.

If the value is not an integer, the right border moves to the right as the number increases to the next integer, but some of the labels may not plot until the number increases to the next integer. The default value of ncol is 1.

The horiz argument takes a logical vector (or a vector that can be coerced to logical) of arbitrary length. If the length is greater than one, a warning is given and only the first element is used. However, the legend plots.

A value of TRUE gives a horizontal legend. A value of FALSE give a vertical legend. The default value of horiz is FALSE.

The title argument takes a one-element character vector containing a title for the legend or the value NULL. The default value is NULL.

The inset argument takes a numeric vector of arbitrary length and is used when the location of the legend is specified by a character string. The argument is measured in units of proportion – where the proportion is of the axis perpendicular to the given axis.

If the location is in the middle of an axis, then only one element is used, even if more elements are given. The legend is moved away from the given axis based on the value of inset and the length of the perpendicular axis.

If the string specifies a corner placement, the first two elements of inset are used if the length of inset is greater than one. The first element gives the distance from the vertical axis as a proportion of the horizontal axis. The second element gives the distance from the horizontal axis as a proportion of the vertical axis.

If only one element is assigned, the distance from an axis is based on that proportion; and, unless the plot is square, this will give differently sized insets on the two axes. The default value of inset is 0.

The xpd argument is the standard xpd from plot(). The argument takes a one-element logical vector that can take on the values TRUE, NA, NULL, and FALSE. If xpd equals TRUE, the legend can plot out to the plotting region boundary. If xpd equals NA, the legend can plot out to the device boundary. If xpd equals NULL or FALSE, legend() stops plotting at the plot border. The xpd argument has no default value – which indicates that xpd is the value set in the call to plot().

The arguments title.col and title.adj give the color and left to right position(s) of the title, respectively. The title.col argument takes a vector of color values (see Section 3.4.1) of arbitrary length. The default value of title.col is text.col.

The title.adj argument takes a numeric vector of arbitrary length. If title.adj equals 0, the title plots to the right of the left border. If equal to 1, the title plots to the left of the right border. If equal to 0.5, the title plots in the center. Negative values and values greater than one are also acceptable.

If the length of title.adj is greater than one, the title plots at each value of adj, and the colors in title.col cycle to the length of title.adj. However, the positions associated with the values of title.adj are different with a multielement vector. Still, the position of the title moves to the right as the values of title.adj increase. The default value of title.adj is 0.5.

The value of seg.len gives the length of the line when the key contains a line and is measured in two character width units. The argument seg.len takes a numeric vector of arbitrary length.

If seg.len is longer than or equal to the length of legend and n is the length of legend, the legend() plots a new legend for each element of seg.len greater than or equal to n. In the case of a multielement vector for seg.len, the values of col, lty, and lwd cycle out to the length of seg.len. If seg.len is shorter than n, the elements of seg.len cycle out to the end of legend. The default value of seg.len is 2.

In Listing 4-22, code is given for some examples of using legend().

Listing 4-22. Code for five examples of using legend()

```
par( cex=0.75 )
plot(
  pop75.ordered, pop15.ordered,
  type="n",
  main="Some Examples of Using legend()"
)

legend(
  "topleft",
  legend=paste("color", 1:3 ),
  fill=grey(
    c( 0.2, 0.5, 0.8 )
  ),
  border=0,
  density=c( 20, NA, NA ),
  bg="grey95",
  box.lwd=3,
  box.lty="dashed",
  box.col="grey20",
  text.col="grey20",
  text.font=3,
  horiz=TRUE,
  title=" Example of fill",
  title.col="grey5",
  title.adj=0,
  inset=c( 0.01, 0.014 )
)
```

```
legend(
  "topright",
  legend=paste("pch", 21:23 ),
  pch=21:23,
  pt.bg="grey80",
  cex = 1.2,
  pt.cex = 1.2,
  pt.lwd = 2,
  bg="grey99",
  box.lwd=2,
  box.col="grey40",
  text.col="grey20",
  text.font=3,
  title="Example of pch",
  title.col="grey5",
  title.adj=0.5,
  inset=c( 0.01, 0.014 )
)

legend(
  0.5,
  40,
  legend=paste("lty", 1:3 ),
  col=grey(
    c( 0.2, 0.5, 0.7 )
  ),
  lty=1:3,
  lwd=1:3,
  bg="grey97",
  box.lwd=2,
  box.col="grey60",
  cex=0.95,
  text.col=grey(
    c( 0.2, 0.5, 0.7 )
  ),
  text.font=1,
```

```
  ncol=2,
  title="Example of lty, lwd & col",
  title.col="grey5",
  title.adj=1,
  seg.len=2.5
)

legend(
  c( 1, 3.5 ),
  c( 26, 33 ),
  legend=paste("example", 1:3 ),
  fill=grey(
    c( 0.7, 0.5, 0.2 )
  ),
  col=grey(
    c( 0.2, 0.5, 0.7 )
  ),
  lty=1:3,
  lwd=2,
  pch=21:23,
  bg="grey96",
  box.lwd=2,
  box.col="grey60",
  pt.bg=grey(
    c( 0.7, 0.5, 0.2 )
  ),
  pt.cex=1.2,
  text.col=grey(
    c( 0.2, 0.5, 0.7 )
  ),
  text.font=1,
  merge=FALSE,
  title="Example of Boxes, pch's, & Lines",
  title.col="grey5",
  seg.len=2.5
)
```

```
legend(
  "bottomr",
  legend=paste( "default", 1:3 ),
  fill=paste0(
    "grey",
    c(75, 60, 45 )
  )
)
par( cex=1 )
```

In Figure 4-21, the code in Listing 4-22 is run.

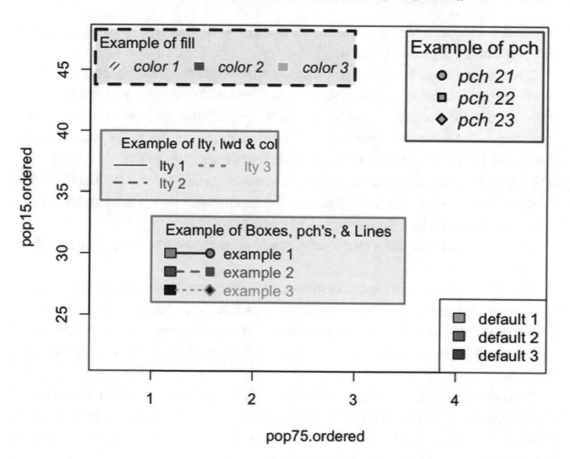

Figure 4-21. *Five examples of using legend()*

In the first legend in Figure 4-21, the first fill box uses fill lines rather than solid color, but the second and third use solid color. The legend is horizontal and the title is on the left. In the legend to the right and high up, plotting characters are used and have been filled with a color. The title is in the center.

In the second box on the left, lines are used for the key. All of line width, line type, and line color vary. The title is on the right and two columns have been used. In the third box on the left, fill boxes, plotting characters, and lines are all used at the same time. Colors, line styles, fill box outlines, and symbol backgrounds are all varied.

In the right of the example, a legend using the default styling arguments is shown. Note, the arguments angle, bty, pt.lwd, xjust, yjust, x.intersp, y.intersp, adj, text.width, trace, and plot were not used in the examples.

4.4.1.2 The mtext() Function

The mtext() function puts text in the margins of a plot. The function takes ten arguments plus many of the arguments from par().

The arguments of mtext() are text, for the text to be plotted; side, for the side on which the text is to be plotted; line, for the line out from the plot on which the text is plotted; outer, for whether the text is to be put in an outer margin or in a margin of the figure (we only cover outer equal to FALSE in this chapter – see Section 6.2.1.1 for outer equal to TRUE); at, for the location at which to put the text; adj, for the text adjustment in the direction parallel to the axis (left/right or down/up); padj, for adjusting the text in the direction perpendicular to the axis; cex, for the character size of the text; col, for the color of the text; and font, for the font weight of the text.

The text argument takes a character vector of arbitrary length. There is no default value for text.

The side argument takes a numeric vector of arbitrary length. If an element of side is not between 1 and 4, inclusive, then no text is plotted for the element. If an element of side is not an integer, the element is rounded up to the next integer. The sides are 1 for the bottom, 2 for the left side, 3 for the top, and 4 for the right side. The default value of side is 3.

The line argument takes a numeric vector of arbitrary length. Negative values are allowed and plot into the plot. Positive values plot out from the plot. Line 0 is just outside of the plot and at the border. If the text takes more than one line, the last line in the text is located at the value of line. The default value of line is 0.

The outer argument takes a logical vector (or a vector that can be coerced to logical) of arbitrary length. The default value of outer is FALSE – that is, the text plots in the margins of the plot.

The at argument takes a numeric vector of arbitrary length and is measured in the units of the x or y axis, depending on the value of side. For a given side by default, the argument gives the location of the start of the text. The default value of at is NA – that is, mtext() uses the value of adj to place the text.

The adj argument takes numeric vectors of arbitrary length. If at is not specified, a value of 0 means the text plots at the left or bottom of the margin depending on the value of side. If adj equals 1, the text plots at the right or top of the margin, depending on the value of side. If at is supplied, adj gives the placement of the text with regard to the location given by at. The adj argument is continuous and can take negative values and values greater than one. The default value of adj is NA – that is, use the value of las in par().

The padj argument takes the same values as adj. For padj equal to 0, the bottom of the text is at the middle of the line, looking perpendicular to the axis. If padj equals 1, the top of the text is at the middle of the line, looking in the perpendicular direction. The default value of padj is NA – that is, use the value of las in par().

The cex, col, and font arguments are the standard arguments from plot(). (See Sections 3.4.3, 3.4.1, and 3.4.2.)

None of the ten arguments of mtext() are necessarily the same length. All cycle out to the length of the longest argument.

In Listing 4-23, code is given for an example of using mtext().

Listing 4-23. Code for the example of using mtext()

```
plot(
  pop75.ordered, pop15.ordered,
  main="Example of Using mtext()"
)

mtext(
  "Source:\nLifeCycleSavings dataset\nin the R datasets package",
  side=1,
  line=4,
  cex=0.8,
  col="grey50",
```

```
font=2,
adj=1
)
```

In Figure 4-22, the code in Listing 4-23 is run.

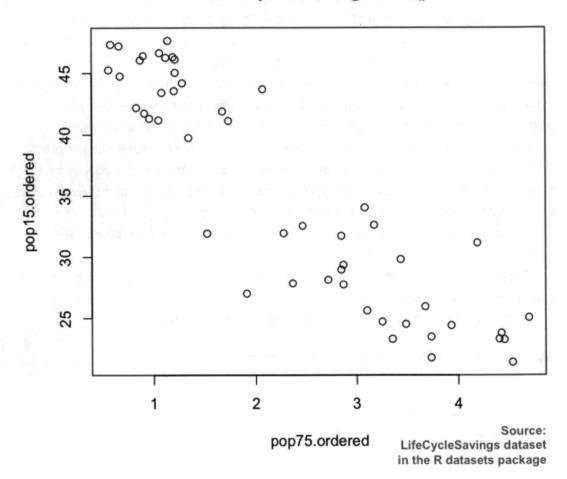

Figure 4-22. *Example of using mtext()*

The source citation is plotted in a shade of gray and in bold font. The character size is smaller than the size of the axis label text. The bottom line of the margin text plots on line 4. There are five lines in the bottom margin by default (including line 0).

4.4.2 The Interactive Functions: identify() and locator()

The functions identify() and locator() make the task of placing things like legends, lines, and labels within a plot easier. The function identify() can label and identify points in a scatterplot (and some other kinds of plots) using the computer pointer. The function locator() allows a person to put things like text or a legend at a location within a plot by using the pointer. The function locator() also allows the freestyle drawing of lines and points.

The functions, when run, wait for the user to click the pointer a specified number of times. To exit either function before the given number of times in Quartz, press the Esc key. For X11 or Windows, click the mouse using any button other than the first. According to the help pages for identify() and locator(), only computers with X11, Quartz, or Windows can use these functions.

4.4.2.1 The identify() Function

The identify() function takes ten specified arguments, plus some of the arguments in par(). The ten specified arguments are x and y, for the locations of the points on the scatterplot; labels, for the labels to assign to the points; pos, for whether to return the position of the label with regard to the point; n, for the maximum number of points to label or identify; plot, for whether to plot the labels or just return index values and – possibly – the values of pos and the order of selection; atpen, to tell identify() to plot the label to the right of and above the clicked pointer; offset, to increase or decrease the offset of the label from the point when atpen equals FALSE; tolerance, for the radius of the circle around a point for which clicking within the circle will choose the point; and order, to say whether to return the order in which the points were chosen.

The function always returns a numeric vector of the indices of the selected points. Sometimes the function returns the vector as the first element of a list containing one or two more vectors – depending on the values of pos and order.

The x and y arguments can be entered in the following ways: x as a numeric vector and y equal to NULL, x as a two-column numeric matrix and y equal to NULL, or x and y as two equal-length numeric vectors. There is no default value for x. The default value of y is NULL.

The labels argument takes a character vector (or a vector that can be coerced to character), usually of length equal to the number of points in the scatterplot. If not equal to the number of points, a warning is given. The default value is seq_along(x).

The pos argument takes a logical vector that should be of length one (otherwise, a warning is given). If set to TRUE, identify() returns a vector of pos values (pos as used in text() – see Section 4.2.2) for the labels assigned to the selected points. The default value of pos is FALSE.

The n argument gives the maximum number of points that can be selected in the call to identify(). The argument takes a numeric vector that should be of length one (otherwise, a warning is given). By limiting n, the function returns control to the console when n points have been selected without any other intervention. The default value of n is length(x).

The plot argument takes a logical vector (or a vector that can be coerced to logical) that should be of length one. No warning is given if the vector is longer than one, but only the first value is used. If set to TRUE, the labels are plotted when control is returned to the console. If set to FALSE, no labels are plotted on the plot. In both cases, information, such as the index value, of the selected points is returned. The default value of plot is TRUE.

The atpen argument takes a logical vector (or a vector than can be coerced to logical) that should be of length one – a longer vector does not give a warning, but only the first value is used. Normally, identify() plots the label to the left, right, top, or bottom of a point based on where around the point that the pointer is clicked. The atpen argument tells identify() to put the lower-left corner of the label at the location of the pointer when the pointer is clicked. The default value of atpen is FALSE.

The offset argument gives the distance of the label from the point in character widths when atpen equals FALSE. If atpen is TRUE, then offset has no effect. The default value of offset is 0.5.

The tolerance argument takes a numeric vector that should be of length one. If longer, no warning is given, but only the first value is used. The argument gives the radius, in inches, of circles around the points for which clicking within the circle tells identify() to identify and – possibly – label the point. If there are no points near enough to where the pointer was clicked, a warning is given, but the function continues – which is also true if there are points with overlapping circles. The default value of tolerance is 0.25.

The order argument takes a logical vector (or a vector that can be coerced to logical) that should be of length one. No warning is given if the length is greater than one, but only the first element is used. If order is set to TRUE, identify() returns where in the order of selection the points were selected. The default value of order is FALSE.

In Listing 4-24, the code for and output from running identify() are given.

Listing 4-24. An example of using identify() multiple times

```
> plot(
pop75.ordered, pop15.ordered,
main="Example of Using identify()"
)

> identify(
pop75.ordered, pop15.ordered, labels=row.names(LifeCycleSavings)[ord],
tol=0.5,
col="grey10"
)
[1] 14 20 22 23 25

> identify(
pop75.ordered, pop15.ordered, labels=row.names(LifeCycleSavings)[ord],
tol=0.5,
pos=TRUE,
order=TRUE,
col="grey40"
)
$ind
[1] 21 24 39 41

$pos
[1] 3 2 3 3

$order
[1] 1 2 4 3

> identify(
pop75.ordered, pop15.ordered, labels=row.names(LifeCycleSavings)[ord],
tol=0.5,
atpen=TRUE,
col="grey50",
font=3
)
[1] 34 45
```

```
> identify(
pop75.ordered, pop15.ordered, labels=row.names(LifeCycleSavings)[ord],
tol=0.5,
offset=0.75,
font=2,
col="grey60"
)
[1] 42 49 50
```

In Figure 4-23 is the plot resulting from the code run in Listing 4-24.

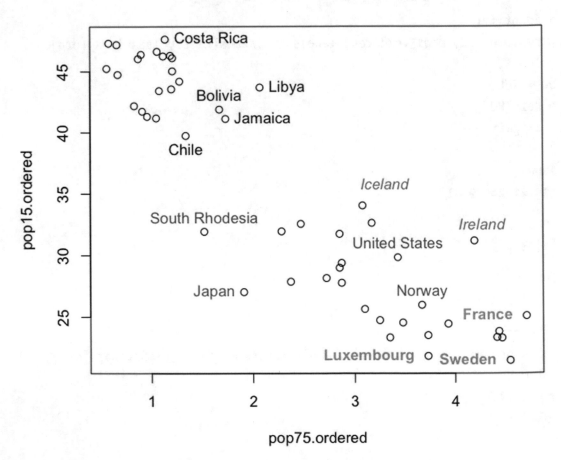

Figure 4-23. *The result of Listing 4-24, examples of running identify()*

The five countries in the upper-left part of the plot were labeled in the first call to identify(). The four countries in the lower part of the plot that are not italicized or bolded were plotted in the second call to identify – for which pos and order were set to TRUE. The two italicized countries were labeled in the third call to identify() – and were located with atpen set to TRUE. The three bolded country names were plotted from the fourth call to identify() – with offset set to 0.75.

4.4.2.2 The locator() Function

The locator() function can be used in two ways. The function can be used to enter x and y values into another function, which then adds information to a plot, or locator() can be used to put freestyle lines and/or points into a plot.

The locator() function takes two specified arguments and many unspecified arguments of par(). The two arguments are n, for the number of points to use, and type, for the type of object to plot.

The n argument should be a one-element numeric vector whose value is greater than or equal to one. If not an integer, the number will be rounded down to an integer. The default value of n is 512.

The argument type is the standard argument type from plot() – see Section 3.3.1. The default value of type is "n" – that is, nothing is plotted – and is useful when locator() is used just to set a location.

In Listing 4-25, an example is given of using locator() to place a legend into the plot originally plotted in Section 4.2.1.

Listing 4-25. An example of using locator() to place a legend

```
> tri1 = quantile( dpi.ordered, 0.33)
> tri2 = quantile( dpi.ordered, 0.67)

> plot(
pop75.ordered, dpi.ordered,
log="xy",
main="Example of locator()",
font.main=1,
type="n"
)
```

155

```
> points(
pop75.ordered, dpi.ordered,
pch=ifelse(dpi.ordered<=tri2,
ifelse( dpi.ordered<=tri1, "L", "M" ),
"H" ),
cex=0.7,
font=2
)
```

```
> legend(
locator( 1, "n" ),
legend=c(
"First Tercile of Income",
"Second Tercile of Income",
"Third Tercile of Income"),
pch=c( "L", "M", "H" ),
pt.lwd=2,
pt.cex=0.7,
cex=0.7,
bg="grey98"
)
```

In Figure 4-24, the result of Listing 4-25 is shown.

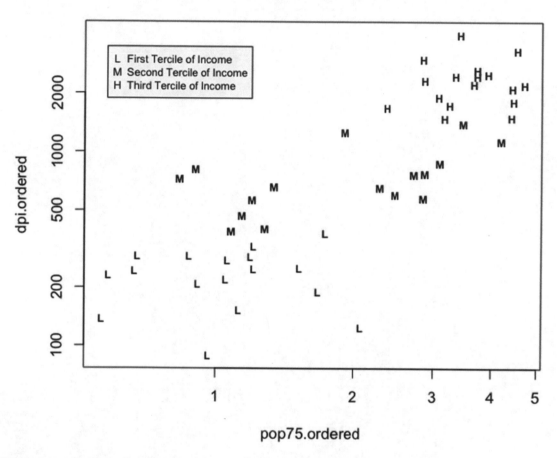

Figure 4-24. *Result of Listing 4-25, an example of using locator()*

In Listing 4-25, n equals 1, so the location of the upper-left corner of the legend was set by the pointer. The argument n could have been set to 2, for which both the upper-left and lower-right corners would have been assigned by the pointer. No other number would have been valid for using locator() in legend().

CHAPTER 5

The Methods of plot( )

For a function like plot(), a method of the function is the version of the function that applies to a specific class of objects – such as the class of numeric vectors or the class of time series objects. In this chapter, we cover those methods of plot() in the graphics and stats packages – other than plot.default(). (The function plot.default() is the subject of Chapter 3.) There are eight methods for plot() in the graphics package, and, in the stats package, there are twenty.

5.1 Methods

When plot() is run, plot() finds the class of the first argument and, based on the class, chooses which method of plot() to use. The first argument is the first argument listed in the call – unless there is an object assigned to x (or formula if the method is formula) elsewhere in the call, which then becomes the first argument. If plot() has a method for the object, a plot, or plots, is (are) created. The graphic created is based on the method and varies with the class of the object.

To see a list of the methods of plot() in an R package when using RStudio, open the Packages tab in the lower-right windowpane and scroll to the package. Open the package (click the name) and scroll down to where plot falls in the alphabetical order of the contents. The methods of plot() start with `plot.` and have an extension describing the method – for example, plot.ts.

Not all functions named `plot.` followed by an extension are methods of plot(). If the function is a method, in the help page for the function, under **Usage,** there will be the expression plot(…) (where the contents between the parentheses vary by the method). Some help pages cover more than one function, so there may be more functions under **Usage** than just plot().

In R, go to the Packages & Data tab in the menu and choose Package Manager. Scroll down to the package, open the package, and then scroll down to plot. Not all packages have methods for plot().

© Margot Tollefson 2021
M. Tollefson, *Visualizing Data in R 4*, https://doi.org/10.1007/978-1-4842-6831-5_5

Given that plot() has a method for a class of objects, the call to plot() does not necessarily include the extension. For some methods, the extension can be included. For other methods, including the extension causes an error. In this chapter, the functions are referred to either as plot() or as plot.*ext*(), where ext is the name of the method. But, with regard to the coding, running plot.*ext*(…) sometimes gives an error.

The arguments to plot() differ as the methods change. On the R help page for a method, arguments specific to the method are located within the parentheses after plot. Some are different from the arguments of plot.default(), and some just have different defaults. In Sections 5.2 and 5.3, the arguments specified on the help page are described, and the kinds of values the arguments take are given. One or more graphic examples are given for each method.

5.2 The Methods for plot() in the graphics Package

The graphics package is one of the R packages that are loaded by default. The package contains many functions that create plots and some that are used in the creation of plots. In Table 5-1, the methods for plot() in the graphics package are given – from RStudio.

Table 5-1. *Methods for plot() in the graphics package*

Function	Description
"plot.data.frame	Plot Method for Data Frames"
"plot.default	The Default Scatterplot Function"
"plot.factor	Plotting Factor Variables"
"plot.formula	Formula Notation for Scatterplots"
"plot.function	Draw Function Plots"
"plot.histogram	Plot Histograms"
"plot.raster	Plotting Raster Images"
"plot.table	Plot Methods for 'table' Objects"

—Help page for the graphics package in R

5.2.1 The data.frame Method

The first method covered is the data.frame method, for objects of the data frame class. A data frame is like a matrix, except that columns can be of different atomic modes. The data frames plotted by plot.data.frame() should be data frames with numeric columns - but columns that are not numeric are converted to numeric. (The mode of a data frame is list, since matrices cannot mix modes across columns.)

According to the help page for plot.data.frame(), the data frame is first converted to a numeric matrix by using data.matrix(). For columns in the data frame that are not numeric, the columns are converted to numeric. Raw data are converted to numeric values, logical values are converted to 0 for FALSE and 1 for TRUE, complex numbers are given the value of the real component, and character values are converted to factors – which have numeric values.

Numeric columns in a data frame can be selected using indices. For example, xx[, c(1, 5, 3)] creates a data frame containing the first, fifth, and third columns of the data frame xx. Selecting a single column does not result in a data frame, but data frames can have just one column by using the function data.frame() with just one vector value. For example, data.frame(xx[, 2]) would create a one-column data frame out of the second column of xx.

After the data frame is converted to a numeric matrix, the function pairs() is used to plot the data frame, except when the data frame contains only one column. When the data frame contains only one column, plot() uses the function stripchart() to plot the data frame.

The only specified argument is x, for the object of the data.frame class. There is no default value for x.

The arguments that can be used by plot.data.frame() are the arguments used by plot.default() and pairs() – also those of stripchart() if the data frame contains a single column.

In Listing 5-1, code is given to demonstrate plot.data.frame() using the LifeCycleSavings data frame.

Listing 5-1. Code for the example of using the data.frame method of plot given in Figure 5-1

```
plot(
  LifeCycleSavings[ , 2:4 ],
  log=3,
```

```
cex=0.5,
main="Example of plot.data.frame()"
)
```

In Figure 5-1, an example of using a data frame in plot() is given.

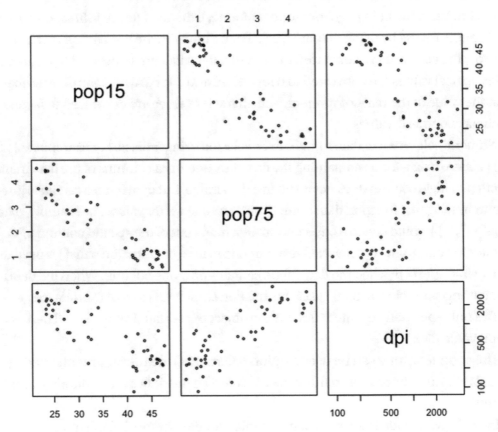

Figure 5-1. *An example of running plot() on the middle three columns of the data frame LifeCycleSavings*

Three columns were selected out of the full LifeCycleSavings dataset. Note that the third variable, dpi, uses a log scale. See the help page for pairs() for information on how to set a log scale.

The plots in the first row are pop15 (y axis) against pop75 (x axis) and pop15 against dpi. In the second row, pop75 is plotted against pop15 and dpi. In the third row, dpi is plotted against pop15 and pop75. The size of the plotting circles was reduced by setting cex equal to 0.5.

5.2.2 The factor Method

R data that is of the factor class is data for which the values are in groups – often the values are names for different factor levels in a designed experiment. The values are usually character strings, but not necessarily. The factor method plots data for which the argument x is a vector of the factor class or a two-column matrix or a data frame whose first column is of the factor class. The value of the argument y is an, optional, vector that can be of the factor or numeric class.

If y is not supplied and x is a vector, the vector is plotted as a bar plot – where the lengths of the bars are the counts (the number of observations) for each factor.

If x is a matrix, the second column of x is a vector of the numeric class, and y is NULL, then the second column of x is plotted against the first column of x. If x is a matrix and y is a vector of the numeric class, then y is plotted against the first column of x. If x is a vector and y is a vector of the numeric class, then y is plotted against x. In all three cases, boxplots are produced for each factor of x, if x is a vector, or for the first column of x, if x is a matrix. The numeric values used for the boxplots are those values associated with the vector in the second column of x or in y – if y is given and numeric.

If y is a vector of the factor class or if y is NULL and x is a matrix for which both columns are of the factor class, then the two factor vectors (x and y, the first column of x and y, or the first and second columns of x) plot against each other in a spline plot. A spline plot puts the first factor vector on the x axis and the second on the y axis.

In a spline plot, for each factor on the x axis, the length along the axis given to the factor depends on the proportion of observations assigned to the factor. On the y axis, for each y axis factor level, a color is assigned to the factor. Then the color is plotted vertically above each x axis factor – with the height of the color based on the proportion of the y axis factor in the x axis factor class.

The specified arguments of plot.factor() are x, for the factor object (if a matrix, the second column can be a numeric vector); y, for an optional numeric or factor vector; and legend.text, to label the factors on the y axis if two factor vectors are supplied to the function – otherwise, the argument is ignored.

The argument x can be a vector of the factor class or a matrix or data frame with two columns, the first of which must be of the factor class and the second of which must be of the numeric or factor class. There is no default value for x.

The argument y can be NULL, a vector of the factor class, or a vector of the numeric class. If a vector, the vector must be the same length as x (or the number of rows of x if x is a matrix). If y is supplied and x is a matrix, only the first column of x is used for the plot. The default value of y is NULL.

The argument legend.text takes a character vector (or a vector that can be coerced to character) of arbitrary length. The character strings in the vector cycle out to the number of factors in y, if y is a factor. If y is NULL, x is a matrix, and the second variable of x is a factor, then legend.text cycles out to the number of factors in the second variable of x. The default value of legend.text is the vector of factor names for y or the second column of x.

The function also takes the arguments used by plot.default(), as well as the arguments of boxplot(), barplot(), and splineplot().

In Listing 5-2, code is given for the example in Figure 5-2 of using plot.factor() for a bar plot, a boxplot, and a spline plot.

Listing 5-2. The code to demonstrate the use of plot.factor() to create a bar plot, a boxplot, and a spline plot

```
LCS = data.frame(
  dpi=dpi.ordered,
  pop75.f=cut(
    pop75.ordered,
    3,
    labels=c( "L", "M", "H" )
  ),
  pop15.f=cut(
    pop15.ordered,
    4
  ),
  sr=LifeCycleSavings$sr[ ord ]
)

plot(
  x=LCS[ ,2 ],
  y=LCS[ ,1 ],
  main="boxplot()",
  xlab="pop75 factor classes",
```

```
  ylab="dpi"
)

plot(
  x=LCS[ , 2 ],
  main="barplot()",
  xlab="pop75 factor classes",
  ylab="count"
)

plot(
  x=LCS[ , 2:3 ],
  legend.text=c("L", "ML", "MH", "H" ),
  main="splineplot()",
  xlab="pop75 factor classes",
  ylab="pop15 factor classes"
)
```

In Figure 5-2, the code in Listing 5-2 is run.

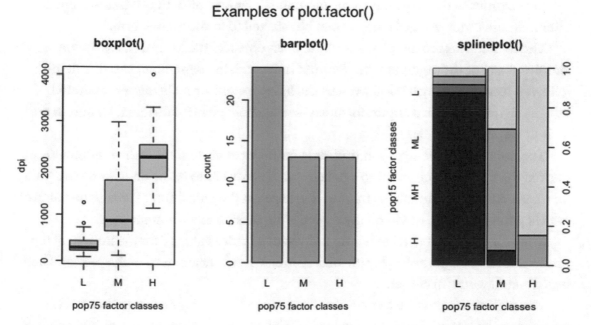

Figure 5-2. *An example of using plot.factor() to create a bar plot, a boxplot, and a spline plot*

Note that the function cut() was used to put the variables for the percentage of the population younger than 15 and the percentage older than 75 into classes. The labels for the percentage over 75 were assigned in the cut function. The labels for the percentage under 15 were assigned by using the argument legend.text.

5.2.3 The formula Method

The formula method for plot() creates plots for objects of the formula class. Objects of the formula class are created by the functions formula() and as.formula() or by explicitly writing out the formula. The dependent variable in the formula is plotted against each independent variable in the formula, each on a separate plot. The type of plot depends on both the class of the dependent variable and the class of the independent variable.

The function takes five specified arguments as well as the arguments used by any other methods called by the function – like plot.default(). The five specified arguments are formula, for the object of the formula class or the explicit formula; data, for the data frame, if one is used; subset, for the set of observations (within the rows) to plot; ylab, for the label on the vertical axis(es); and ask, for whether to pause before going to the next plot if there is more than one independent variable.

In the order of the arguments, the argument ... comes third. In general, arguments after ... in the order of arguments cannot be referred to in shortened form.

The formula argument takes a formula or an object of the formula class. In the simplest form of the argument, the formula starts with the dependent variable name, followed by a tilde, which is followed by the independent variable names separated by plus signs. For more complex formulas, see the help page for formula(). There is no default value for formula.

The data argument takes a matrix, data frame, or environment. If the argument is a matrix, the matrix is converted to a data frame. The variables in the data frame can then be referred to in the formula by the variable name in the data frame. The default value of data is parent.frame(), which on my device is the session environment.

The subset argument takes a numeric vector of index values – for the indices of the observations to be plotted. Only the observations in subset are used in the plot(s). There is no default value for subset.

The ylab argument takes a one-element character vector (or a vector that can be coerced to character). The default value of ylab is varnames[response] – which, on my device, uses the variable name of the dependent variable.

The ask argument takes a logical vector (or a vector that can be coerced to logical) of arbitrary length. Only the first value is used. The default value of ask is dev.interactive() – which on my device gives a value of TRUE since I can interact with my device.

In Listing 5-3, code is given for an example of using plot.formula(). All of the five arguments are used, as well as the arguments las and xlab.

Listing 5-3. Code to demonstrate plot.formula() using formula, data, subset, ylab, ask, las, and xlab

```
plot(
  dpi ~ .,
  data=LCS,
  subset=11:40,
  ylab="Disposable Income",
  ask=FALSE,
  las=3,
  xlab=""
)
```

In Figure 5-3, the code in Listing 5-3 is run.

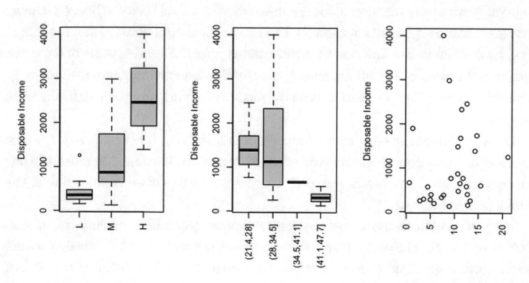

Figure 5-3. *An example of using formula, data, subset, ylab, ask, las, and xlab in plot()*

The argument formula takes the form `dpi ~ ..` Since the argument data is set to LCS, the period after the tilde tells R that all of the variables in LCS are to be used as independent variables except the assigned dependent variable.

Only the middle 30 observations are plotted, since subset equals `11:40`. The y axis label has been changed to "Disposable Income". The argument ask is set to FALSE, since the plots are plotted together in one graphic (which is done by setting mfrow in par() and will be covered in Section 6.2.1). Note that the x labels have been suppressed and the x axis tick labels are plotted vertically.

The three plots are against the percentage of the population over age 75, the percentage of the population under age 15, and the ratio of aggregate personal savings to disposable income. Since the first two variables are factor variables in the data frame LCS, the first two plots contain boxplots.

5.2.4 The function Method

The function method for plot() plots an object of the function class. Objects of the function class are either canned R functions or created with the function() function. The function plot.function() is similar to the function curve(), and the two functions share the same help page. The arguments of plot.function() are a bit simpler than those of the function curve(), but the method gives essentially the same result.

The plot.function() function takes six specified arguments as well as the arguments of curve() – with the exception of the argument expr in curve() (see Section 4.3.2 for a discussion of the arguments of curve()). The six specified arguments of plot.function() are x, for the function definition or function name; y, for the starting value of the variable input into the function; to, for the ending value of the variable input into the function; from, an alias of y; xlim, for the limits on the x axis of the plot; and ylab, for the label on the y axis.

The x argument can be a written function definition (e.g., `function( z ) z +1)` or the name of a function – including user-defined functions. The function must take only one argument and must return only one value for each value of the input variable. There is no default value for x.

The y, to, and from arguments take logical, numeric, complex, or character vectors of arbitrary length. The vectors are coerced to mode numeric, and only the first value is used. If from is specified, then from takes precedence over y. The default value of y is 0, of to is 1, and of from is y. (If from is specified as equal to y in the call to plot(), then plot() looks in the workspace for a value for y; and if y is not found, an error is given.)

The xlim argument takes a two-element vector of the raw, logical, numeric, or character mode. If not numeric, the vector is converted to the numeric mode. If y and to are not specified and xlim is, the values in xlim are used for y and to. The default value of xlim is NULL – that is, use the (possibly default) values of y and to for the x limits.

The ylab argument takes a character vector (or a vector that can be coerced to character) of arbitrary length. The elements of ylab are plotted on consecutive lines in the plot margin, starting at the default line used for axis labels. The default value of ylab is NULL – which plots the value of the argument x as the y label.

In Listing 5-4, code for an example using x (as a function definition), y, to, xlim, and xlab in plot.function() is given.

Listing 5-4. Code to demonstrate the use of x, y, to, xlim, and xlab in plot() when x is a function definition

```
plot(
  x=function( z ) z^2 + 2*z + 1,
  y=-5,
  to=5,
  xlim=c( -5.5, 5.5 ),
  xlab="z",
  main="Example of using x, y, to,\nxlim, & xlab in plot.function()"
)
```

In Figure 5-4, the code in Listing 5-4 is run.

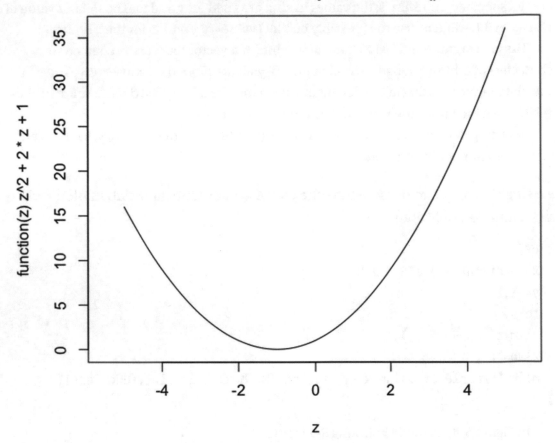

Figure 5-4. *An example of using x, y, to, xlim, and xlab in plot(), where x is a function definition*

Note that the y axis label is the function definition and, since the variable z was used for the function definition, the x axis label has been changed to "z". By default, the x axis label is "x". The range of xlim is wider than the range of y and to, so the parabola does not plot as far as the x axis limits.

5.2.5 The histogram Method

Histograms are plots of the number of observations that fall into numeric classes, usually of equal width, within the range of a numeric vector. The numeric variable can be on the horizontal or vertical axis. The histogram method of plot() plots a histogram when x is set equal to an object of the histogram class or is set equal to a list with the correct structure for a histogram. Objects of the histogram class are created by a call to hist().

The plot.histogram() function takes 17 specified arguments plus many unspecified graphical parameters. Of the specified arguments, the values of only three are specific to plot.histogram().

The first seven arguments are x, for a list containing the specifications of the histogram; freq, for whether to plot frequencies or a probability density function; density, for lines per inch in the histogram rectangles if the rectangles are filled with lines; angle, for the angles of the lines in the histogram rectangles; col, for the colors of the histogram rectangles; border, for the colors of the borders of the rectangles; and lty, for the line type of the borders of the rectangles.

The argument x takes a list with six elements. The first element is named breaks and contains an increasing numeric vector of break points for the histogram rectangles. There is one more break point than there are rectangles.

The second element is named counts and is a numeric vector containing the number of observations that fall between each two break points. There should be one value for each rectangle.

The third element is named density and is a numeric vector with a value for each rectangle giving the height of the rectangle. The value that R calculates for the density is the count for a rectangle divided by this quantity: the total number of observations multiplied by the width of the rectangle. The values have the property that the areas of the rectangles sum to one – a fundamental property of a probability density.

The fourth element is mids, a numeric vector of the midpoints along the x axis of the rectangles. The fifth element is xname and is a one-element character vector containing the name of the object for which the histogram is drawn.

The sixth element is equidist and is a one-element logical vector. The value should be TRUE if the rectangles are all of the same width. Otherwise, the value should be FALSE.

An appropriate list for x can be generated by a call to the function hist(), for example, by setting x equal to `hist( pop75.ordered, plot=FALSE )`.

The second argument, freq, takes a single-element logical vector. If set equal to TRUE, the counts values are used for the histogram heights. If FALSE, the density values are used.

The third through seventh arguments density, angle, col, border, and lty are as in the ancillary function rect(). See Section 4.3.4.1 for more information.

The last ten arguments, except labels, are standard arguments from plot.default(), but some have default values specific to plot.histogram(). The arguments are main, sub, xlab, and ylab, for the title, subtitle, x axis label, and y axis label; xlim and ylim, for the limits of the x and y axes; axes, for whether to plot axes; labels, for whether to plot and what to put for labels above the histogram rectangles; add, for whether to add to an existing plot; and ann, for whether to plot the titles and axis labels. See Sections 3.2.1, 3.2.2, and 4.1 or the help pages for plot.default(), title(), and axis() for more information.

The default value of main is `paste( "Histogram of", paste( x$xname, collapse="\n" ) )`. The default value of xlab is `x$xname`. The default value of xlim is `range( x$breaks )`. The default values of axes, add, and ann are TRUE, FALSE, and TRUE, respectively.

The labels argument can be either logical or a character vector of arbitrary length. If set to TRUE and freq is also set to TRUE, then the number of observations falling in the class of a rectangle (the count) is plotted above the rectangle.

If set to TRUE and freq is set to FALSE, then plotted above the rectangle is the count in a rectangle divided by the quantity: the total number of observations multiplied by the width of the rectangle. The result is taken out to three decimal places at most – depending on the width of the rectangles. If labels is FALSE, no labels are plotted.

If labels is a character vector and if the length of labels is less than the number of rectangles, then the elements of labels cycle out to the last rectangle. If the length of labels is the same as or larger than the number of rectangles, the elements will continue cycling through the rectangles until reaching the end of labels – overplotting the labels that were already above the rectangles as the cycling continues. The default value of labels is FALSE.

In Listing 5-5, code is given for an example of running plot() with a histogram list as the value for x.

Listing 5-5. Code and output for an example of using x, freq, labels, and ylim in plot.histogram()

```
pop75=hist(
  pop75.ordered,
  plot=FALSE
)
```

```
> pop75
$breaks
 [1] 0.5 1.0 1.5 2.0 2.5 3.0 3.5 4.0 4.5 5.0

$counts
[1]  9 11  4  4  5  7  4  4  2

$density
[1] 0.36 0.44 0.16 0.16 0.20 0.28 0.16 0.16 0.08

$mids
[1] 0.75 1.25 1.75 2.25 2.75 3.25 3.75 4.25 4.75

$xname
[1] "pop75.ordered"

$equidist
[1] TRUE

attr(,"class")
[1] "histogram"

plot(
  x=pop75,
  freq=FALSE,
  labels=c( "nine", "eleven", "four", "four", "five", "seven", "four",
    "four", "two" ),
  ylim=c( 0, 0.5 ),
  main="Example of using\nx, freq, labels & ylim in plot.histogram()"
)

box(
  bty="l"
)
```

In Figure 5-5, the code in Listing 5-5 is run.

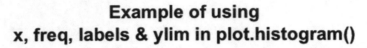

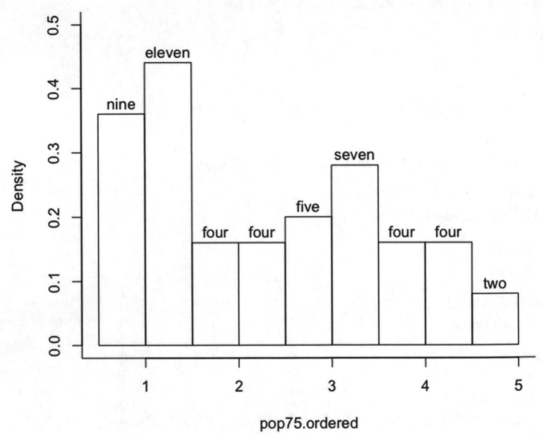

Figure 5-5. *Example of using x, freq, labels, and ylim in plot.histogram()*

Note that the y axis has been extended, because the top of the el in eleven was cut off with the default value of ylim. Also, the labels plot out the numbers in letter form. The size of the labels is determined internally. On the y axis, the values are for a probability density. An L-shaped box was added to the plot.

5.2.6 The raster Method

Raster objects are used in plotting images and are created out of rectangular grids – in the form of a vector or matrix of color values in R. The function plot() plots objects of the raster class. Objects of the raster class are created by the function as.raster(). The function as.raster() takes a vector or matrix and assigns color values based on the values in the object. By default, as.raster() gives a raster object with a gray scale. (See the help page for as.raster() for more information.)

When using plot.raster(), the matrix or vector to be plotted must be of the raster class. Otherwise, nothing plots. No annotation can be done in the call to plot(), but it can be added by using ancillary functions.

The plot.raster() function takes eight specified arguments, plus unspecified arguments used by plot.default() and rasterImage() (see Chapter 3 and Section 4.2.4.2). The arguments are x, for the raster object; y, which is ignored; xlim and ylim, for the limits of the x and y axes; xaxs and yaxs, for the style of edge spacing on the x and y axes; asp, for the aspect ratio; and add, for whether to add to an existing plot.

The x argument takes an object of the raster class. There is no default value for x.

The xlim and ylim arguments give the limits of the plotting region on which the raster object is plotted. Usually, only one is used by plot(); the other limits are calculated internally by plot(). The axis limits can be used to select a portion of an image, to resize an image, and/or to place an image at a specific place on a graphic. The default values of xlim and ylim are `c( 0, ncol( x ) )` and `c( 0, nrow( x ) )`.

The xaxs and yaxs arguments are as in Section 3.4.5. By default, xaxs and yaxs are equal to "i", that is, there is no margin between the edge of the plot and the limits of the plot.

The asp argument gives the ratio of a unit on the y axis to a unit on the x axis. By default, asp equals 1. That is, the actual length of a unit on the y axis equals the length of a unit on the x axis.

The add argument tells plot() whether to add to an existing plot or to create a new plot. The default value is FALSE, that is, create a new plot.

If the raster object is a vector, the object is always plotted vertically. If the object is a matrix with one row or column, the object is plotted vertically. If the object is a matrix with one row or one column and is transposed, the object is plotted horizontally.

The values used for locating the cells of a raster matrix (the x and y coordinates) are the values of the row and column indices minus one-half. That is, for a nr by nc raster matrix, the image plots from zero through nc on the x axis and zero through nr on the y axis. The arguments xlim and ylim can be set to affect the placement of the image in the plotting region.

The size of the plotting region is set by the pin argument of par(). The pin argument is a two-element numeric vector containing the lengths of the sides of the plotting region in inches – the length of the horizontal sides is given first and the length of the vertical sides second. The argument pin can only be set by a call to par() (see Chapter 6, Section 6.2.1.3).

How the raster image plots depends on the row and column dimensions of the matrix (or vector) and the ratio of the width and height of the plotting region. The function plot() figures which of xlim or ylim to extend to the horizontal or vertical limits of the plotting region based on whether the limits given for the other axis fit within the plotting region.

Say xlim is used for the limits of the x axis. To find the limits of the y axis, the range of the x axis is divided by two and then multiplied by the ratio of the height of the plotting region to the width of the plotting region. The result is then subtracted from and added to the mean of ylim. The two results give the limits of the y axis. That is, the limits on the y axis equal mean(ylim) minus and plus (max(xlim) - min(xlim)) / 2 * par("pin")[2] / par("pin")[1]. The process gives an image that is centered on the mean of ylim.

If the ylim is extended, the y axis limits are set by ylim. The x axis limits are then mean(xlim) minus and plus (max(ylim) - min(ylim)) / 2 * par("pin") [1] / par("pin")[2]. The placement of the image also depends on the argument asp.

For example, the volcano dataset is a matrix with 87 rows and 61 columns. Each row is one unit, and each column is one unit. Assume that the plotting region is such that the top and bottom of the image are at the edge of the plot. That is, the vertical axis goes from 0 to 87. Assume that, for the plotting region, the vertical to horizontal ratio is 0.86. Then 87 divided by 0.86 gives the range of the horizontal axis limits. The range would be 101 units. For the default value of xlim (c(0, 61)), the mean of xlim is 30.5, so the image is centered at 30.5 on the x axis, which gives a lower limit of -20 and an upper limit of 81 on the x axis. The image does not fill out to the left and right edges of the plot if asp equals 1.

To plot the volcano dataset so that the image completely fills the plotting region, the following code works: plot(as.raster(250-volcano, max=195), asp=(par("pin")[2]/87)/(par("pin")[1]/61)). The argument asp is then the inches per unit on the y axis divided by the inches per unit on the x axis. Given that the ratio of height to width for the plotting region is 0.86, for the preceding value of asp, a unit on the y axis would be about 0.6 the size of a unit on the x axis.

In Listing 5-6, code is given for an example of not setting and setting asp.

Listing 5-6. Code to plot the volcano dataset with and without setting asp in plot.
raster()

```
plot(
  as.raster(
    250-volcano,
    max=195
  )
)

{ box(); axis(1); axis(2) }

title(
  "Default Plot"
)

plot(
  as.raster(
    250-volcano,
    max=195
  ),
  asp=
    ( par( "pin" )[ 2 ]/87 )/
    ( par( "pin" )[ 1 ]/61 )
)

{ box(); axis(1); axis(2) }

title(
  "asp Set"
)

mtext(
  "Default Plot & Plot with asp Set",
  outer=TRUE,
  font=1,
  side=3
)
```

In Figure 5-6, the code in Listing 5-6 is run.

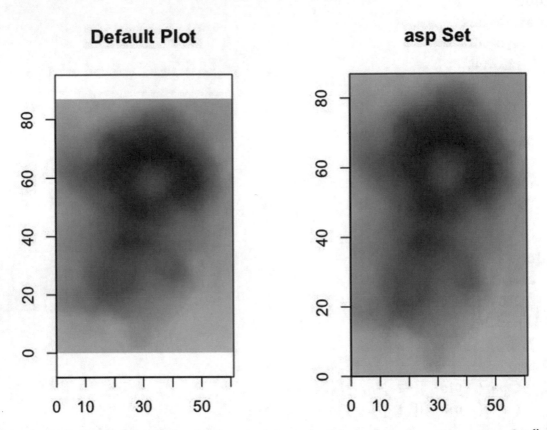

Figure 5-6. *Example of plotting a raster image of the volcano matrix using plot()*
without and with setting asp

Note that the axes and boxes were added to the plots to clarify how plotting works in
plot.raster(). The function plot.raster() plots raster images without axes or annotation.
Because the width and height of the individual plotting regions are not the same, the
second plot is not to the scale of the matrix.

Figure 5-7 gives a demonstration of how a raster matrix is plotted. The code for
Figure 5-7 is given in Listing 5-7.

Listing 5-7. Code for the demonstration of plotting a raster matrix in Figure 5-7

```
plot(
  as.raster(
    1-( volcano[ 87:1, 61:1 ] - 76 )/140
  ),
  interpolate=FALSE
)

title(
  main="Example of Using plot.raster()",
  line=2.6
)

title(
  sub="The Maungawhau Volcano Data\nRows and Columns in Reverse Order",
  line=3.6,
  font=2
)

mtext(
  "S\ntop of volcano matrix",
  side=1,
  line=1
)

mtext(
  "right side\nof volano matrix",
  side=2,
  las=1,
  line=-5.9
)

mtext(
  "W",
  side=2, ,
  las=1,
  line=-7
)
```

```
mtext(
  "bottom of volcano matrix\nN",
  side=3
)

mtext(
  "left side\nof volano matrix",
  side=4,
  las=1,
  line=-5.9
)

mtext(
  "E",
  side=4,
  las=1,
  line=-7
)
```

In Figure 5-7, the code in Listing 5-7 is run.

Example of Using plot.raster()

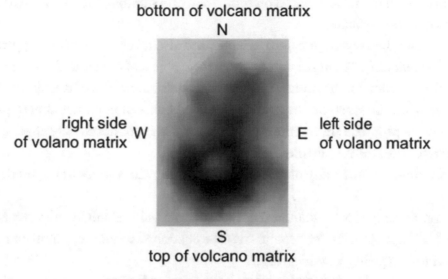

bottom of volcano matrix

The Maungawhau Volcano Data
Rows and Columns in Reverse Order

Figure 5-7. *Example of using plot.raster() on the matrix volcano, where as.raster() is run a function of volano*

In Figure 5-7, the matrix in the volcano dataset has been put in reverse order for both the rows and the columns and then plotted. So the top of the plotted matrix is the bottom of the original matrix, and the left of the plotted matrix is the right of the original matrix. The reversal was done to put north on the top and west on the left.

5.2.7 The table Method

Tables tabulate or cross-tabulate data that is in columns. A table contains the number of observations in each group within the columns of the dataset. If there is more than one column, the columns are crossed with each other to find the unique groups. Cells of the table can contain zero. Tables are often used with data that contains measurements of the presence, absence, or class of a property of the observations.

The table method for plot() plots objects of the table class. An object of the table class can be created by using the table() function on classified data or by using the function as.table() on a numeric vector, matrix, or array. The function table() creates a contingency table, and as.table() gives an object of the numeric mode (with nonnegative values) the table class.

The function plot.table() draws bars for the count in each class if the table is based on one variable. If the table is based on more than one variable, the function plots a mosaic plot of the variables.

The function has seven specified variables and also takes many of the arguments used by plot.default(). The arguments are x, for the object of the table class; type, for the type of plot; ylim, for the limits of the y axis; lwd, for the width of the plotted lines; xlab and ylab, for the labels on the x and y axes; and frame.plot, for whether to put a box around the plot. The arguments type, ylim, lwd, and plot.frame only affect plots of a single variable, not the mosaic plots.

The argument x can be any object of the table class. The argument has no default value.

The argument type is the standard argument from plot.default() and can take the values "p", "l", "b", "c", "o", "h", "s", "S", and "n". (See Section 3.3.1 for more information.) The default value of type in plot.table() is "h".

The arguments ylim, lwd, xlab, and ylab are the standard arguments from plot. default(). (See Sections 3.2.1 for ylim, xlab, and ylab and 3.4.4 for lwd.) The default value of ylim equals c(0, max(x)). The default value of lwd equals 2. The default values of xlab and ylab equal NULL.

The argument frame.plot takes a logical vector (or a vector that can be coerced to logical) of arbitrary length. Only the first value is used. If set to TRUE and the plot is of bars, the argument bty can be used to set the box type (see Section 3.2.2). The default value of frame.plot is is.num – which takes the value of TRUE when the names of the variables can be coerced to numeric. Otherwise, the value is FALSE.

In Listing 5-8, code is given for an example of plotting single-variable and two-variable contingency tables, using x, ylim, lwd, lend, main, xlab, ylab, frame.plot, and bty.

Listing 5-8. Code for the example, in Figure 5-8, of plotting single-variable and two-variable contingency tables with plot(), using x, ylim, lwd, lend, main, xlab, ylab, frame.plot, and bty

```
LCSf = data.frame(
  apply(
    LifeCycleSavings,
    2,
    cut,
```

```
      breaks=3,
      labels=c( "few", "half", "many" )
    )
)

plot(
    table( LCSf$pop15 ),
    lwd=10,
    lend=1,
    ylim=c( 0, 25 ),
    frame.plot=TRUE,
    bty="l",
    main="One Variable",
    xlab="pop15 factors",
    ylab="count"
)

plot(
    table(
      LCSf$pop15,
      LCSf$pop75
    ),
    main="Two Variables",
    xlab="pop15 factors",
    ylab="pop75 factors"
)

mtext(
    "Example of using x, lwd, ylim,\nframe.plot, bty, main, xlab, and ylab
    in plot.table()",
    outer=TRUE,
    side=3
)
```

In Figure 5-8, the code in Listing 5-8 is run.

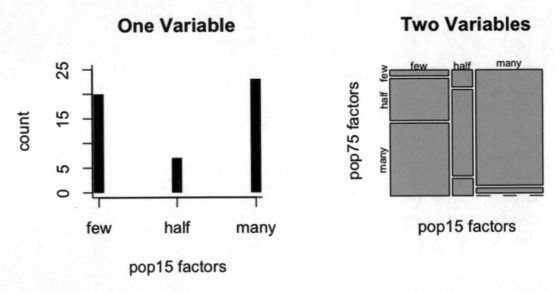

Figure 5-8. *An example of using x, ylim, lwd, lend, main, xlab, ylab, frame.plot, and bty in two calls to plot.table()*

Note that in the first plot there is a space between the bars and the axis. Setting xaxs to "i" would move the axis up to 0 and eliminate the gap. Also, for the bars, lwd was set to 10, and lend was set to a square line end. The default gives rounded line ends. Since frame.plot was set to TRUE in the first plot, the box type was set to "l" for an L-shaped box.

5.3 The Methods for plot() in the stats Package

The methods for the plot() function in the stats package are used to plot output from a variety of functions used for statistical analysis. For example, there are methods for linear regression, dendrograms, and principal component analysis. In all, there are 20 methods for plot() in the stats package.

In Table 5-2, the methods for plot() in the stats package are given. The table is from the help page for the stats package in R.

Table 5-2.   *The methods for plot() in the R stats package*

Function	Description
"plot.acf	*Plot Autocovariance and Autocorrelation Functions"*
"plot.decomposed.ts	*Classical Seasonal Decomposition by Moving Averages"*
"plot.dendrogram	*General Tree Structures"*
"plot.density	*Plot Method for Kernel Density Estimation"*
"plot.ecdf	*Empirical Cumulative Distribution Function"*
"plot.hclust	*Hierarchical Clustering"*
"plot.HoltWinters	*Plot function for HoltWinters objects"*
"plot.isoreg	*Plot Method for isoreg Objects"*
"plot.lm	*Plot Diagnostics for an lm Object"*
"plot.ppr	*Plot Ridge Functions for Projection Pursuit Regression Fit"*
"plot.prcomp	*Principal Components Analysis"*
"plot.princomp	*Principal Components Analysis"*
"plot.profile.nls	*Plot a profile.nls Object"*
"plot.spec	*Plotting Spectral Densities"*
"plot.spec.coherency	*Plotting Spectral Densities"*
"plot.stepfun	*Plot Step Functions"*
"plot.stl	*Methods for STL Objects"*
"plot.ts	*Plotting Time-Series Objects"*
"plot.tskernel	*Smoothing Kernel Objects"*

—Help page in R for the stats package

Each of the methods in the table is covered in this chapter. Examples are given for the methods.

5.3.1 The acf Method

Autocorrelation and autocovariance plots and partial autocorrelation and partial autocovariance plots (or cross-correlation and cross-covariance plots) are used in time series analysis to visually assess the amount of autocorrelation within a vector of numbers (or cross-correlation for two vectors). Usually the vector(s) contains observations that are equally spaced in time or space.

The acf method of plot() plots objects of the acf class. Objects of the acf class are created by the functions acf(), pacf(), and ccf(). The functions acf(), pacf(), and ccf() calculate and plot autocorrelations and autocovariances (acf()), partial autocorrelations and partial autocovariances (pacf()), and cross-correlations and cross-covariances (ccf()) for numeric (usually time series) vectors or matrices – that is, objects of the numeric class or mode (usually of the ts class).

The plot.acf() function takes 17 specified arguments, plus many of the arguments that plot.default() takes. The first nine arguments are x, for the object of the acf class; ci, for the level(s) of the confidence of the confidence interval(s) that is (are) plotted; type, for the plot type; xlab and ylab, for the labels on the x and y axes; ylim, for the limits on the y axis; main, for the title of the plot; ci.col, for the confidence interval color(s); and ci.type, for the type of confidence interval.

The x argument takes an object of the acf class. There is no default value for x.

The ci argument takes a numeric vector with elements that are greater than or equal to zero and less than one. A confidence interval is plotted for each value. A value of 0 suppresses the confidence interval. The default value of ci is 0.95.

The type argument is the standard argument from plot.default() (see Section 3.3.1). The default value of type is "h".

The xlab, ylab, ylim, and main arguments are the standard arguments from Section 3.2.1. The default value of xlab is "Lag". The default values of ylab, ylim, and main are NULL.

The ci.col argument takes a vector of color values (see Section 3.4.1) of arbitrary length. The colors cycle in the following way: The first color is assigned to the first confidence level line above the line at zero. The second to the second confidence level line. And so on until all of the lines above zero are assigned a color. Then, the lines below zero are assigned colors starting with the line closest to zero. The default value of ci.col is "blue".

The ci.type argument takes NULL or a one-element character vector that can take on the value "white" or "ma". The values NULL and "white" tell plot to use the assumption that the errors are white noise to generate the confidence intervals and multiple intervals do not cause a problem.

The value "ma" tells plot() to assume a moving average time series with the order of the time series being one less than the lag being calculated (see the help page for plot. acf()). Only one interval can be calculated if ci.type equals "ma". The default value for ci.type is c("white", "ma"), that is, use "white".

The tenth through sixteenth arguments are used to make the plotting of acf objects with multiple time series easier. The arguments cannot be changed – at least on my device.

The seven arguments are max.mfrow, to tell plot() how many series to plot on a page if there are multiple series; ask, to tell plot() whether to ask the user for a response before going on to a new plotting page; mar, for setting the margins of the plot(s); oma, for setting the outer margins of the page; mgp, for setting the lines on which the axis labels and subtitles plot; xpd, for whether to expand the plotting region; and cex.main, for the character size of the plot titles. The arguments are included because the arguments have special default values in plot.acf().

For max.mfrow, the value is 6, for a maximum of 36 plots per page – six rows and six columns. (The mfrow argument is covered in Section 6.2.1.5.)

For ask, the default value is Npgs > 1 && dev.interactive(), that is, if there is more than one page and the device allows interaction with the user, then ask is set to TRUE. Otherwise, ask is FALSE.

For mar, oma, and mgp, the arguments take the respective values in par() if the number of time series is less than three. Otherwise, the respective values are c(3, 2, 2, 0.8), c(1, 1.2, 1, 1), and c(1.5, 0.6, 0). Both mar and oma are covered in Sections 6.2.1.1 and 6.2.1.2, and mgp is covered in Sections 4.1 and 4.2.1.

The argument xpd takes the value of xpd in par(). The argument cex.main takes a value of 1 if the number of time series is greater than two. Otherwise, cex.main has the value of cex.main in par().

The 17th argument is verbose, for the level of information to return. The default value is the value of verbose in options() – which on my device is FALSE (found by running getOption("verbose")).

Most of the arguments to plot.default() in Chapter 3 can be set. However, font.main, col.main, and cex.main cannot be set.

For the examples in Figure 5-9, the dataset sunspot.year from the datasets package is used. The data run from 1700 to 1988 and are the average over the year of daily sunspot numbers. Currently, the source is WDC-SILSO, at the Royal Observatory of Belgium.

In Listing 5-9, the code used in the examples of plot(), using output from acf(), pacf(), and ccf(), is given.

Listing 5-9. Code for the examples of plotting output from acf(), pacf(), and ccf() using plot(). The arguments x, ci, type, ci.col, ci.type, and main are set

```
par(
  oma=c( 1, 1, 3, 1),
  mfrow=c( 3, 1 )
)

acf.m=acf(
  sunspot.year,
  lag=150
)

pacf.m=pacf(
  sunspot.year,
  lag=10
)

ccf.m=ccf(
  sunspot.year[ 1:278 ],
  sunspot.year[ 12:289 ],
  lag=150
)

plot(
  acf.m,
  ci=c( 0.966 ),
  type="l",
  ci.col=grey( 0.4 ),
  ci.type="ma",
  main="ci=c(0.966), type=\"l\", ci.col=grey(0.4), ci.type=\"ma\""
)
```

```
plot(
  pacf.m,
  ci=c( 0.8, 0.966 ),
  type="h",
  ci.col=grey(
    c(0.4, 0.6)
  ),
  ci.type="white",
  main="ci=c(0.8,0.966), type=\"h\", ci.col=grey(c(0.4,0.6),   ci.
  type=\"white\""
)

plot(
  ccf.m, ci=c( 0.8, 0.966 ),
  type="h",
  ci.col=grey(
    c( 0.4, 0.6 )
  ),
  ci.type="white",
  main="ci=c(0.8,0.966), type=\"h\", ci.col=grey(c(0.4,0.6)),
  ci.type=\"white\""
)

mtext(
  "Examples of Using ci, type, ci.col, and ci.type in plot.acf()",
  outer=TRUE,
  line=1
)

par(
  oma=c( 0, 0, 0, 0 ),
  mfrow=c( 1, 1 )
)
```

In Figure 5-9, the code in Listing 5-9 is run.

Examples of Using ci, type, ci.col, and ci.type in plot.acf()

ci=c(0.966), type="l", ci.col=grey(0.4), ci.type="ma"

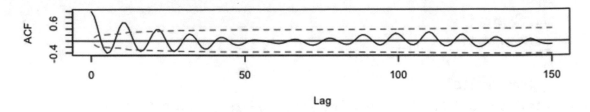

ci=c(0.8,0.966), type="h", ci.col=grey(c(0.4,0.6), ci.type="white"

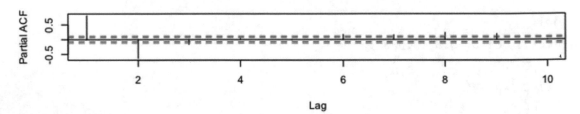

ci=c(0.8,0.966), type="h", ci.col=grey(c(0.4,0.6)), ci.type="white"

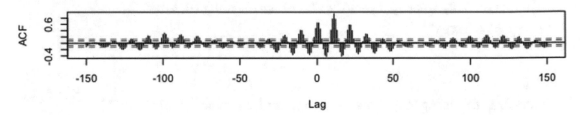

Figure 5-9. *Examples of using plot() to plot output from acf(), pacf(), and ccf(). The first plot is of output from acf(), the second from pacf(), and the third from ccf(). The arguments x, ci, type, ci.col, ci.type, and main were set*

Sunspots have a known cycle of slightly less than 11 years. In the third plot, the cross-correlations between the sunspot series lagged by 11 years and the current sunspot series are given – just for an example. Note that, for the first and third plots, the lags are over 150 years and, for the second plot, the lags are over 10 years.

For the first plot, type is set to "l" – for a line plot. In the second and third plots, type is set to "h" – for histogram bars (the default value). For the first plot, ci.type is set to "ma" – for moving average – so only one confidence interval can be calculated. In the second and third plots, ci.type takes the value "white" – for white noise – so two confidence intervals can be and are calculated.

5.3.2 The decomposed.ts Method

For seasonal time series data with a trend, the time series can be decomposed into three time series. The three time series give the trend within the data, the seasonal component of the data based on the given frequency of the time series, and the residuals found by subtracting the combined trend and seasonal components from the original series.

The decomposed.ts method for plot() plots objects of the decomposed.ts class. Objects of the decomposed.ts class are created by the decompose() function. The decompose() function decomposes a time series, based on the frequency of the time series, using an autoregressive method.

The decomposition returns a list containing the original data, the trend in the data, the seasonal component of the data, the random component of the data, and the type of decomposition. The function plot() plots the first four elements of the list in four separate plots and gives the type of decomposition in the title.

The help page for plot.decomposed.ts() and the help page for decompose are the same page. However, there is no function plot() under **Usage** on the help page, so no specific plotting parameters are set.

The function decompose() takes three arguments, x, for the time series; type, for the type of decomposition; and filter, to manually enter numeric values to filter the seasonal component.

The x argument is the time series and takes an object of the ts class. The frequency of the time series must be greater than or equal to two. The value of x can contain more than one time series, but plot() does not perform well in the case of more than one time series. There is no default value for x.

The type argument takes a one-element character vector that has the value "additive" or "multiplicative". If type equals "additive", then an additive model is used. If type equals "multiplicative", a multiplicative model is used. (The strings "additive" and "multiplicative" can be shortened and still be recognized by decompose().) The default value of type is c("additive", "multiplicative"), that is, the additive method is used.

The filter argument takes a numeric vector of a length less than the following quantity: two plus the length of the time series minus the frequency of the time series. The filter should be in reverse of the time order. If filter is given the value of NULL, then a symmetric moving average model is used to find the seasonal component. The default value of filter is NULL.

For an object created by decompose(), no changes can be made to main, sub, and ylab in the call to plot(), but xlab can be set. Most of the other arguments in Chapter 3 can be set. However, the font weight for a plotting character cannot be set. The family argument and the other font arguments can be set. The ancillary function mtext() can be used to put information about the plot onto the figure.

See the help page for decompose() for more information. In Listing 5-10, code is given for the example in Figure 5-10 of using plot() and decompose() together, with lwd, lty, col, and xlab set.

Listing 5-10. Code for the example of running plot() and decompose() together – lwd=2, lty=3, col=grey(0.25), and xlab="Eleven Year Cycles"

```
plot(
  decompose(
    ts(
      sunspot.year,
      freq=11
    ),
    type="mult"
  ),
  lwd=2,
  lty=3,
  col=grey( 0.25 ),
  xlab="Eleven Year Cycles"
)

mtext(
  "The sunspot.year Dataset - Yearly Data: 1700 to 1988",
  side=1,
  line=3.7,
  font=3
)
```

In Figure 5-10, the code in Listing 5-10 is run.

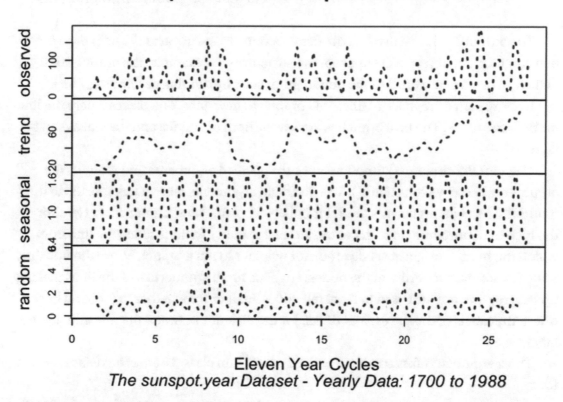

Figure 5-10. *Example of using plot() and decompose() together. The arguments to plot(), lwd, lty, col, and xlab, are set*

Note that only the x axis label could be changed and that mtext() is used to include the information about the dataset. A line width of 2 and a line type of "dotted" are used. The color in the plots is grey(0.25). The method of decomposition is the multiplicative method.

5.3.3 The dendrogram Method

Dendrograms are used as a method of clustering a dataset. Observations in the dataset are grouped together based on the values of variables within the dataset. The rows of the dataset are usually named. The dendrogram method for plot() plots objects of the dendrogram class. To quote from the help page for dendrogram in R

193

The dendrogram is directly represented as a nested list where each component corresponds to a branch of the tree.

—The help page for dendrogram in R

The structure of a list that has the dendrogram class is given at the help page for dendrogram. An object of the appropriate structure – for example, the output from hclust() – can be converted to the dendrogram class by running as.dendrogram().

Dendrograms are made of lines that branch to new lines. The places where the lines branch are nodes. The final branches are leaves. Both the nodes and the leaves can be labeled.

The plot.dendrogram() function takes 16 specified arguments and many of the arguments used by plot.default(). The first eight arguments take values specific to the method. The eight arguments are x, for the object of the dendrogram class; type, for the type of dendrogram to plot; center, for the location of a node along the line from which the branch originates; edge.root, for whether to put a branch above the first line; nodePar, for the properties of the nodes; edgePar, for the properties of the lines making up the tree and any text used to label the nodes; leaflab, for whether to plot and how to orient the labels of the leaves; and dLeaf, for the distance between the tree and the leaf labels.

The x argument takes an object of the dendrogram class. There is no default value for x.

The type argument is a character vector and can take one of two values – "rectangle" or "triangle". The choice of "rectangle" plots a rectangular tree. The choice of "triangle" plots a triangular tree. The default value is `c( "rectangle", "triangle" )`, which gives a rectangular tree.

The center argument takes a single-element logical vector (or a vector that can be coerced to logical). The value TRUE tells plot() to use the position of the leaves to locate a node on a line. The value FALSE tells plot() to position the nodes at the center of the line containing the node. The choice of TRUE gives a narrower plot. The default value is FALSE.

The edge.root argument takes a one-element logical vector (or a vector that can be coerced to logical). A value of TRUE tells plot() to plot a branch into the first line. The value FALSE tells plot() to not plot the branch. The default value is `is.leaf(x) || !is.null( attr(x, "edge.text" ) )`.

The nodePar argument takes a list, if used, and the value of NULL otherwise. The argument tells plot() what to plot at the nodes and leaves. There can be up to five elements in the list which are each named one of the following: pch, col, cex, xpd, or bg – for the plotting character, the outline color for the plotting character, the character size, the expansion choice, and the fill color for the plotting characters 21–25 (see Sections 3.2, 3.3, and 3.4).

The elements of the list can have one or two values. If one value long, the property is applied to both the nodes and the leaves. If there is a second value, the first value affects the nodes, and the second value affects the leaves. The default value of nodePar is NULL, that is, do not annotate the nodes.

The edgePar argument takes a list, if edgePar is used, and otherwise takes the value NULL. The list is up to seven elements long, and each element is named one of the following – col, lty, lwd, p.col, p.lty, p.lwd, and t.col.

Each element can take one or two values. If only one value is supplied, and depending on the name of the value, the setting is applied to all of the lines, node label polygons, or node labels. If two values are supplied, the first value applies to all of the nodes down to the lines to the leaves, while the second value applies to the leaves and the lines into the leaves.

The values named col, lty, and lwd apply to the lines making up the tree and are the standard col, lty, and lwd of plot.default(). The values named p.col, p.lty, and p.lwd affect the polygons that are drawn around labels for the nodes – if the nodes are labeled – and act like the standard col, lty, and lwd.

The value named t.col gives the color of the text if the nodes are labeled and takes color values. The default value of edgePar is list() – that is, segments and polygons are black, with solid lines of width 1, and the text is black.

The leaflab argument takes a character vector with one of three possible values – "perpendicular", "textlike", or "none". If the value is "perpendicular", the leaf labels are plotted perpendicularly to the tree. If leaflab is set to "textlike", the leaf labels are plotted parallel to the tree and in polygons. If set equal to "none", no labels are plotted. The default value of leaflab is c("perpendicular", "textlike", "none"), that is, the labels are plotted perpendicularly.

The dLeaf argument takes a numeric vector of arbitrary length. If dLeaf is longer than one, each label is plotted n times – where n is the length of dLeaf – each time at the distance given by the respective value in dLeaf. Usually, just one value is used in dLeaf. A large value – like 100 – is necessary to see the effect of dLeaf. The default value of dLeaf is NULL – which gives a space of about three-quarters of a character size in the direction perpendicular to reading (height for text parallel to the tree and width for text perpendicular to the tree).

The ninth through sixteenth arguments of plot.dendrogram() are xlab and ylab, for the x and y axis labels; xaxt and yaxt, for the x and y axis types; horiz, for the orientation of the tree; frame.plot, for whether to frame the plot; and xlim and ylim, for the x and y axis limits. Most of the arguments are the standard arguments to plot.default() but have different default values than in plot.default().

The xlab and ylab arguments take character vectors of arbitrary length. The default value for the arguments is " ".

The xaxt and yaxt arguments take character vectors of arbitrary length. Only the first element is used which must take on a value of "s", "l", "t", or "n". The first three values give the same result – a standard axis. The value of "n" suppresses the axis. The default value of xaxt is "n" and of yaxt is "s".

The horiz argument takes a logical vector (or a vector that can be coerced to logical) of arbitrary length. If the length is greater than one, a warning is given and only the first value is used. If set to TRUE, a horizontally oriented tree is plotted. If FALSE, a vertically oriented tree is plotted. The default value is FALSE.

The frame.plot argument is a logical vector (or a vector that can be coerced to logical) of arbitrary length. If the value of frame.plot is longer than one element, only the first element is used and a warning is given. If set to TRUE, a box is plotted around the tree. If set to FALSE, no box is plotted. The default value is FALSE.

The xlim and ylim arguments take numeric vectors of length two. The maximum values of x and y are found by entering the dendrogram at the R prompt. The maximum values are given. For example:

```
> as.dendrogram( hclust( dist( LifeCycleSavings[ , 2:4 ] ) ) )
'dendrogram' with 2 branches and 50 members total, at height 3912.968.
```

For the example, there are 50 leaves, and the x values of the leaves go from 1 to 50. Also, the height is given as 3912.968, so the maximum value of y is 3912.968. The minimum value of y is 0. There are no default values for xlim and ylim – R chooses good values.

In Listing 5-11, code is given for the example in Figure 5-11 of using plot() to plot an object of the dendrogram class. Default values were used in dist(), hclust(), and as.dendrogram(). The only argument set in plot() is axes.

Listing 5-11. Code for the example of using plot() to plot an object of the dendrogram class. The argument axes is set to FALSE

```
par(
  mar=c( 7, 0, 4, 0 ) + 0.1
)

plot(
  as.dendrogram(
    hclust(
      dist(
        LifeCycleSavings[ , 2:4 ]
      )
    )
  ),
  axes=FALSE
)

title(
  main="50 Countries: Average Over Years 1960 to 1970 of
  Disposable Income, Population Under 15, and Population Over 75
  Euclidean Distance used in dist()",
  font.main=1
)

par(
  mar=c( 5, 4, 4, 2 ) + 0.1
)
```

In Figure 5-11, the code in Listing 5-11 is run.

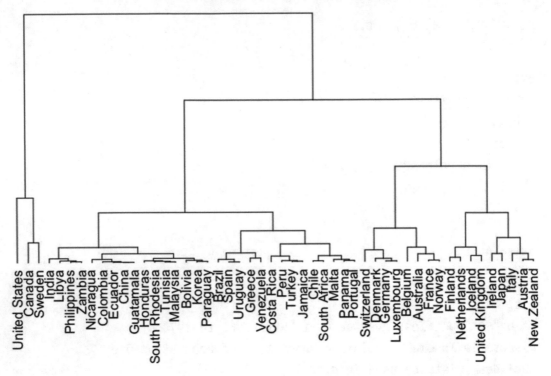

**50 Countries: Average Over Years 1960 to 1970 of
Disposable Income, Population Under 15, and Population Over 75
Euclidean Distance used in dist()**

Figure 5-11. *Example of creating and plotting a dendrogram using the defaults of dist(), hclust(), and as.dendrogram(). The plot() argument axes is set to FALSE*

The bottom margin of the plot is increased by two lines to accommodate the labels on the leaves. The left and right margins are reduced to 0.1 line width for the plot. The margins are reset to the default values after the plot is plotted. The left axis is suppressed.

5.3.4 The density Method

Probability distribution functions, also called probability densities, are the basis of inferential statistics. There are many probability densities that are based on mathematical functions. The densities are estimated by estimating parameters of the mathematical functions. Density functions can also be estimated directly from the data. The density method of plot() plots probability densities estimated directly from the data. Probability densities have the property that the area under the curve is equal to one.

The density method for plot() plots objects of the density class. Objects of the density class are created by the density() function. The density() function estimates probability densities using the kernel method of density estimation.

The plot.density() function takes six specified arguments plus many arguments used by plot.default(). The six arguments are x, for the output from density(); main, xlab, and ylab, for the title and x and y axis labels; type, for the plot type; and zero.line, for whether to plot a line at y equal to zero.

The x argument takes objects of the density class. There is no default value for x.

The main, xlab, and ylab arguments take character vectors of arbitrary length. The default value for main is NULL, for which plot() plots the value of x as the title. For xlab the default value is NULL, for which the number of observations and the kernel bandwidth are plotted as the label of the x axis. For ylab, the default value is "Density".

The type argument is the standard argument from plot.default(). In plot.density() the default value is "l", that is, a line is plotted.

The zero.line argument takes a logical vector (or a vector that can be coerced to logical) of arbitrary length. If longer than one element, only the first element is used and a warning is given. If set to TRUE, plot() should put a line at y equal to 0. On my device, no line is plotted. The default value is TRUE.

In Listing 5-12, code is given for an example of using the default values in plot. density() and density().

Listing 5-12. Code for the example given in Figure 5-12 of using the defaults in plot.density() and density() to plot an estimated probability density of the variable pop75.ordered

```
plot(
  density(
    pop75.ordered
  )
)
```

In Figure 5-12, the code in Listing 5-12 is run.

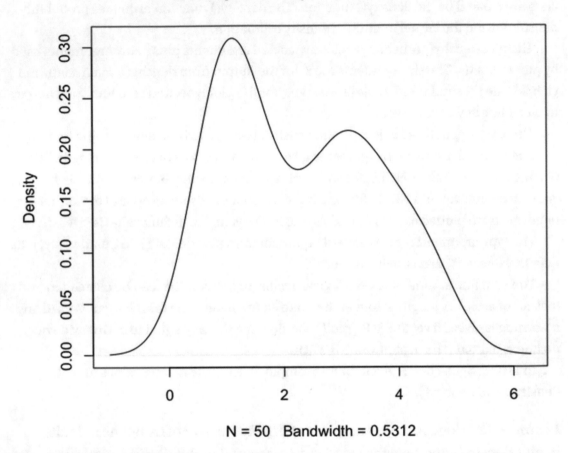

Figure 5-12. *Example of using the defaults for plot.density() and density() to plot an estimated probability density of the variable pop75.ordered*

Note than no line is drawn at y equal to 0, even though the default value for zero.line is TRUE.

5.3.5 The ecdf Method

The cumulative distribution function, plotted against x, is the integral from minus infinity to x of the probability density function. The values of the cumulative distribution function go from zero to one, and the function is nondecreasing. (The integral is done over some combination of the real line and the counting measure, depending on the underlying measure of the probability density.)

The ecdf method for plot() plots objects of the ecdf class. Objects of the ecdf class are created by the ecdf() function. The ecdf() function creates an empirical cumulative density function out of a numeric vector. An empirical cumulative density function is a nondecreasing function that steps from zero to one over the range of the data. The function steps up where there is a data point.

In ecdf(), the data is a numeric vector (or an object that can be coerced to a numeric vector) and is sorted internally before the step function is created. See the help page for ecdf() for more information.

The plot.ecdf() function takes five specified arguments plus arguments used by the plot.stepfun() function. The five specified arguments are x, for the object of the ecdf class; ylab, for the y axis label; verticals, for whether to plot the vertical parts of the steps; col.01line, for the colors of lines at y equal to 0 and 1; and pch, for the plotting character at the top of each step. In the order of the arguments, … is the second argument.

The x argument takes an object of the ecdf() class. There is no default value for x.

The ylab argument is the standard argument from plot.default(). The default value of ylab in plot.ecdf() is "Fn(x)".

The verticals argument takes a logical vector (or a vector that can be coerced to logical) of arbitrary length. If longer than one element, only the first element is used and a warning is given. If set to TRUE, the vertical parts of the steps are drawn. If FALSE, the vertical parts are not drawn. The default value of verticals is FALSE.

The col.01line argument takes a vector of color values of arbitrary length (see Section 3.4.1 for kinds of color values). Only the first and second values are used if the length of col.01line is greater than 2. If there is only one color, both the zero line and the one line are the given color. Otherwise, the zero line takes the first color, and the one line takes the second color. The default value in ecdf() is "gray70".

The pch argument takes a vector of plotting character values (see Section 3.3.2) of arbitrary length and is the standard argument used in plot.default(). The values of pch cycle through the plotted points. In plot.ecdf(), the default value of pch is 19.

In Listing 5-13, a line of code is given for the example in Figure 5-13. The function plot() is run with an ecdf object, and the arguments verticals, col.01line, pch, and cex are set.

Listing 5-13. Code to demonstrate plot.ecdf() with verticals, col.01line, pch, and cex set

```
plot(
  ecdf(
    pop75.ordered
  ),
  verticals=TRUE,
  col.01line=grey(
    c( 2, 6 )/10
  ),
  pch=".",
  cex=4
)
```

In Figure 5-13, the code in Listing 5-13 is run.

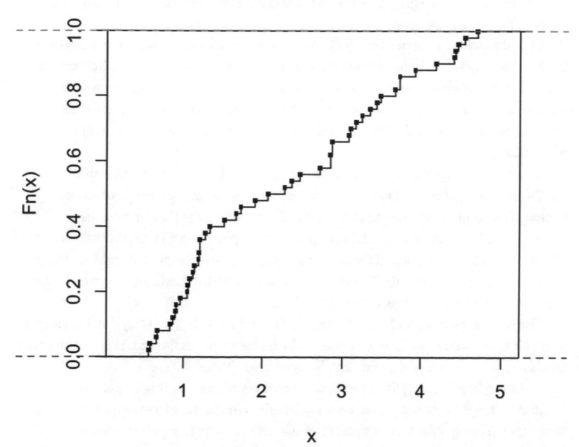

Figure 5-13. *Example of running plot.ecdf() and ecdf(), with verticals=TRUE, col.01line=grey(c(2, 4)/10), pch=".", and cex=4 in plot.ecdf()*

Note that the line at 1 is lighter than the line at 0. Also, solid lines extend from the distribution to the left at y equal to 0 and to the distribution from the right at y equal to 1. Setting pch to "." and increasing cex is a useful way to plot small points – as has been done in the figure.

5.3.6 The hclust Method

Hierarchical clustering is a method of putting observations into clusters based on a dataset of variables associated with the observations. The hclust method for plot() plots objects of the hclust class. Objects of the hclust class are created by the hclust() function or by running as.hclust() on an object with an appropriate structure. (The help pages for hclust() and as.hclust() give the structure and other information.) The function hclust() does hierarchical clustering.

The plot.hclust() function takes 11 specified arguments plus many of the arguments used by plot.default(). The specified arguments are x, for the object of the hclust class; labels, for the labels of the leaves on the tree; hang, for the length of the branch that branches to a leaf label; check, to check if x has a valid format; and the standard axes, frame.plot, ann, main, sub, xlab, and ylab from plot.default() – with defaults specific to plot.hclust().

The x argument takes an object of the hclust class. There is no default value for x.

The labels argument takes a character vector (or a vector that can be coerced to character) that must be NULL, FALSE, or of a length equal to the number of observations being clustered. If labels equals NULL, plot.hclust() uses the row names of the observations as labels, if the row names exist, or else the index numbers of the observations. If labels equals FALSE, no labels are plotted. Otherwise, the given labels are plotted. The default value of labels is NULL.

The hang argument takes a numeric vector of arbitrary length. Only the first value is used. Negative values for hang cause all of the leaves to end at the zero line and all of the labels to line up in a row at a constant distance below the zero line.

A value of 0 tells plot() to use leaves of zero length. The resulting leaf locations can be at different heights. As hang increases, the length of the leaves increases proportionately to the size of hang. When hang equals 1, the length of the leaves plus the distance from the end of the leaves to the labels equals the length of the y axis. The default value of hang is 0.1.

The check argument takes a logical vector (or a vector that can be coerced to logical) of arbitrary length. Only the first value is used. If set to TRUE, plot.hclust() checks to see if the structure of x is a valid hclust class structure. If set to FALSE, the function does not check. The default value is TRUE (see the help page for hclust() for more information).

The default value of axes is TRUE – that is, axes are plotted. The default value of frame.plot is FALSE – that is, no box is drawn around the plotting region. The default value of ann is TRUE – that is, titles and axis labels are drawn. The default value of main is "Cluster Dendrogram". The default values of sub and xlab are NULL. The default value of ylab is "Height".

In Listing 5-14, code is given for the example of using plot() with an hclust class x value. The arguments labels and hang are set.

Listing 5-14. Code for the example in Figure 5-14 of using plot() with an hclust
class x value. The arguments labels and hang are set

```
plot(
  hclust(
    dist(
      pop75.ordered
    )
  ),
  labels=row.names( LifeCycleSavings )[ ord ],
  hang=0
)
```

In Figure 5-14, the code in Listing 5-14 is run.

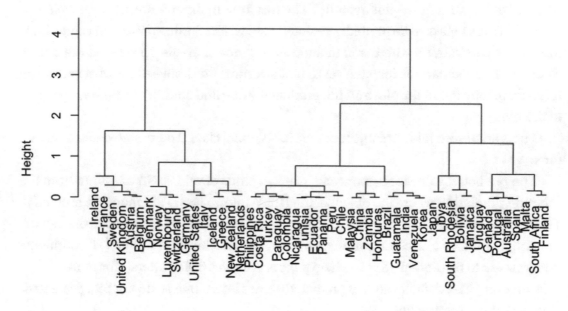

Figure 5-14. *Example of using plot.hclust(), hclust(), and dist(), with labels and
hang set in plot.hclust() and default values used in hclust() and dist(). The source
of the data is the LifeCycleSavings dataset in the R datasets package*

Note that the clustering differs from the clustering in the dendrogram in Section 5.3.3. Only one column of the LifeCycleSavings dataset was used in Figure 5-14, whereas three were used in Figure 5-11. In the preceding plot, hang was set to 0, so the leaves are of zero length.

5.3.7 The HoltWinters Method

Holt-Winters filtering is a technique used to model time series data. The HoltWinters method for plot() plots objects of the HoltWinters class. Objects of the HoltWinters class are created by running the function HoltWinters(). The function HoltWinters() performs Holt-Winters filtering on time series objects for which the frequency is greater than or equal to two. The observations and the fitted values from the Holt-Winters model are plotted by plot(). Values predicted into the future can also be plotted, with or without confidence intervals.

The function plot.HoltWinters() takes 15 specified arguments, as well as taking many of the arguments of plot.default(). The first four arguments are x, for the object of the HoltWinters class to be plotted; predicted.values, for plotting predicted values into the future; intervals, for whether to include confidence intervals if predicted values are calculated; and separator, for whether to plot a vertical line between the observation and fitted value portion of the plot and the predicted value and confidence interval portion of the plot.

The x argument takes an object of the HoltWinters class. There is no default value for x.

The predicted.values argument can take two kinds of values, NA or output from the function predict() – where the object of the HoltWinters class is the model in predict(). The number of time periods into the future to be found must be included in the call to predict(). Whether to include confidence intervals must be set in predict() if confidence intervals are to be plotted. (See the help page for predict.HoltWinters() for more information.) The default value of predicted.values is NA, that is, do not plot predicted values or the separator line.

The intervals argument takes a logical vector (or a vector that can be coerced to logical) of arbitrary length. Only the first value is used. If intervals is set to TRUE and predicted values have been calculated and calculated with confidence intervals, then confidence intervals are plotted. Otherwise, no confidence intervals are plotted. The default value of intervals is TRUE.

The separator argument takes a logical vector (or a vector that can be coerced to logical) of arbitrary length. Only the first value is used. If set to TRUE and predicted values have been calculated, then the separator line is plotted. Otherwise, no line is plotted. The default value of separator is TRUE.

The fifth through twelfth arguments are col, col.predicted, col.intervals, col. separator, lty, lty.predicted, lty.intervals, and lty.separator. The first four specify the color of the observation line, the line of fitted values, the line of predicted values, and the separator line, respectively. The four arguments take vectors of color values of arbitrary length. Only the first value is used. The respective default values are 1, 2, 4, and 1. (See Section 3.4.1 for color value formats.)

The second four arguments specify the line type of the observation line, the fitted value and predicted value line, the confidence interval lines, and the separator line. The arguments take vectors of line type arguments of arbitrary length. Only the first value is used. The respective default values are 1 (or "solid"), 1, 1, and 3 (or "dotted"). (See Section 3.3.2 for information about line type formats.)

The 13th through 15th arguments are the standard ylab, main, and ylim (see Section 3.2.1 for more information). The default value of ylab is "Observed/Fitted" and of main is "Holt-Winters filtering". According to the help page for plot.HoltWinters(), if ylim is set to NULL, the function chooses limits that contain the observations, fitted values, and predicted values. The default limits may not be large enough for the confidence intervals. The default value of ylim is NULL.

In Listing 5-15, a line of code for the example in Figure 5-15 is given. The example is of using plot() with x equal to an object of the HoltWinters class.

Listing 5-15. Code for the example in Figure 5-15 is given. The functions plot(), HoltWinters(), predict(), and ts() are used. The frequency is set in ts(); the number of time periods to predict and to calculate prediction intervals is set in predict(); and col, col.predicted, col.intervals, and ylim are set in plot()

```
HW = HoltWinters(
  ts(
    sunspot.year,
    freq=11
  )
)
```

```
plot(
  HW,
  predict(
    HW,
    100,
    prediction.interval=TRUE
  ),
  col="grey60",
  col.predicted="grey40",
  col.intervals = "grey70",
  ylim=c( -300, 700 )
)
```

In Figure 5-15, the code in Listing 5-15 is run.

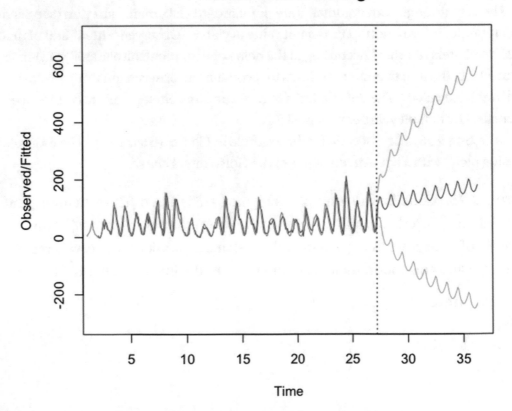

Figure 5-15. *An example of using plot() on an object of the HoltWinters class. The functions ts(), predict(), HoltWinters(), and plot() are run*

Note that the frequency of the time series is set to eleven in ts() – the function that creates time series objects. The number of predicted values is set to 100 in predict(). The observations are plotted in a mid-gray, the fitted and predicted values in a dark gray, and the confidence interval in a light gray.

The y axis limits are set to -300 and 700 so that both confidence intervals are included in the plot. Since 0 is the minimum possible value of y for this dataset, the lower confidence limit is not sensible.

5.3.8 The isoreg Method

Isotonic regression is a form of nonparametric regression for two variables that are positively correlated. The isoreg method of plot() plots objects of the isoreg class. Objects of the isoreg class are created by the function isoreg(). From the help page for isoreg(), the function does isotonic regression – which is a nonparametric technique that fits a monotonically increasing series of horizontal lines (with the endpoints connected by vertical lines).

The isoreg() function fits a regression model by finding the model that minimizes the sum of residual squares. The data can be a numeric vector, which is fit against an index value, or two numeric vectors with the second vector fit against the first. If the data tends to decrease instead of increase, just one horizontal line is fit – at the y value equal to the mean of the y values.

The plot.isoreg() function takes ten specified arguments plus many of the arguments that plot.default() takes. The first two arguments are x, for the object of the isoreg class; and plot.type, for the kind of page to plot.

The x argument takes an object of the isoreg class. There is no default value for x.

The plot.type argument takes a one-element character vector that can take three possible values. The values are "single", "row.wise", or "col.wise". The value of "single" tells plot() to plot a single plot containing the data and the regression fit.

For both "row.wise" and "col.wise", a second plot is plotted – of the cumulative data and fit. For "row.wise", the two plots are in two rows. For "col.wise", the two plots are in two columns. (The values of the arguments can be shortened to a unique identifier – e.g., "col" instead of "col.wise".) The default value of plot.type is c("single", "row.wise", "col. wise"), which tells plot() to plot a single plot.

The third through sixth arguments are main, for the title of the regression plot; main2 for the title of the cumulative data plot, if the plot is included; xlab for the x axis labels on the plot(s); and ylab for the y axis labels on the first plot and part of the y axis label on the second plot – if the second plot is included.

The types of values that the four arguments take are the standard types for main, xlab, and ylab in plot.default() (see Section 3.2.1.). The default value of main is paste("Isotonic regression", deparse(x$call)), of main2 is "Cumulative Data and Convex Minorant", of xlab is "x0", and of ylab is "x$y".

The seventh through tenth arguments are par.fit, for formatting the regression lines and points; mar, for the size of the margins of the plot(s); mgp, for the placement of the axis labels, axis tick mark labels, and axis line within the margins; and grid, for whether to plot a grid in the first plot and some vertical lines in the second plot.

The par.fit argument takes a list of arbitrary length. The function plot.isoreg() will ignore any element that is not named col, cex, pch, or lwd. The elements are the standard col, cex, pch, and lwd of plot.default(), but are applied to the regression line and the points on the regression line, not the data points. All can have multiple values, and all cycle through the lines and points. The default value of par.fit is list(col = "red", cex = 1, pch = 13, lwd = 1.5).

The mar argument (which is covered in Section 6.2.1.2) gives the size of the four margins in units of margin lines. The argument takes a numeric vector of length four. The default value in par() is c(5.1, 4.1, 4.1, 3.1). In plot.isoreg(), the default value is if (both) c(3.5, 2.1, 1, 1) else par("mar").

The mgp argument takes a three-element numeric vector. In par(), the default value is c(3, 1, 0). In plot.isoreg(), the default value is if (both) c(1.6, 0.7, 0) else par("mgp").

If two plots are run, then the values for mar, mgp, and mfrow in par() are changed. To return the default values to par(), enter par(mar=c(5, 4, 4 , 2) + 0.1, mgp=c(3, 1, 0), mfrow=c(1, 1)) at the R prompt.

The grid argument takes a logical vector (or a vector that can be coerced to logical) of arbitrary length. If longer than one, only the first value is used and a warning is given. If set to TRUE, a light gray grid is plotted on the first plot, and light gray vertical lines are plotted on the second plot at the regression steps (see the help page for plot.isoreg() for more information). If set to FALSE, the grid or line(s) is not plotted. The default value of grid is length(x$x) < 12.

In Listing 5-16, code for the example of running plot() with an object of the isoreg class, found in Figure 5-16, is given.

Listing 5-16. Code for the example of using an object of the isoreg class in plot(). The arguments par.fit, col, plot.type, cex, and grid are set

```
plot(
  isoreg(
    pop75.ordered,
    dpi.ordered
  ),
  par.fit = list(
    col=1,
    cex=1,
    pch=23,
    lwd=1.2
  ),
  col=grey( 0.5 ),
  plot.type="row",
  cex=0.75,
  grid=TRUE
)

par(
  mar=c( 5, 4, 4 ,2 ) + 0.1,
  mgp=c( 3, 1, 0 ),
  mfrow=c( 1, 1 )
)
```

In Figure 5-16, the code in Listing 5-16 is run.

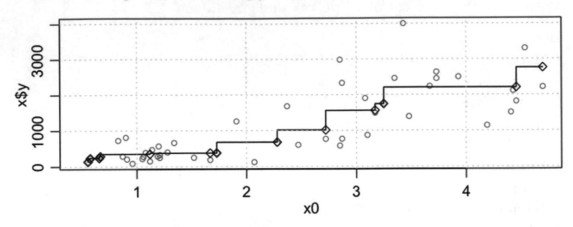

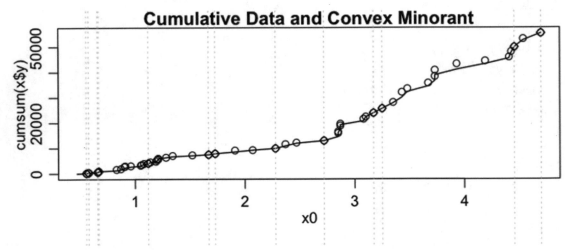

Figure 5-16. *Example of running plot on an object of the isoreg class*

Note that in the second plot, light gray vertical lines are drawn where the steps in the first plot occur. For the styling of the regression line, col is set to 1, cex is set to 1, pch is set to 23, and lwd is set to 1.2. For the styling of the observations, col is set to grey(0.5), and cex is set to 0.75. The plot type is set to "row" and grid is set to TRUE.

5.3.9 The lm Method

Linear models are models for which a dependent variable is set equal to a sum of independent variables multiplied by constants, for example, y=b0 + b1 x1 + b2 x2. In linear regression models, an error term is added to make the linear model exact for the data.

The lm method for plot() plots objects of the class lm. The functions in the stats package that create objects of the lm class are lm(), glm(), and aov(). The functions lm(), glm(), and aov() fit linear models – that is, a variable y is fit to a number of x variables, which can be just one x variable, based on a linear model. Usually, an intercept is fit.

The lm() function fits ordinary least squares models. The glm() function fits binomial, gaussian, gamma, inverse gaussian, poisson, quasi, quasibinomial, and quasipoisson models by various methods (see the help page for family for more information). The aov() function fits analysis of variance models.

The plot() function returns up to six plots when the value of x is of the lm class. The six plots are the plot of the residuals against the fitted values, the plot of the observed quantiles vs. the theoretical quantiles based on the normal distribution, the plot of the square root of the studentized Pearson residuals against the fitted values, the Cook's distance plotted against the observation number, the plot of the studentized Pearson residuals against the leverage, and the plot of the Cook's distance vs. the leverage divided by one minus the leverage.

The plot() function takes 17 specified arguments plus many of the arguments of plot. default(). The argument ... is the eighth argument in the order of the arguments. The total number of listed arguments is 18, if ... is included.

The first seven arguments are x, for the object of the lm class; which, for which plots to plot; caption, for the captions on the plots; panel, for whether to include a smoothed line in some of the plots; sub.caption, for the subtitle on the plots (the same for all plots if the plots are plotted separately – otherwise, a title in the outer margin on the third side if multiple plots are plotted on a page and the outer margin on the third side is greater than zero, but only on the last page if there are multiple pages); main, for a title to be plotted on all of the plots; and ask, for whether to ask to continue between pages when more than one page is plotted.

The x argument takes an object of the lm class. There is no default value for x.

The which argument takes a numeric vector of arbitrary length. The elements can take on values between 1 and 6, inclusive. If a value of an element is not an integer, the value is rounded down to an integer. If more than one element rounds down to the same integer, the plot associated with the integer is only plotted once. The plots are always plotted in the same order, irrespective of the order of the values assigned to which. The default value of which is c(1, 2, 3, 5).

The caption argument takes a list of single-element character vectors (or single-element vectors that can be coerced to character) or a single vector that can be coerced to character. Both the list and the single vector can be of arbitrary length. (The elements of the list can be of length greater than one too, but each new element of the character

213

vector plots over the previous element if the length is greater than one.) Only the first six elements are used.

Depending on the plots selected in which, the corresponding captions are used, where each title is placed above the correct plot. The default value of caption is `list(`
`"Residuals vs Fitted"`, `"Normal Q-Q"`, `"Scale-Location"`, `"Cook's distance"`,
`"Residuals vs Leverage"`, `expression("Cook's dist vs Leverage. " * h[ii] /`
`(1 - h[ii])))`.

The panel argument takes an object of the function class. Two possible functions can be used, panel.smooth() and points(). If the argument is set to panel.smooth, a smoothed line is plotted in plots 1, 3, 5, and 6 – by default in the color red (the color can be changed by changing the palette). If set to points, the smoothed line is not plotted. The default value of panel is `if(add.smooth) function(x, y, ...) panel.smooth(x,`
`y, iter=iter.smooth, ...) else points`, that is, if add.smooth is TRUE, add smoothed lines and otherwise do not. For both options, the points are plotted.

The sub.caption argument takes a vector that can be coerced to character and is of arbitrary length. The sub-caption is plotted either at the top of the last page if there are multiple plots on a page or below the label on the x axis if there is just one plot on a page. (The arguments mfrow and mfcol in par() control the number of plots on a page and are covered in Section 6.2.1.5.)

If there is more than one element in the value of sub.caption, the elements overplot on the same line. With text that has more than one line, the lowest line in the string plots on the line below the label of the x axis. (The text "\n" in a string causes a line feed and can be used to move text in an element up or down.) The default value of sub.caption is NULL, that is, a (possibly) abbreviated version of `deparse(x$call) is plotted`.

The main argument takes a vector that can be coerced to character and that can be of arbitrary length. The value of main plots above the caption on all of the plots. For vectors with multiple elements, each element of the vector plots on a different line. The default value of main is " ", that is, no title is plotted.

The ask argument takes a logical vector (or a vector that can be coerced to logical) of arbitrary length. If longer that one value, only the first value is used and a warning is given. A value of TRUE tells plot() to ask before going to a new page if more than one page is plotted. A value of FALSE plots all of the plots without pausing. The default value of ask is `prod(mfcol) < length(which) && dev.interactive()`, that is, ask whether to go to the next page if the number of plots on a page is less than the number of plots to be plotted. Note that if which contains duplicates, the default logic can fail.

The ninth through eighteenth arguments of plot.lm() are id.n, for the number of extreme points to label; labels.id, for the labels to assign to the observations; cex.id, for the character size used in the labels; qqline, for whether to plot the 45-degree line on the quantile-quantile plot; cook.levels, for the values of the Cook's distance at which to draw contour lines; add.smooth, for whether to plot a smoothed line on plots 1, 3, 5, and 6; iter.smooth, for the value of iter to be supplied to the function panel.smooth() if panel equals panel.smooth; label.pos, for the position of the labels in the first three plots; cex. caption, for the character size used in the caption; and cex.oma.main, for the character size used in the sub-caption if there are multiple plots on a page.

The id.n argument takes a numeric vector of arbitrary length. If longer than one element, only the first element is used and warnings are given. The argument must be greater than -1 and less than or equal to the number of observations. If between -1 and 1 and not equal to either, no labels are plotted. If greater than 1 and not an integer, the number is rounded down to the next lowest integer. The default value of id.n is 3.

The labels.id argument takes the value NULL or any vector that can be coerced to the character mode and which can be of arbitrary length. If labels.id equals NULL, the index values of the observations are assigned as the labels. If the value of labels.id is longer than the number of observations, then only the labels with indices up to the number of observations are used. If shorter than the number of observations, only those observations with indices up to the length of labels.id are given labels if the observations are extreme. The default value of labels.id is `names(residuals(x))`.

The cex.id argument takes a numeric vector. The vector must be of length one if the fifth plot is plotted. Otherwise, the vector can be of arbitrary length; and the labels on the extreme values can be of different sizes, where the order of assignment is based on the order of extremity. The default value of cex.id is 0.75.

The qqline argument takes a logical vector (or a vector that can be coerced to logical) of arbitrary length. If longer than one element, only the first element is used and a warning is given. If set to TRUE, the line is drawn in the quantile-quantile plot (the second plot). If FALSE, no line is drawn. The default value is TRUE.

The cook.levels argument takes a nonnegative numeric vector of arbitrary length. Contours are drawn for each value in cook.levels if the contours are within the limits of the plot. The default value for cook.levels is `c(0.5, 1.0)`.

The add.smooth argument takes a logical vector (or a vector that can be coerced to logical) of arbitrary length. If longer than one element, only the first element is used and a warning is given. If set to TRUE, the argument tells plot() to add (in plots 1, 3, 5, and 6) a line based on the smoothed y values. If FALSE, the lines are not plotted. The default value is getOption("add.smooth"), which on my device has a value of TRUE. (The first option in options() is add.smooth.)

The iter.smooth argument takes a numeric vector of arbitrary length. Only the first value is used. The default value of iter.smooth is if(isGlm) 0 else 3, that is, if x is a result from the glm() function, then set iter.smooth to 0. Otherwise, set iter.smooth to 3.

The label.pos argument takes a numeric vector (or a character vector that can be coerced to numeric) of length greater than one. Only the first two values are used; and those values can only take the numbers 1, 2, 3, or 4. The first value gives the position with respect to the point of the odd-numbered labels and the second value of the even-numbered labels. A value of 1 puts the label below the point, of 2 to the left, of 3 above, and of 4 to the right. The default value of label.pos is c(4, 2), that is, labels are plotted to the right of points whose index values are odd and to the left for the points whose index values are even.

The cex.caption argument takes a numeric or logical vector of arbitrary length. Logical vectors are coerced to numeric. The value gives the character size used in the caption. If more than one value is set for cex.caption, the caption is plotted in the same place for each of the values. So using just one value makes the most sense. The default value of cex.caption is 1.

The cex.oma.main argument takes a numeric or logical vector of arbitrary length. Logical values are coerced to numeric. The argument has an effect only if multiple plots are plotted and the outer margin is set larger than 0 on side 3 (with the amount larger depending on the character size used for sub.caption). Then cex.oma.main operates on sub.caption like cex.caption operates on caption. The default value of cex.caption is 1.25.

In Listing 5-17, the code to generate Figure 5-17 is given. The example is of using plot() on an object of the lm class. Before running plot(), the palette is changed to a gray scale, and oma and mfrow are changed in par(). After plot is run, the palette, oma, and mfrow are changed back to default values.

Listing 5-17. Code for the example of using plot() on an object of the lm class. The arguments x, caption, which, labels.id, sub.caption, main, cex.id, cook.levels, iter.smooth, label.pos, cex.caption, and cex.oma.main are set

```
palette(
  grey(
    0:10/14
  )
)
```

```
par(
  mfrow=c( 2, 2 ),
  oma=c( 2, 2, 2, 2 )
)

plot(
  glm(
    sr ~ .,
    data=LifeCycleSavings
  ),
  caption=paste( "plot", 1:6 ),
  which=c( 1, 2, 4, 5 ),
  labels.id=NULL,
  sub.caption="sub.caption",
  main="main",
  id.n=2,
  cex.id=0.9,
  cook.levels= c( 0.33, 0.67, 1 ),
  iter.smooth=5,
  label.pos=c( 4, 4 ),
  cex.caption=1.15,
  cex.oma.main=1.4
)

par(
  mfrow=c( 1, 1 ),
  oma=c( 0, 0, 0, 0 )
)

palette(
  "default"
)
```

In Figure 5-17, the code in Listing 5-17 is run.

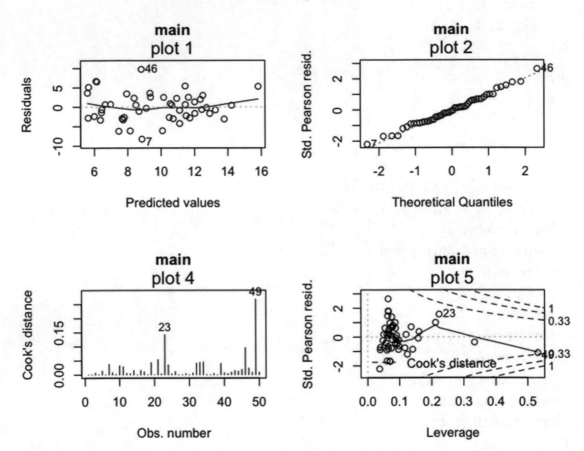

Figure 5-17. *An example of running plot() with an object of the lm class. The arguments that were set were x, caption, which, labels.id, sub.caption, main, id.n, cex.id, cook.levels, iter.smooth, label.pos, cex.caption, and cex.oma.main*

Only four of the six possible plots are plotted in the example. The captions on the six plots are assigned the values "plot 1", "plot 2", ... "plot 6". The labels argument is set to NULL, so the index values are used for the labels. In Figure 5-17, since there are multiple plots on the page and only one page, the sub-caption appears above the plots. The value of the argument main, "main", is plotted above the caption on each plot.

Two labels are plotted, for the two most extreme y values in each plot, since id.n was set to 2. The character size for the labels is set to 0.9. There are three contour levels for the Cook's distance, and six contour lines are plotted. The smoothing is strong since iter. smooth is set to 5. Since both lab.pos values are set equal to 4, both labels plot to the right of the points. The character size for the captions is 1.15 and for the sub.caption is 1.4.

In order to plot four plots on a page, the argument mfrow was set to c(2, 2) in par(). After the plots were plotted, mfrow was set back to c(1, 1) to reset R to plotting one plot on a page. The outer margins were set to two lines deep by setting oma to c(2, 2, 2, 2) in par() and then set back to zero width by setting oma equal to c(0, 0, 0, 0) after the plotting was done. To change those lines and text that plot red by default to the color gray, the palette was changed to a gray scale. After plot() was run, the palette was changed back to the default palette. (See Section 6.2 for information about par() and multiple plots on a page.)

5.3.10 The ppr Method

Projection pursuit regression is a form of regression. The regression estimates a model for one or more dependent variables using one or more independent variables. The ppr method of plot.ppr() plots objects of the ppr class. Objects of the ppr class are created by the function ppr(). The function ppr() does projection pursuit regression of a y on an x, where either can be a matrix or vector and both have the same length and/or number of rows. The plots are done for each of the terms found in ppr() and are of the ridge functions for the terms. See the help page for ppr() for more information.

The plot.ppr() function takes seven specified arguments, plus many of the arguments used by plot.default(). All of the arguments are standard arguments for plot.default() but have different default values in plot.ppr(). The arguments are x, for the object of the ppr class; ask, for whether to ask before plotting a new plot; type, for the kind of plot; cex, for the character size of the plotting characters; main, for the title of the plot; and xlab and ylab, for the x and y axis labels. See Section 6.2.1.5 for information about ask; Section 3.3.1 for type; Section 3.4.3 for cex; and Section 3.2.1 for main, xlab, and ylab.

The x argument takes an object of the ppr class. There is no default value for x.

The ask argument takes the value of ask in par() by default, which on my device is FALSE.

The type argument takes the value of "o" by default, that is, plot the lines over the points.

The cex argument takes a value of ½ by default. The ½ is relative to the value of cex in par().

The main argument takes the value quote(bquote("term"[.i]*"i" -- hat(beta[.i]) == .(bet.i))) by default.

The xlab argument takes the default value quote(bquote(bold(alpha)[.(i)]^T * bold(x))).

The y argument takes the default value of "".

In Listing 5-18, code is given for the example, in Figure 5-18, of running plot() with x set to an object of the ppr class. Four ridge function plots are drawn.

Listing 5-18. Code for an example of using an object of the ppr class in plot(). Four terms are used in ppr()

```
par(
  mfrow=c( 2, 2 ),
  oma=c( 1, 1, 3, 1 )
)

plot(
  ppr(
    x=LifeCycleSavings[ , 2:5 ],
    y=LifeCycleSavings[ , 1 ],
    nterms=4,
    max=5
  )
)

mtext(
  "Example of Using a ppr Class Object in plot()\nPlots of the Ridge
  Functions",
  side=3,
  font=1,
  outer=TRUE
)

par(
  mfrow=c( 1, 1 ),
  oma=c( 0, 0, 0, 0 )
)
```

In Figure 5-18, the code in Listing 5-18 is run.

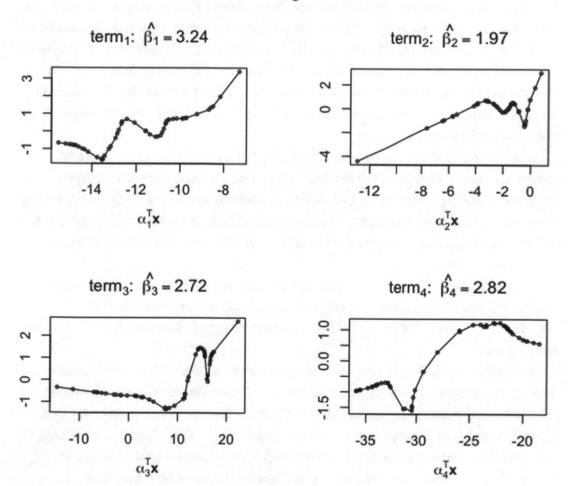

Figure 5-18. *Example of using an object of the ppr class in plot()*

Note that the number of terms is four (nterms=4), so four ridge function plots are drawn. In main and xlab, the functions quote() and bquote() allow the index to be changed for each plot. Inside bquote(), the expression .(i) returns the current value of i in the function.

5.3.11 The prcomp and princomp Methods

Principal components are properties of matrices. Given a matrix, the matrix containing the principal components of the original matrix in the columns, when multiplied by the original matrix on the left, creates a new matrix with the same information as the original matrix but for which the columns of the matrix are linearly independent. Principal component analysis is sometimes used in data modeling to reduce the dimensionality of correlated variables. The other main use of principal component analysis is to cluster the observations in a dataset.

The prcomp and princomp methods of plot() plot objects of the prcomp and princomp classes. Objects of the prcomp and princomp classes are created by the functions prcomp() and princomp(). Both functions do a principal component analysis of a numeric matrix or data frame. The functions differ in the R functions used in the calculations and in the divisor of the covariance matrix of the matrix or data frame containing the data.

For prcomp(), the eigenvalues and eigenvectors are found using singular value decomposition, that is, using the svd() function. Also, in the estimation of the covariance – if done – the divisor of the covariance matrix is the number of observations minus one.

For princomp(), the eigenvalues and eigenvectors are found by inputting the output from the function cor() into the function eigen(). If the covariance matrix is used in the calculations, the divisor for the covariance matrix is the number of observations rather than the number of observations minus one. According to the help pages for prcomp() and princomp(), the method used by prcomp() is the preferred calculation method.

The function plot() creates a scree plot from the output of both functions. A scree plot plots the amount of the total variance each principal component contains. If the analysis is done with standardized variables, then the variance of each column of the standardized original matrix is one, so the total variance is just the number of columns.

There are no specified arguments, other than x, for plot() if x is an object of the prcomp or princomp class. (The functions plot.prcomp() and plot.princomp() both take the arguments that screeplot() takes.)

In Listing 5-19, the code for the examples of using plot() on objects of the prcomp and princomp classes is given.

Listing 5-19. Code for the example, in Figure 5-19, of using plot() on objects of the prcomp and princomp classes

```
par(
  mfrow=c( 1, 2 ),
  oma=c( 2, 0, 3, 0 )
)

plot(
  prcomp(
    LifeCycleSavings,
    scale=TRUE
  ),
  main="prcomp()"
)

plot(
  princomp(
    LifeCycleSavings,
    cor=TRUE
  ),
  main="princomp()"
)

mtext(
  "Example of Using plot() on Output\nfrom prcomp() and princomp()",
  side=3,
  outer=TRUE
)
mtext(
  "2 Scree Plots",
  side=1,
  outer=TRUE
)
```

```
par(
  mfrow=c( 1, 1 ),
  oma=c( 0, 0, 0, 0 )
)
```

In Figure 5-19, the code in Listing 5-19 is run.

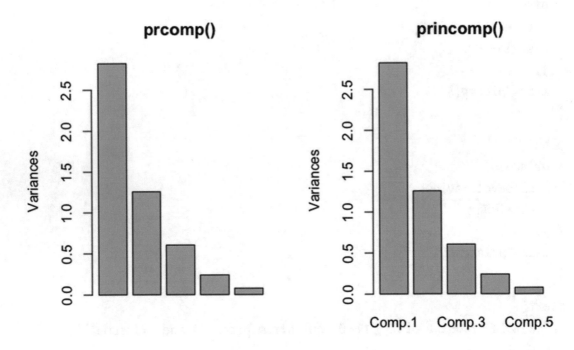

Figure 5-19. *Scree plots, which are produced by plot() when x is set equal to objects of the prcomp and princomp classes*

Note that the plots are very similar. The only major difference is that no bar labels are plotted by default for the output from prcomp(), while the output from princomp() plots bar labels by default.

5.3.12 The profile.nls Method

Nonlinear least squares modeling is an approach used to model a data vector with a model in which the relationship between the independent variables is nonlinear. The least squares criterion is used to evaluate how well the model fits the data.

The profile.nls method for plot() plots objects of the profile.nls class. Objects of the profile.nls class are created by running profile() on objects created by nls(). The nls() function does least squares fitting for nonlinear models.

The plot.profile.nls() function creates diagnostic plots. According to the help page for the function, on the vertical axis of the plots is the statistic tau – which is the square root of the change in the sum of the squares of the residuals divided by the standard error of the residuals. (The value of the residual sum of squares changes as the value of the coefficient being estimated is changed in the fitting process.) On the horizontal axis are the values that the coefficient takes as the size of the coefficient is changed. A plot can be generated for every coefficient that is estimated or for a subset of the coefficients.

The plot.profile.nls() function takes six specified arguments, plus many of the arguments of plot.default(). However, according to the help page for the function, the arguments xlab, xlim, ylim, and type cannot be set. The arguments that are specified are x, for the object of the profile.nls class; levels, for the levels of the confidence contours measured in the units of tau; conf, for the levels of the confidence contours measured in levels of confidence; absVal, for whether to use the absolute value of tau in the plot; lty, for the line type of the confidence contours and the vertical line at the estimated coefficient; and ylab, for the label on the y axis.

The x argument takes an object of the profile.nls class. There is no default value for x.

The levels argument takes a numeric vector of arbitrary length. The values should be reasonable values for tau. There is no default value for levels.

The conf argument takes a numeric vector of arbitrary length. The values must be between 0 and 1, but not equal to either. (If both levels and conf are set, levels is used.) The default value of conf is c(99, 95, 90, 80, 50)/100.

The absVal argument takes a logical vector (or a vector that can be coerced to logical) of arbitrary length. If longer than one, only the first element is used and a warning is given. If set to TRUE, the absolute values of the tau's are plotted. If FALSE, negative values of tau are plotted as negative. The default value of absVal is TRUE.

The lty argument takes a line type vector of arbitrary length (see Section 3.3.2). Only the first value is used. The default value of lty is 2, that is, a dashed line.

Colors in the plot are based on the color values in the color palette (see Section 3.4.1.3). According to the help page for plot.profile.nls(), the color of the axes is based on the first element of the color palette. On my device, the axis color is not affected by setting the first element of the palette – the axes are plotted in black.

The color of the vertical line at the estimate of the parameter is based on the third element in the color palette. The color of the line representing tau is based on the fourth element. The color of the confidence contours is based on the sixth element.

There is no element in plot.profile.nls() to tell the function which parameters to select for plotting. All profiles that are generated in profile() are plotted. The which argument in profile() controls which profiles are generated.

In Listing 5-20, the code for the example in Figure 5-20 is given. The example demonstrates using the functions palette(), par(), mtext(), nls(), and profile() and the arguments levels, lty, and ylab.

Listing 5-20. Code for the example of running plot() on an object of the profile. nls class

```
palette(
  grey(
    c( 7, 0, 3, 0, 0, 6 )/8
  )
)
par(
  mfrow=c( 2, 2 ),
  oma=c( 0, 0, 4, 0 ) + 0.1
)

sr.ordered=LifeCycleSavings$sr[ ord ]

plot(
  profile(
    nls(
      sr.ordered ~ y_center +
        y_scale*cos( pi/angle_divisor*( pop15.ordered + angle_shift ) ) ),
      start=list(
        y_center=10,
        y_scale=3,
```

```
        angle_divisor=20,
        angle_shift=-20
      )
    )
  ),
  levels=c( 0.5, 1, 1.5, 2 ),
  lty=5,
  ylab="| tau |"
)

mtext(
  "Example of a profile.nls Class Object in plot()\nTau Plots for 4
  Parameters",
  side=3,
  outer=TRUE,
  line=1
)

par(
    mfrow=c( 1, 1 ),
    oma=c( 0, 0, 0, 0 )
)

palette(
    "default"
)
```

In Figure 5-20, the code in Listing 5-20 is run.

Example of a profile.nls Class Object in plot()
Tau Plots for 4 Parameters

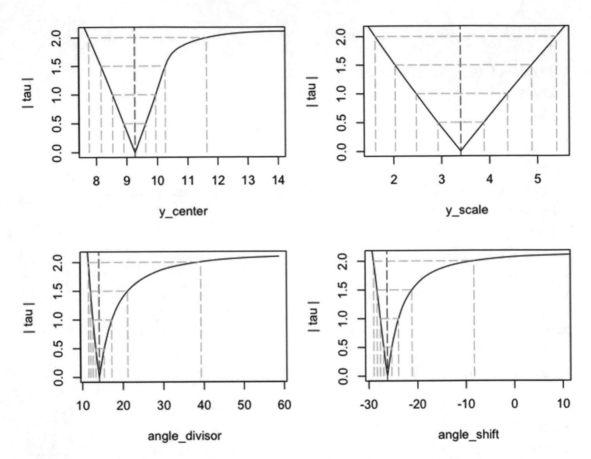

Figure 5-20. *Example of using plot() on an object of the profile.nls class. The functions par(), mtext(), plot(), nls(), profile(), and palette() are run. In plot() the arguments levels, lty, and ylab are set*

Note that the x labels are the names of the parameters. Also, plots are plotted for all of the parameters. The which argument in profile() is not set, so the default value (generating profiles for all of the parameters) is used.

The arguments levels, lty, and ylab in plot() are set to c(0.5, 1, 1.5, 2), 5, and "| tau |", respectively. The colors in the color palette are changed to colors on the gray scale by running palette() with gray scale colors set. The confidence contours are spaced evenly on the tau scale. With type set equal to 5, the line type is a long dash.

5.3.13 The spec, spec.coherency, and spec.phase Methods

In time series analysis, two common approaches are the time domain approach and the frequency domain approach. The time domain approach looks for patterns that repeat in time by looking at plots of a time series over time (such as looking at the 11-year cycles in the sunspot data over time). The approaches in Sections 5.3.1, 5.3.2, 5.3.7, 5.3.15, and 5.3.16 are in the time domain.

The frequency domain involves plotting the data against frequencies, rather than against time, in order to look for frequencies at which cycles occur. The function spectrum() creates plots of the data against frequency. The methods used to create the plots given by spectrum() are based on calculating periodograms, either on the raw data or on a fit by an autoregressive model.

In the sunspot data, there is approximately one cycle every 11 years. Using spectrum(), in a plot of the data against the frequency, there is a peak at 0.091. (The value of 0.091 is 1/11. Since the frequency in the sunspot.year object is 1, not 11, the value 1 divided by 0.091 gives the period of the cycle in years.)

The spec, spec.coherency, and spec.phase methods of plot() plot objects of the spec class. Objects of the spec class are outputted from the function spectrum(). The function spectrum() fits either a periodogram on the data or a periodogram on an autoressive fit to the data – where the data is a times series object. (The autoregressive modeling is not up and running yet for multiple time series.)

In spectrum(), the method argument tells spectrum() to either create a periodogram from the raw data or to fit an autoregressive model first. If the first method is chosen, the raw periodogram can be plotted, or the periodogram can be smoothed. If smoothing is done, according to the help page for spectrum(), the argument spans sets the smoothing width(s) and a modified Daniell smoother is used to do the smoothing. Smoothing is not done on the periodogram for the second method.

Three types of plots are generated by the three versions of plot.spec(). The first type is the marginal plot, which plots the marginal periodogram(s) for the time series. The second type plots the coherence between multiple time series, two at a time. The third type plots the phase shift between multiple series, two at a time.

The plot.spec() function takes 11 specified arguments, plus many of the arguments of plot.default(). The arguments are x, for the object of the spec class; add, for whether to plot a new plot or add to an existing plot; ci, for the level of the confidence interval; log, for the type of scale on the y axis; xlab and ylab, for the labels on the x and y axes; type, for the type of plot; ci.col, for the color of the confidence contour; ci.lty, for the line type of the confidence contour; main and sub, for the title and subtitle of the plot; and plot. type, for which of the three types of plots to plot.

The x argument takes an object of the spec class. There is no default value for x.

The add argument takes a logical vector (or a vector that can be coerced to logical) of arbitrary length. The argument appears not to affect the plot(s) on my device. The default value of add is FALSE, that is, start a new plot.

The ci argument takes a numeric vector of length one. The value of ci must be between 0 and 1, exclusive, and gives the level of the confidence interval. Confidence intervals are only plotted for smoothed coherency or phase plots.

The log argument takes a character vector of length one and, according to the help page for plot.spec(), only affects plots if the plots are marginal plots. Logical vectors are not accepted (unlike what is written on the help page for plot.spec()). The four possible values of log are "no", for a linear scale on the y axis; "dB", for a log scale, with the powers in base ten as the labels on the y axis; "yes", for a log scale, with 1, 2, and 5 times the powers of ten as the labels on the y axis; and NULL, for the same result as "yes". The default value of log is c("yes", "dB", "no"), that is, the value used is "yes".

The xlab, ylab, and type arguments are the standard arguments from plot.default() (see Sections 3.2.1 and 3.3.1). The default values in plot.spec() for marginal plots are "frequency" for xlab, NULL for ylab, and "l" for type. For coherency plots, the values are "frequency", "squared coherency", and "l". For phase plots, the values are "frequency", "phase", and "l".

The ci.col and ci.lty arguments take color and line type vectors of arbitrary length (see Sections 3.4.1 and 3.3.2 for the kinds of values). For both arguments, only the first value is used. The default values are "blue" for ci.col and 3 (for a dotted line) for ci.lty.

The main and sub arguments are the standard arguments from plot.default() (see Section 3.2.1). The default values in plot.spec() are NULL for both arguments.

The plot.type argument takes a character vector of length one. The possible values of plot.type are "marginal", "coherency", and "phase", for the three types of plots. (The values can be shortened to "m", "c", and "p".) The values of "coherency" and "phase" give an error if x contains a single time series. The default value of plot.type is c("marginal", "coherency", "phase"), that is, a marginal plot is plotted.

Both coherency and phase plots take a different default ylim from plot.default(). Coherency plots take ylim equal to c(0, 1) by default. Phase plots take ylim equal to c(-pi, pi) by default. (See Section 3.2.1 for information about ylim.)

The number of possible basic figures for objects of the plot.spec classes is seven, given that method and spans can vary in spectrum() and that the plot.spec functions generate three types of plots. For the example in Figure 5-21, in spectrum(), method is set to "pgram" and spans is set to 3 and, in plot.spec(), ci is set to 0.966 and plot.type is set to "coherency".

The times series used in the example are lkhu, from the LakeHuron dataset; nile, from the Nile dataset; and snpt, from the sunspot.year dataset. The LakeHuron, Nile, and sunspot.year datasets are in the datasets package and are accessible for most users, since the datasets package is loaded by default in R. The years 1875–1970 were selected from the three datasets by using the function window().

In Listing 5-21, code is given for the example in Figure 5-21.

Listing 5-21. Code for an example of using an object of the spec.coherency class in plot(). The method and spans arguments are set in spectrum(), and the ci and plot.type arguments are set in plot.spec()

```
snpt = window(
  sunspot.year,
  start=1875,
  end=1970,
  freq=1
)

nile =  window(
  Nile,
  start=1875,
  end=1970,
  freq=1
)
```

```
lkhu = window(
  LakeHuron,
  start=1875,
  end=1970,
  freq=1
)

plot(
  spectrum(
    ts(
      cbind(
        lkhu,
        nile,
        snpt
      ),
      start=1,
      freq=11
    ),
    method="pgram",
    spans=3
  ),
  plot.type="coherency",
  ci=0.966
)
```

In Figure 5-21, the code in Listing 5-21 is run.

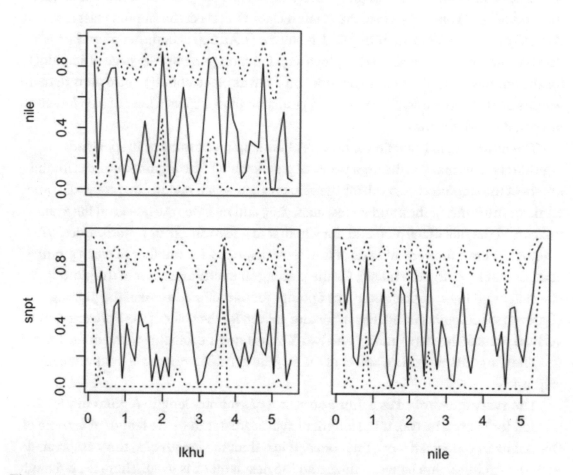

Figure 5-21. *Example of running plot() with an object of the spec class. In spectrum(), method and spans are set. In plot(), plot.type and ci are set. The frequency is one cycle per 11 years*

Note that smoothed periodograms are used in the figures, since method is set to "pgram" in spectrum() and spans is set to 3. The coherency between each pair of periodograms is plotted, along with a 96.6% confidence interval, since plot.type is set to "coherence" in plot() and ci is set to 0.966. The frequency that is set in ts() is eleven.

(Note that the labels on the x axis ticks give the frequency of the time series object divided by a sequence from 0 to 0.5. That is, if the frequency of the time series object equals 11, then the frequencies on the x axis go from 0 to 5.5. Also, the x and y axis labels are the names of the time series.)

5.3.14 The stepfun Method

A step function plot is a kind of plot that creates steps from point to point. The stepfun method of plot() plots objects of the stepfun class. Objects of the stepfun class are created by the functions stepfun() and as.stepfun(). An object of the stepfun class is a list with the information needed to plot a step function (see the help page of stepfun() for the components of the list). The function – run as plot.stepfun() – also plots numeric vectors as step functions. (The plot.ecdf() function plots a special kind of step function out of a numeric vector.)

The function plot() applied to objects of the stepfun class takes 18 specified arguments, plus many of the arguments of plot.default(). The arguments are x, for the object of the stepfun class; xval, for the values of x at which to find and plot y; xlim and ylim, for the limits of the x and y axes; xlab, ylab, and main for the labels on the x and y axes and the title of the plot; add, for whether to add to an existing plot; verticals, for whether to draw the vertical parts of the steps; do.points, for whether to plot a plotting character at a point; pch and col, for the plotting character and color of the plotting character and lines; col.points and cex.points, for the color and size of the plotting characters if do.points is TRUE; col.hor and col.ver, for the color of the horizontal and vertical parts of the steps; and lty and lwd, for the line type and line width of the lines.

The x argument takes an object of the stepfun class. There is no default value for stepfun.

The xval argument takes a numeric vector of arbitrary length. A point in y is plotted for every x in xval. If the length of xval is greater than the length of x, some of the points in y are used more than once. If less than the length of x, the y associated with the middle value between the x and the next larger x is used. There is no default value for xval.

The arguments xlim and ylim are the standard arguments from plot.default() (see Section 3.2.1). There is no default value of xlim. The default value of ylim is `range(c(y, Fn.kn))`.

The xlab, ylab, and main arguments are the standard arguments from plot.default() (see Section 3.2.1). The default value of xlab is "x", of ylab is "f(x)", and of main is NULL.

The add argument takes a logical vector (or a vector that can be coerced to logical) of arbitrary length. If longer than one, only the first value is used and a warning is given. If set to TRUE, the plot is added to the previous plot. If FALSE, a new plot is opened. The default value of add is FALSE.

The verticals argument takes a logical vector (or a vector that can be coerced to logical) of arbitrary length. If longer than one, only the first value is used and a warning is given. If set to TRUE, vertical lines are drawn at the steps. If FALSE, no vertical lines are drawn. The default value of verticals is TRUE.

The do.points argument takes a logical vector (or a vector that can be coerced to logical) of arbitrary length. If longer than one, only the first value is used and a warning is given. If set to TRUE, points are plotted. If FALSE, points are not plotted. The default value of do.points is (n < 1000), that is, TRUE if the number of points is less than 1000 and otherwise FALSE.

The col.hor and col.ver arguments take a color vector of arbitrary length (see Section 3.4.1 for possible color values). The color vectors cycle as the function goes through the points. The default values of col.hor and col.ver are the color set by col.

The lty and lwd arguments are the standard arguments from plot.default() (see Sections 3.3.2 and 3.4.4). The default values of lty and lwd are the values in par() of lty and lwd – "black" and 1 on my device.

In Listing 5-22, code is given for using plot() on output from stepfun(). The xval, verticals, pch, col.points, cex.points, and lwd arguments are set.

Listing 5-22. Code for the example in Figure 5-22 for using plot() on an object of the stepfun class. The xval, verticals, pch, col.points, cex.points, and lwd arguments are set

```
plot(
  stepfun(
    1:50,
    c(
      pop15.ordered[1],
      pop15.ordered
    )
  ),
  xval=1:100/2,
  verticals=FALSE,
  pch=23,
  col.points=grey( 0.4 ),
  cex.points=0.9,
  lwd=2.5
)
```

In Figure 5-22, the code in Listing 5-22 is run.

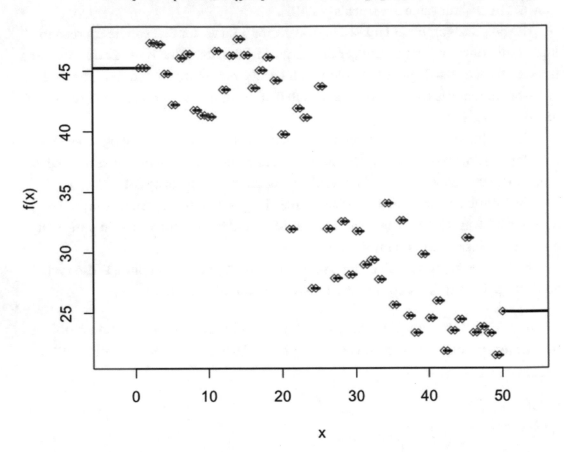

Figure 5-22. *An example of using an object of the stepfun class in plot(). The xval, verticals, pch, col.points, cex.points, and lwd arguments are set*

In stepfun(), the value plotted on the x axis must be an increasing vector (which 1:50 in Figure 5-22 is). Note that for y, the first element of pop15.ordered is repeated. To plot the points at the correct place, a point must be added to the beginning of y. Since the step function starts at the beginning of the x axis, setting the first and second values of y to the first value of the vector to be plotted makes good graphical sense.

The xval argument has been set to even steps of width 1/2 between 1 and 50. Each of the points is plotted twice at the height of the respective element of pop15.ordered. The steps are drawn toward the right of the points. (The direction can be changed in stepfun().)

The plotting character is 23 – an open diamond – and plotted in a mid-gray color at a size of 0.9 the size of a character width. The line width of the steps is 2.5. The vertical parts of the steps are not plotted.

5.3.15 The stl Method

Seasonal time series decomposition can be done using a loess method rather than by an autoregressive method. The plotting in this section is much the same as the plotting in Section 3.3.2, but the method of finding the values used in the plots is different in this section – using a loess method.

The stl method of plot() plots objects of the stl class. Objects of the stl class are created by the stl() function. The stl() function does seasonal time series decomposition using the loess method – as opposed to the function decompose(), which does seasonal time series decomposition using an autoregressive method (see Section 3.3.2 for plots from the autoregressive method).

The plot.stl() function takes six specified arguments, one of which takes four sub-arguments, plus many of the arguments of plot.default(). The ... argument is in the sixth place in the order of arguments, so the last argument cannot be shortened. The specified arguments are x, for the object of the stl class; labels, for the y axis labels for the four plots of the components; set.pars, for setting parameters for the plots (contains mar, oma, tck, and mfrow, which are arguments of par()); main, for the title over the four plots; range.bars, for whether to put a bar that represents a standard size measurement for the y scales of the plots; and col.range, for the color of the range bar.

The x argument takes an object of the stl class. There is no default value for x.

The labels argument takes a character vector (or a vector that can be coerced to character) of arbitrary length. If there are more than four elements, only the first four are used. If less than four, the elements do not cycle. Those plots without labels are not given a label. The default value for labels is colnames(X), that is, "data" for the top plot, "seasonal" for the next plot, "trend" for the third plot, and "remainder" for the bottom plot.

The set.pars argument sets the parameters for mar, oma, tck, and mfrow (all except tck are covered in Section 6.2; tck is covered in Section 3.4.5). The default values for the parameters are c(0, 6, 0, 6) for mar, c(6, 0, 4, 0) for oma, -0.01 for tck, and c(nplot, 1) for mfrow.

The main argument is the standard argument from plot.default() (see Section 3.2.1). The default value of main is NULL in plot.stl(), that is, no title is plotted.

The range.bars argument takes a logical vector (or a vector that can be coerced to logical) of arbitrary length. If longer than one, only the first element is used and a warning is given. If set to TRUE, range bars are plotted. If FALSE, range bars are not plotted. The default value of range.bars is TRUE.

The col.range argument takes a vector of color values of arbitrary length (see Section 3.4.1 for kinds of color values). If longer than one, only the first value is used. The default value of col.range is "light gray".

In Listing 5-23, code is given for the example in Figure 5-23 of using an object of the stl class in plot().

Listing 5-23. Code for the example of using an object of the stl class in plot. The arguments labels, main, and col.range are set

```
plot(
  stl(
    ts(
      sunspot.year,
      start=1,
      freq=11
    ),
    "per"
  ),
  labels=c( "DATA", "SEASONAL", "TREND", "REMAINDER" ),
  main="Example of Using a stl Class Object in plot()",
  col.range="grey70"
)
```

In Figure 5-23, the code in Listing 5-23 is run.

Example of Using a stl Class Object in plot()

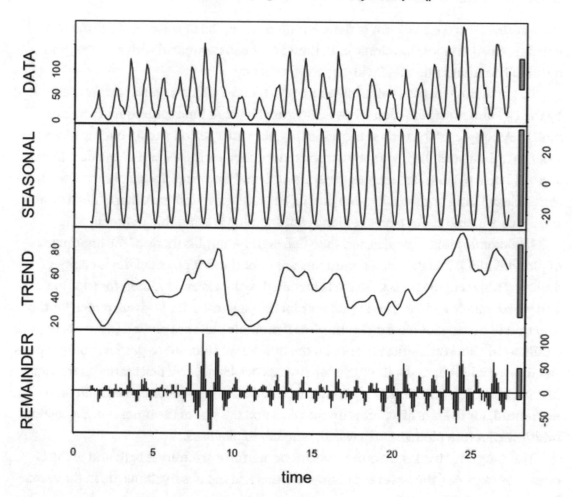

Figure 5-23. *An example of using an object of the stl class in plot(). The arguments labels, main, and col.range are set. The dataset is the sunspot.year dataset from the datasets package in R*

Note that the labels on the four plots are changed to uppercase letters from lowercase letters. A title is added to the plot, using the default plot settings for titles. The color of the range bars is changed from "light gray" to "grey70".

The ranges of the scales on the y axes for the data and the remainder are much larger than for the trend and the seasonal components, as can be seen from the range bars. The dataset used for the plot is the same dataset used in the example for the decomposed.ts method (see Section 3.3.2), so the plots can be directly compared.

239

5.3.16 The ts Method

Time series are a specific form of data. For time series, the observations are made at evenly spaced times or locations. In R, time series can be created with starting (and optionally ending) times and with a given frequency.

The ts method of plot() plots objects of the ts class. Objects of the ts class are created by the ts() and as.ts() functions. The ts function creates a time series out of a vector or matrix. An object of the ts class has a starting place in a period and an ending place in a period and a periodic frequency associated with the series, as well as the data in the series. (The tsp() function returns the start, end, and frequency for an object of the time series class.) Running the full name plot.ts() with a vector or matrix that is not a time series plots a time series plot where the starting value is 1 and the frequency is 1.

The plot.ts() function takes ten specified arguments plus many of the arguments of plot.default(). The specified arguments are x, for the first object of the ts class; y, for a second object of the ts class, if one is included; xy.labels and xy.lines, for whether and which labels and/or lines to plot for plots of x against y, if y is given; panel, for the function to use to plot the data in the plots if multiple plots are plotted (does not appear to affect the plots on my device); nc, for the number of columns to use for multiple plots; yax.flip, for whether to put the y axis labels, axis tick labels, and tick marks on the right instead of the left on alternate plots when multiple plots are plotted; mar.multi and oma.multi, for the size of margins on the plots and the size of the outer margin, again if multiple plots are plotted; and axes, for whether to plot axes.

The x argument takes a numeric vector or matrix of arbitrary length and of the ts class. For matrices, the series are in the columns and the observations are in the rows. There is no default value for x.

The y argument takes either the value of NULL or a numeric vector. If a vector, according to the help page for plot.ts(), x must also be a vector, and x and y must be the same length. The function then plots a scatterplot of y against x. The default value of y is NULL, that is, x is plotted against time.

The plot.type argument takes a character vector of length one. The argument affects the plot when x is a matrix. The argument can take the value "multiple" or "single" – for creating separate plots for each time series or for plotting the multiple time series on one plot.

The xy.labels argument takes either a logical vector or a character vector of arbitrary length. If logical and longer than one, only the first element is used and warnings are given. If character and the length is less than the length of x and y, the values cycle out to the ends of x and y. If longer than x and y, the excess values are ignored. There is no default value for xy.labels, that is, the time values for x and y are plotted at the points.

The xy.lines argument takes a logical vector of arbitrary length. If longer than one, only the first element is used and a warning is given. If set to TRUE, lines are plotted of the type "c" (see Section 3.3.1). If set to FALSE, no lines are plotted. There is no default value for xy.lines, that is, according to the help page for plot.ts(), if xy.labels is logical, xy.lines takes the same value. If xy.labels is character, xy.lines is set to TRUE.

The panel argument takes a function name as a value. The argument has no effect on my device. The default value of panel is lines.

The nc argument takes a positive numeric vector of length one. If not an integer, the value is rounded down to an integer, except for values between 1.5 and 2, which can do unusual things. There is no default value for nc, that is, according to the help page for plot.ts(), if the number of time series is less than or equal to four, one column is used and otherwise two columns are used.

The yax.flip argument takes a logical vector (or a vector that can be coerced to logical) of arbitrary length. If longer than one, only the first element is used and a warning is given. If set to TRUE, the y axis label, axis tick labels, and tick marks flip to the right side on alternate plots. If FALSE, the y axis annotation does not flip. The default value of yax.flip is FALSE.

The mar.multi and oma.multi arguments take nonnegative numeric vectors of length four, giving the number of line widths in the bottom, left, top, and right margins. The default value of mar.multi is `c(0, 5.1, 0, if (yax.flip) 5.1 else 2.1)`. The default value of oma.multi is `c(6, 0, 5, 0)`.

The axes argument takes a logical vector (or a vector that can be coerced to logical) of arbitrary length. If longer than one, only the first element is used and a warning is given. If set to TRUE, axes are plotted. If FALSE, axes are not plotted. The default value of axes is TRUE.

In Listing 5-24, an example is given of running plot() with two time series vectors for x and y. The data are from the sunspot.year, Nile, and LakeHuron datasets in the R package datasets.

Listing 5-24. Code to demonstrate using x and y time series vectors in plot()

```
snpt = window(
  sunspot.year,
  start=1875,
  end=1970,
  freq=1
)
nile  = window(
  Nile,
  start=1875,
  end=1970,
  freq=1
)
lkhu = window(
  LakeHuron,
  start=1875,
  end=1970,
  freq=1
)

labels=1875
for ( i in seq( 1879, 1971, 4 ) ) labels=c( labels, rep( NA, 3 ), i )
labels=c( labels[ 1:95 ], 1970 )
labels[45]=NA

plot(
  x=lkhu,
  y=nile,
  xy.labels=as.character( labels ),
  xy.lines=FALSE,
  cex=0.68,
  main="Annual Flow Over the Aswan Dam\nagainst Lake Huron Elevation\n1875
  to 1970 (selected years)",
  xlab="Elevation in Feet",
  ylab="100 Million Cubic Meters"
)
```

In Figure 5-24, the code in Listing 5-24 is run.

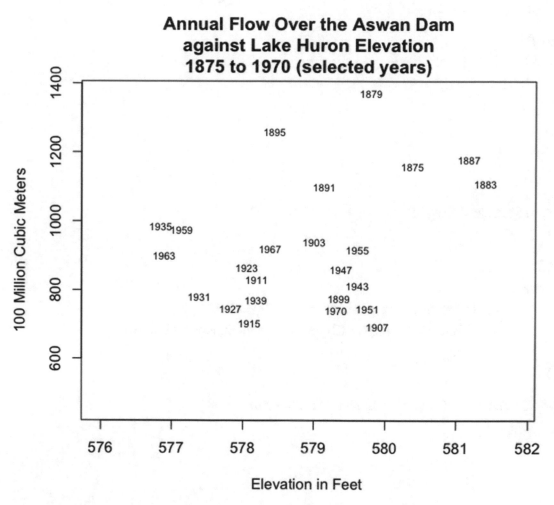

Figure 5-24. *An example of running plot() with x and y set equal to vectors of the ts class*

Note that only a selection of the years are plotted. The selection is done externally to the plot() call. Also, xy.lines is set to FALSE, so no lines are plotted.

In Listing 5-25, code is given for an example of running plot() on a matrix of the ts class with plot.type set to "single".

Listing 5-25. Code for the example of using plot() on a time series matrix with plot.type set to "single"

```
plot(
  as.ts(
    cbind(
      lkhu,
      nile,
      snpt
    )
  ),
  plot.type="single"
)

title(
  main=c(
    "Example of Setting plot.type to \"single\"",
    "Aswan Flow, Lake Huron Elevation, and Sunspot Numbers"
  )
)
```

In Figure 5-25, the code in Listing 5-25 is run.

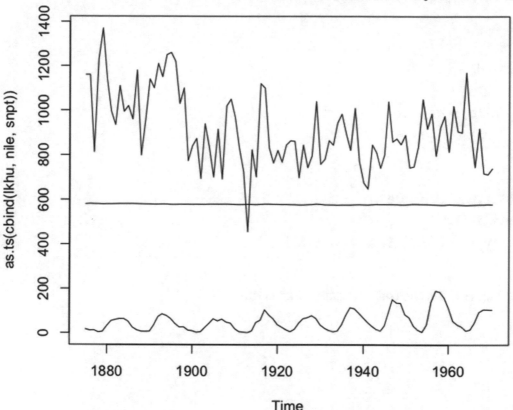

Figure 5-25. *Example of using plot() on a matrix of the ts class with plot.type set to "single"*

Note that, for the scale on the y axis, there is little variation in the Lake Huron elevations, so the data looks like a straight line. The labels on the x and y axes are the labels plotted by default – Time and the value of the x argument.

In Listing 5-26, code is given for an example of running plot() on a matrix of the ts class with plot.type equal to "multiple" and mar equal to c(0.3, 5.1, 0.3, 5.1) (see Section 6.2.1.2).

Listing 5-26. Code for the example, in Figure 5-26, of setting plot.type to "multiple" in plot.ts(). The argument mar.multi is also set

```
plot(
  as.ts(
    cbind(
      lkhu,
      nile,
      snpt
    )
  ),
  plot.type="multiple",
  yax.flip=TRUE,
  mar.multi=c( 0.3, 5.1, 0.3, 5.1 )
)
```

In Figure 5-26, the code in Listing 5-26 is run.

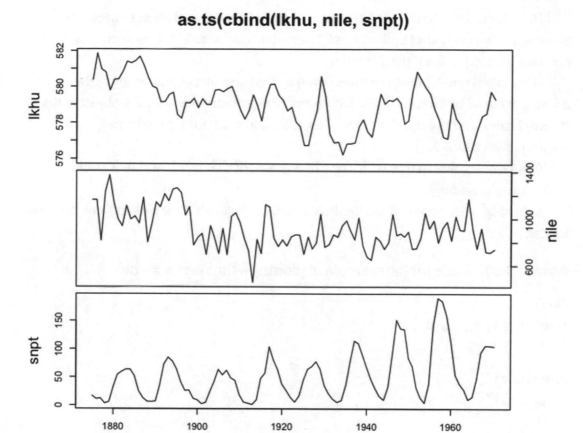

Figure 5-26. *An example of running plot() on a matrix of the ts class with plot. type set equal to "multiple" and mar.multi set*

Note that plot type is "multiple" (the default). The argument yax.flip has been set to TRUE, so the y axis annotation is on the right side of the second plot. A small margin has been added between the plots by setting the first and third values of mar.multi to 0.3.

There is no way to change the y axis labels – the labels are set equal to the names of the time series in x. The title is the default title and is the value of the argument x.

5.3.17 The tskernel Method

Kernels are used to smooth numeric vectors, usually vectors with data that is evenly spaced in space or time. Kernels consist of a vector of numbers used to weight consecutive data points in the smoothing process. The numbers are generated by specific kinds of processes.

The tskernel method of plot() plots an object of the tskernel class. Objects of the tskernel class are created by the kernel() function. The kernel() function creates kernels that can be used to smooth time series.

The plot.tskernel() function takes five specified arguments plus many of the arguments used by plot.default(). The specified arguments are x, for the object of the tskernel class, and the standard type, xlab, ylab, and main from plot.default() (see Sections 3.2.1 and 3.3.1).

The default value of type is "h", for a histogram; of xlab is "k"; of ylab is "W[k]"; and of main is attr(x,"name").

In Listing 5-27, code is given for the example in Figure 5-27 of plotting a time series kernel.

Listing 5-27. Code for the example of plotting a time series kernel

```
par(
  oma=c( 1, 1, 2, 1 )
)

exa=kernel(
  "daniell",
  m=5,
  name="exa"
)

plot(
  exa
)

mtext(
  "Example of Using plot() on an Object of the tskernel Class",
  outer=TRUE
)
```

In Figure 5-27, the code in Listing 5-27 is run.

Example of Using plot() on an Object of the tskernel Class

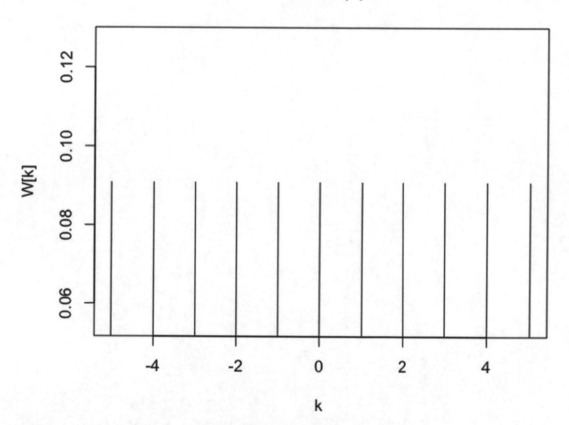

Figure 5-27. Example of running plot() on an object of the tskernel class. A Daniell kernel with m equal to 5 is plotted

Note that the Daniell kernel gives a kernel with a width that is two times m plus one and that every weight in the kernel has the same value. The kernel weights sum to one. (The preceding kernel is appropriate for yearly sunspot data since the kernel has a width of eleven.)

CHAPTER 6

Graphics Devices and Laying Out Plots

In R, plots are plotted on graphics devices. Given that a graphics device is chosen, figures with multiple plots can be plotted on the device. In this chapter, we list the graphics devices and give some functions that work with the devices. Then, we give a few ways to set up a graphics device to plot multiple plots in one figure by using par(), layout(), or split.screen(). Any arguments of par() not covered in earlier chapters are covered, most of which are related to device regions, figure regions, plotting regions, margins, and multiple plot layouts.

6.1 Graphics Devices and Working with Graphics Devices

There are several graphics devices available in R. Some are operating system dependent. Some create files in standard plot formats. Some are internal to RStudio. For example, some of the devices available are the standard device for Microsoft Windows, a device that creates a pdf file, and the default RStudio device on an Apple MacBook. In Section 6.1.1, the various kinds of devices currently available in R are described. In Section 6.1.2, ways of working with devices are given.

6.1.1 The Graphics Devices

Graphics devices specify where a plot is created. Some of the graphics devices open on the screen of the computer, and others open a file (or files) that is written to a location when the device is closed. The location can be a URL, a folder on a computer, a pipe, a socket, or a printer.

© Margot Tollefson 2021
M. Tollefson, *Visualizing Data in R 4*, https://doi.org/10.1007/978-1-4842-6831-5_6

The default graphics device is the graphics device that opens when a plotting function is called but a graphics device has not been specifically opened. The default device is given by the value returned when `options("device")` is entered at the R console. (In RStudio on my computer, the graphics device is `"RStudioGD"`, and the device opens a plot in the lower-right window of RStudio.)

Links to graphics devices, other than the default, are listed on the help page for Devices. Links to 14 functions that open graphics devices are listed. A few of the links include more than one function. Some of the graphics devices are operating system dependent. Others depend on the presence of Ghostscript website (an interpreter for pdf files and the PostScript language) or access to an X Window System server. Some others require that R has been compiled with cairo (a library of graphics programs) or X Window System (X11) support.

The operating system–dependent functions are windows() (also win.graph(), win. metafile(), and win.print()), for MS Windows systems; quartz() (and quartz.save()), for current OS X systems; and X11() (or x11()), for systems that use X Window System graphics (which include MS Windows and UNIX-like systems – e.g., UNIX, LINUX, and earlier OS X systems). The functions windows(), X11(), and quartz() open a graphics device window on the computer screen.

Functions that should run on any system and that create external files are pdf(), for portable document format files, and postscript(), for PostScript files. Also, the function xfig() creates files in the format used by Xfig, and pictex() creates TeX/PicTeX files. The function bitmap() (also dev2bitmap()) uses the Ghostscript interface and creates bmp files.

Functions that run if R has been compiled with cairo are cairo.pdf(), for pdf files; cairo.ps(), for PostScript files; and svg(), for scalable vector graphics files. My version of R – the most current default version when loaded in mid-2020 – does not run the cairo functions.

The functions bmp() for bitmap files, jpeg() for Joint Photographic Experts Group files, png() for portable network graphics files, and tiff() for tagged image files run on systems that support cairo, X11, or Quartz – which are most systems. By default, first, the function checks to see if cairo is available. If not, the function checks for X11. If X11 is not available, the function checks to see if Quartz windows are available. Which option to use can be set in the call to the functions. My version of R runs the four functions.

6.1.2 Working with Graphics Devices

In this section, we cover how to work with graphics devices, including the default plotting device. Most functions that manage and interact with graphics devices begin with *dev.*, and functions that begin with *dev.* all affect graphics devices. One other function that affects graphics devices is graphics.off().

In RStudio, the default graphics device opens a plot in the plot window (under the Plots tab in the lower-right window). Given that a plot has been opened, there are a number of options for what to do with the plot.

The window can be resized by dragging the left and/or top handle of the window. (The handles appear as double arrows when hovering over the center of the left or top side. The arrow only appears at the top if the window has not been expanded to the maximum height.)

The window can be zoomed to a standalone window on the screen by selecting the *Zoom* tab above the plot. The plot can then be resized by dragging the handles. (If the window is maximized to the full screen, the handles do not appear. Otherwise, top, bottom, left-side, right-side, and corner handles appear.)

The plot can be exported to an image file. To export to an image file, select the *Export* tab above the plot in the plot windowpane, and then select *Save as Image* .... In the window that opens, select *Update Preview* to see the plot.

Choices are given for changing the size of the plot. If the width and/or height is changed, update the plot by selecting *Update Preview*. (Otherwise, the window can close.) Six choices are given for the format of the image file: PNG, JPEG, TIFF, BMP, SVG, and EPS. The file extension is added automatically to the file name when the file is saved.

To export to a pdf file, select the *Export* tab and then select *Save as PDF* .... The choices for the pdf format are of the orientation (portrait or landscape) and of the size of the pdf (in inches). Size options include *US Letter*, *US Legal*, and *A4*. To preview the resulting pdf, select *Preview*. Select the *Save* button to save the plot. The file extension, pdf, is added automatically to the file name.

To copy the plot to the clipboard, select Export, and then select *Copy to Clipboard*. The options are the same as for *Save as Image* ..., except there is no file name to be assigned. The copied image is in the tiff format.

The plot can be saved or copied as is by right-clicking the plot. The extension must be added manually and can be bmp, jpeg, png, or tiff.

If more than one plot has been generated, step backward or forward through the plots by using the arrows to the left of the *Zoom* tab. A plot can be removed from the plot windowpane by selecting the white cross in the red circle to the right of the *Export* tab. To erase all open plots, select the little broom to the right of the white cross in the red circle.

In the top menu for the RStudio program, there is a tab, *Plots*. The selections under the *Plots* tab are the same selections that are found in the plot windowpane.

In R, on my MacBook Air, plots open in a Quartz window by default. To save the plot to a file, the function quartz.save() can be run after the plot is created. The name to be assigned to the file must be set in quartz.save(). From the help page for windows(), the functions win.metafile() and win.print() are similar to quartz.save(), except the functions are for the MS Windows operating system.

The devices that are open are assigned names and, sequentially, numbers (on my device, the numbers 3–8 are skipped). The device with number 1 is a null device and is not used. Open devices start numbering at 2 and can have numbers as large as 63. Devices are referenced by number.

The dev.cur() function returns the current device name and number. The dev.list() function lists the names and numbers of all open devices.

The dev.next() and dev.prev() functions return the name and number of the next or previous device. The two functions have one argument, which – for the number of the device from which to start looking for the number of the next or previous device. (The default value of the argument is dev.cur().) The numbers of the devices cycle, excluding device 1. If no devices are open, dev.next() and dev.prev() return *null device* and *1*, respectively.

The dev.set() function tells R which device to make the current device. The function has one argument, which, for the number of the device to set as current. The default value of which is dev.next().

The dev.off() function closes a device. The function has one argument, which – for the number of the device to be closed. The default value is dev.cur(), that is, the current device. The graphics.off() function closes all open devices.

The dev.new() function opens a new device. The function takes one specified argument plus several unspecified plotting arguments that are to be applied to the device opened. The one specified argument is noRStudioGD, for whether to use the device RStudioGD if RStudioGD is the default device. (The default device is the value of getOption("device").) The default value of noRStudioGD is FALSE, that is, use RStudioGD if RStudioGD is the default device.

The dev.copy() function copies the settings and contents of the current device to a new device. After the copying, if the plot is changed, most of the settings are not affected. While most of the arguments of the original device are copied, width and height are not.

The function has two specified arguments – device and which – but takes one or the other, not both. The argument device takes the name of a function that plots. Just the name of the function is entered. Arguments to the function are added by name and are separated by commas from the other arguments and from the value of device.

The argument which takes a numeric vector of length one. The value of the argument is a device number. The contents of the current device are copied to the device assigned by which. The device must have been opened before the copying can be done, and the device cannot copy to itself.

Other than the two possible specified arguments, the arguments of the function set by device, if device has been set, can be set. If which has been set, the arguments of the device that is being copied can be set. After the device is copied, the device to which the settings and contents were copied becomes the current device.

The dev.copy2pdf() and dev.copy2eps() functions copy the contents of a device to a pdf, Quartz, cairo, or PostScript file. See the help page for dev.copy() for more information.

The dev.print() function copies the contents of a graphics device to a printer, by default in PostScript form. The file is sent to the default printer connected to the computer on which R is run. See the help page for dev.copy() for more information.

If memory is an issue and the plot is not ever resized, then running `dev.control(displaylist="inhibit")` uses less memory. See the help page for dev.copy() for more information.

In Figure 6-1, an example of using quartz(), dev.cur(), dev.copy(), dev.set(), and dev.list() is given. Note that the numbers of the devices are in the headings above the plots.

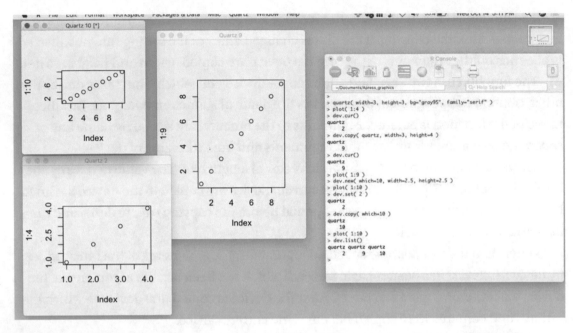

Figure 6-1. *A screenshot of the console of R with examples of using dev.cur(),*
dev.copy(), dev.new(), dev.set(), and dev.list()

The dev.capabilities(), dev.interactive(), and dev.size() functions query the current
graphics device. The dev.capabilities() function returns the capabilities of the device and
behaves like the function options(). The dev.interactive() function returns whether the
device is interactive. The dev.size() function returns the size of the device in inches.

There are five device capabilities: transparentBackground (with values "no", "fully",
and "semi"), rasterImage (with values "no", "yes", and "non-image"), capture (logical,
TRUE if the graphics device can capture raster images), locator (logical, TRUE if the
functions locator() and identify() are supported), and events (with possible values
"MouseDown", "MouseMove", "MouseUp", and "Keybd".)

The orNone argument (taking values TRUE and FALSE) is used by dev.interactive().
If set to TRUE, the function also checks if the value of getOption("device") is
interactive. The units argument (with possible values "in", "cm", and "px" – for inches,
centimeters, and pixels) can be set in dev.size().

The dev.capture() function creates a raster image out of the contents of the graphics
device. Not all graphics devices support the creation of raster images; and, if not, the
graphics device returns NULL when dev.capture() is run.

The function takes one argument, native. The argument takes a logical vector of length one. If set to FALSE, a matrix of color values is returned. If set to TRUE, an object of the nativeRaster class is returned.

The functions dev.hold() and dev.flush() can be used if the graphics device has a stack of hold levels. The function takes one argument, level, which should take a nonnegative integer. See the help page for dev.hold() for more information.

6.2 The par(), layout(), and split.screen() Functions

The par() function sets plotting parameters. There are 72 parameters listed on the help page for par(). Most of the parameters have been covered already – in Chapter 3. The ones covered in this section are parameters that can only be set in par(), those that can only be queried, and those that have a different effect in par() than in the plot() function.

Some of the arguments of par(), the layout() function, and the split.screen() function provide for multiple plots to be plotted on a graphics page. Section 6.2.1 goes over the arguments of par() that behave differently when set in par() or that are not covered in Chapter 3. Section 6.2.2 covers the function layout(). Section 6.2.3 describes the function split.screen().

6.2.1 The par() Function

Many of the arguments used by plot(), and other plotting functions, get default values from the arguments of par(). By using par(), arguments can be set for an entire plotting session rather than within the call for each plot.

The arguments in par() can be queried by entering the names of the arguments in quotes, separated by commas, within the parentheses in the call to par(). For example, running par("bg", "fg") returns $bg [1] "white" and $fg [1] "black". If par() is called with no arguments, all of the 72 arguments are returned, along with the values of the arguments.

To set arguments in par(), set the arguments equal to the values to be set, separated by commas. For example, par(lwd=2, lty="dotted") sets the line width to 2 and the line type to a dotted line.

The graphics device is sectioned into three sections, the device, the figures within the device, and the plots within the figures. The size of the margin between the device edge and the figures can be set. Each figure has margins that surround the plot. The sizes of the margins around the plot can be set.

This section is split into five subsections. The subsections cover the device region, the figure region, the plotting region, character properties, and multiple plots on a page.

6.2.1.1 The Device Region

The arguments of par() that query or set values controlling the graphics device region are din, oma, omi, omd, and bg. The din argument is an argument that can only be queried, not set. The argument gives the width and height of the graphics device in inches.

The oma, omi, and omd arguments – which can only be set in par() – use three different types of units to set the sizes of the outer margins. The oma argument takes a numeric vector of length four and gives the size of the margins in line widths. The four values are for the bottom margin, left margin, top margin, and right margin, respectively. The default value of oma is c(0,0,0,0), that is, no outer margin.

The omi argument is similar to oma, except that the units are in inches. The default value of omi is also c(0,0,0,0).

The omd argument sets the inner corners of the device region in normalized device coordinate (NDC) units. The argument takes a four-element numeric vector, where the values are between 0 and 1, inclusive.

The first number is the distance between the left side of the graphics device and the left side of the figure region, measured as a proportion of the bottom of the graphics device (i.e., in normalized device coordinates). The second number is the distance from the left side of the graphics device to the right side of the figure region, measured in normalized device coordinates.

The third number is the distance from the bottom of the graphics device to the bottom of the figure region, measured in normalized device coordinates. The fourth number is the distance from the bottom of the graphics device to the top of the figure region, measured in normalized device coordinates. The default value of omd is c(0,1,0,1), that is, no margins.

The bg argument gives the background color of the graphics device. The color covers the entire device. (The argument behaves differently in par() than in the function(s) that creates the plot.) According to the help page for par(), if bg is set in par, then the new argument is set to FALSE (see the last part of Section 6.2.1.5). The default value of bg is "transparent" or "white" (see the help page for par() for more information).

6.2.1.2 The Figure Region

There can be one or more figures within the inner limits of the outer margins. In this section, we only cover the case of one figure. Multiple figures are covered in Section 6.2.1.5.

The figure region is the region in which a plot and, usually, the annotation of the plot are plotted. Within the figure region, there is, often, a margin around the plotting region (which is between the outer figure limits and the region where the plot is plotted). The plot annotation is, by default, within the figure margins.

The arguments that affect the figure region and the margins of the figure region are fig, fin, mar, and mai. The arguments can only be set in par().

The fig argument gives the locations of the left side, right side, bottom, and top of the plotting region with respect to normalized figure region coordinates (referenced to the outer sides of the figure region). The argument takes a four-element numeric vector, with values between 0 and 1, inclusive. For a single plot, the default value of fig is c(0,1,0,1).

The fin argument gives the size of the figure region in inches. The argument takes a two-element numeric vector. The first value gives the width of the figure region, and the second value gives the height. For a single plot, the default value of fin is the value of din.

The mar argument gives the sizes of the figure margins measured in line widths. The argument takes a four-element numeric vector giving the sizes of the bottom, left, top, and right margins. The default value of mar is c(5.1, 4.1, 4.1, 2.1).

The mai argument gives the sizes of the figure margins measured in inches – bottom, left side, top, and right side. The default value of mai is c(1.02, 0.82, 0.82, 0.42).

6.2.1.3 The Plotting Region

The plotting region contains the plot. The arguments that affect the plotting region and the plot are pty, plt, usr, pin, xlog, ylog, ylbias, and fg. All but fg can only be set in par().

The pty argument gives the type of plotting region shape to use. The argument takes a one-element character vector. The possible values are "m" and "s". The value "m" tells R to maximize the plot within the margins of the figure region. The value "s" tells R to use a square plotting region. The default value of pty is "m".

The plt argument gives the locations of the left side, right side, bottom, and top of the plotting region in normalized device coordinates (x1, x2, y1, and y2), referenced to the figure region. The argument takes a numeric vector of length four with values between 0 and 1, inclusive. The default value of plt, for a single plot, depends on the aspect ratio of the plot.

The usr argument gives the locations of the left side, right side, bottom, and top of the plotting region in the units of the plot (user units). For example, if the x axis of a plot goes from 0 to 10 and the y axis from 0 to 5, under default conditions, the value of usr would be c(-0.4, 10.4, -0.2, 5.2).

To get the plot limits, 0.04 is multiplied by 10, then subtracted from the lower x limit, and added to the upper x limit, while 0.04 multiplied by 5 is subtracted from the lower y limit and is added to the upper y limit. (See the description of xaxs and yaxs in Section 3.4.5 for more information.) The value of usr is constant given the data and the axis limits, that is, usr does not depend on the aspect ratio or the size of the plot.

The pin argument gives the size of the plotting region in inches. The argument takes a two-element positive numeric vector, giving the width and the height. The default value of pin depends on the size of the figure region and the margins. The value of par("pin")[1] added to the sum of par("mai")[c(2, 4)] gives par("fin")[1]. Similarly, par("pin")[2] added to the sum of par("mai")[c(1, 3)] gives par("fin")[2].

The xlog and ylog arguments are used to set the x axis and the y axis to a log scale instead of a linear scale. (The log scale is to base 10, not base *e*.) If set to TRUE, the respective log scale is used by default for all functions that do not create a new plot. However, if a new plot is called, the value of xlog is set to FALSE. The default value of xlog and ylog is FALSE. In Listing 6-1, code is given for an example of using xlog.

Listing 6-1. An example of changing xlog to TRUE in par()

```
> par( xlog=TRUE )
> par( "xlog" )
[1] TRUE
> plot( c( 0, 2.5 ), c( 1, 200 ), type="n" )
> par( "xlog" )
[1] FALSE
> par( xlog=TRUE )
> lines( 1:200, 1:200 )
> lines( 1:200, 200:1 )
> title( main="Example of Setting xlog in par()")
```

In Figure 6-2, the result from the code in Listing 6-1 is given.

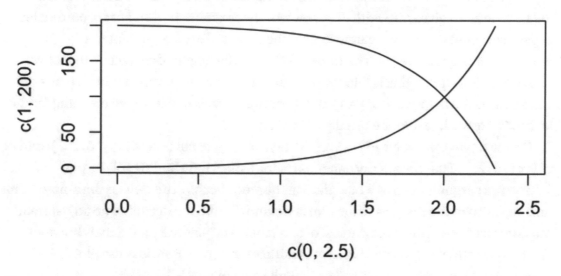

Figure 6-2. *Example of setting xlog in par()*

The ylbias argument gives a measure of the offset of text entered through axis() or mtext(). For text on the bottom and top sides, smaller values for ylbias plot below where larger values plot. For text on the left and right sides, smaller values of ylbias plot to the right of where larger values plot. The default value of ylbias is 0.2.

The fg argument if set in par() and if col is not set in par() gives the color of the tick marks, axes, points, lines, and text. (If both fg and col are set in par(), then the tick marks are the color given by fg and the axes, points, lines, and text are the color given by col.) The argument takes a one-element vector of color values (see Section 3.4.1 for information about color values). The default value of fg is usually "black", depending on the kind of device opened.

6.2.1.4 Text and Line Width Arguments

The arguments in this section are related to the size of characters and the height of the lines on which the characters are plotted. There are seven arguments covered in this section: cra, for the character size in rasters; cin, for character size in inches; csi, for the height of characters in inches; cxy, for character size in user coordinates; mex, for the level of the conversion from line widths to inches in the margins; lheight, for the line height used by multiline text; and ps, for the point size of text. The cra, cin, csi, and cxy arguments can only be queried, not set. The mex, lheight, and ps arguments can only be set in par().

The values of the cra, cin, and cxy arguments are two-element numeric vectors. The first element gives the width of characters, in rasters, inches, and user coordinates, respectively, and the second element gives the height. The csi argument is a one-element numeric vector. The value of csi gives the height of characters in inches.

A raster is a square that is filled with a color. Graphic images are made up of rasters. According to the help page for par(), in R rasters are pixels if pixels have meaning for the device. Otherwise, rasters are usually 1/72 of an inch.

On my device, the value of cra is c(10.8, 14.4), of cin is c(0.15, 0.20), and of csi is c(0.2). The value of cxy depends on the aspect ratio and size of the plot.

The mex argument takes a one-element numeric vector. The value is the amount that the line width in the margins of the plot is expanded from the default of no adjustment. The argument does not affect the size of axis labels and axis tick mark labels but does affect the length of tick marks. If the line width is increased, R shrinks the plot to accommodate the larger margins. The default value of mex is 1.

The lheight argument takes a one-element numeric vector. The value is the line height for text generated by text() (and, according to the help page for par(), measured by strheight()). The default value of lheight is 1. The argument only has an effect if set between the call to plot() and the call to text().

The ps argument gives the point size, in rasters, of the text in axis labels, axis tick mark labels, and the title – also, text generated by the function text(). For points, the size of the plotting character is not affected. The default value of ps is 12.

6.2.1.5 Using par() to Generate Multiple Plots

The par() function can be used to set up the graphics device to plot multiple plots. A grid to contain the plots is set up by using the mfcol or mfrow argument. Each plot is plotted in a square in the grid.

Before going over the relevant arguments in par(), a discussion of plot.new() is in order. Functions that create standalone plots, such as plot() or curve(), call the function plot.new() at some point. The function plot.new() closes the previous plot and opens a new one. The function does not take any arguments. When working with multiple plots, using plot.new() sometimes makes sense. For example, when generating multiple plots by setting mfcol or mfrow, calling plot.new() without adding a plot will skip a block of the plot grid.

The arguments for multiple plots are fig (from Section 6.2.1.2); mfcol, for the number of rows and columns in a grid of plots where the plots are plotted down the columns first; mfrow, same as mfcol except that the plots are plotted across the rows first; mfg, for where the last plot was plotted or where the next plot will be plotted, when mfcol or mfrow is set; page, for whether a new page will be plotted on the next call to plot.new(); ask, for whether to pause when a new page is to be opened and ask for a response before going to the next page; and new, for whether to open a new plot or to overplot an existing plot. The argument page can only be queried, not set. The other arguments can only be set in par().

The fig argument can be used to put multiple plots on a graphics device. Setting fig, which is a four-element vector giving the position of the figure on the graphics device in normalized device coordinates, puts a figure at a limited location on a graphics device. By calling par() with a new location and with new set to TRUE (see the last part of Section 6.2.1.5) in par(), more figures can be plotted. In Listing 6-2, code is given for an example of plotting three figures on a graphics device.

Listing 6-2. Code for an example of plotting three figures on a graphics device using fig and new in par()

```
par(
  ps=9,
  mar=c( 4, 4, 2, 1 ),
  oma=c( 0, 0, 2, 0 )
)

par(
  fig=c( 0.1, 0.49, 0.1, 0.8 )
)

plot(
  1:10,
  main="Plot 1"
)
```

```r
par(
  fig=c( 0.5, 0.85, 0.5, 0.95 ),
  new=TRUE
)

plot(
  1:10,
  main="Plot 2"
)

par(
  fig=c( 0.6, 0.9, 0.0, 0.45 ),
  new=TRUE
)

plot(
  1:10,
  main="Plot 3"
)

mtext(
  "Example of Using fig and new in par()",
  outer=TRUE,
  cex=1.5,
  font=2
)
```

In Figure 6-3, the code in Listing 6-2 is run.

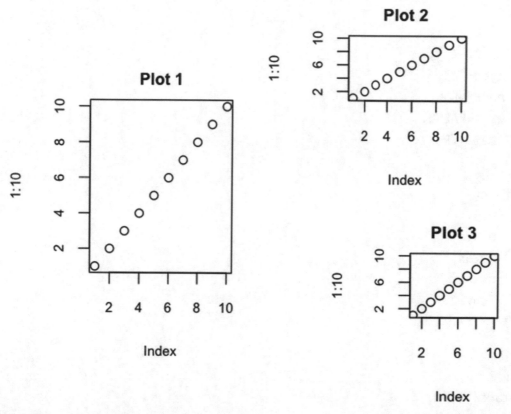

Figure 6-3. *An example of putting multiple plots on a page by using fig and new in par()*

Note that, in the example, the point size has been reduced to 9 and the margins have been reduced to 4 line widths for the bottom margin, 4 line widths for the left margin, 2 line widths for the top margin, and 1 line width for the right margin. When plotting multiple figures in the preceding manner, figures can overlap.

The mfcol and mfrow arguments take a two-element integer vector, with the first element set equal to the number of rows in the plot grid and the second element set equal to the number of columns. Only one of the two is set. The default value of both mfcol and mfrow is c(1, 1).

In Listing 6-3, code is given for the examples in Figure 6-4 of setting mfcol and mfrow.

Listing 6-3. Code for the examples of setting mfcol and mfrow

```
plotter = function( words ) {
  plot(
    c( 0, 1 ),
    c( 0, 1 ),
    type="n",
    ann=FALSE,
    axes=FALSE,
    frame=TRUE
    )

    text(
      0.5,
      0.5,
      words,
      cex=2,
      font=2
    )
}

par(
  oma=c( 0, 0, 4, 0 ),
  mfcol=c( 2, 2 )
)

plotter(
  "PLOT ONE"
)
plotter(
  "PLOT TWO"
)
plotter(
  "PLOT THREE"
```

```
)
plotter(
  "PLOT FOUR"
)

mtext(
  "Example of Setting mfcol",
  outer=TRUE,
  font=2,    cex=2
)

box(
  which="outer",
  lwd=4
)

par(
  mfrow=c( 2, 2 )
)

plotter(
  "PLOT ONE"
)
plotter(
  "PLOT TWO"
)
plotter(
  "PLOT THREE"
)
plotter(
  "PLOT FOUR"
)

mtext(
  "Example of Setting mfrow",
  outer=TRUE,
  font=2,
  cex=2
```

```
)
box(
  which="outer",
  lwd=4
)
```

In Figure 6-4, the two figures generated by the code in Listing 6-3 are shown.

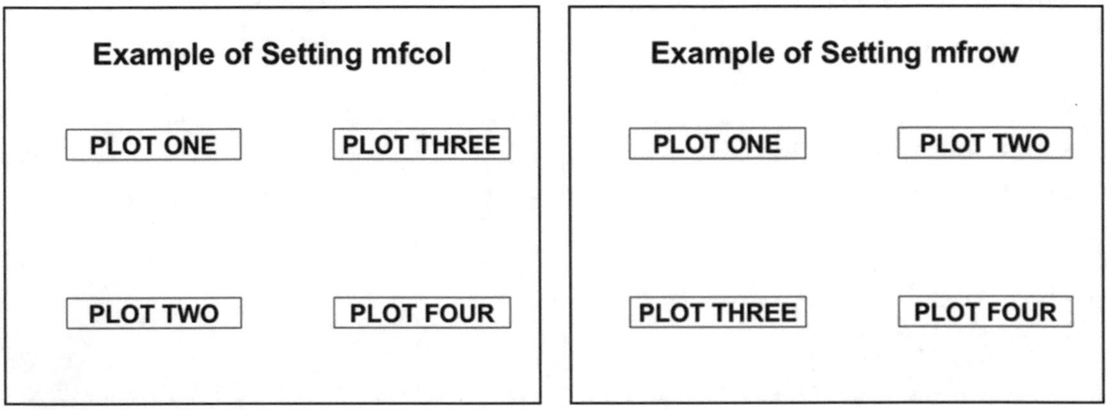

Figure 6-4. *Examples of setting mfcol and mfrow in par()*

The mfg argument takes a two- or four-element integer vector. If queried (par("mfg")), the row and column of the last plot that was plotted, along with the number of rows and the number of columns in the plot grid, are returned. If set, the row and column for the next plot are set. Both numbers must be included. Optionally, the number of rows and the number of columns in the plot grid can be included. For example, for mfrow set equal to c(3, 2), to enter the next plot into the grid at row 2 and column 1, mfg would be set to c(2, 1) or c(2, 1, 3, 2) in a call to par().

The argument only affects the placement of the plots that are plotted after the first plot in the grid is plotted – which is always placed in the first cell of the matrix irrespective of the value of mfg. If the matrix is filled out without the last plot in the last cell of the matrix, a new page is not opened if a new plot is plotted. Instead, R overplots cells in order from the last cell used to the last cell in the matrix. The default value for mfg is c(1, 1, 1, 1).

The page argument is a logical vector of length one. If the value is FALSE, the next call to plot.new() does not open a new plot. If the value is TRUE, then a new plot is opened on the next call to plot.new(). As noted in the preceding text, page can only be queried.

The ask argument takes a logical vector of length one. If set to TRUE, when a new page is plotted, R asks to go on to the next page before going on. If set to FALSE, R does not ask. According to the help page for par(), the argument ask is deprecated and should be replaced by the devAskNewPage() function. The default value of ask is FALSE.

The new argument takes a logical vector of length one. If set to TRUE, R does not go to a new page when a new call to plot.new() occurs. If set to FALSE, a call to plot.new() resets the page. The default value of new is FALSE.

6.2.2 The layout(), layout.show(), and lcm() Functions

The layout() function provides another way to create pages containing multiple plots. The plots are placed in a grid set up by a matrix that has the dimensions of the grid. The main difference from using mfcol and mfrow is that a plot can be spread over multiple cells of the matrix.

The layout.show() function can be used, after layout() has been called, to show the structure of the cells. The lcm() function can be used within layout() to give absolute dimensions, in centimeters, to the cells.

The layout() function takes four arguments. The arguments are mat, for the matrix containing the grid; widths, for the widths of the columns; heights, for the heights of the rows; and respect, for whether or how the horizontal and vertical scales relate.

The mat argument takes an integer matrix structured as the plot grid is to be structured. If there are n plots to be plotted in the grid, the cells must contain all of the integers from 1 to n.

The matrix can also contain 0s in cells, for which no plot is plotted in the cell. Also, more than one cell can contain the same number. If the cells are adjacent, then the plot expands to fill out the cells. There is no default value for mat.

The widths argument gives the widths of the cells and takes a numeric vector of length equal to the number of columns in the matrix mat. Unless lcm() is used when setting the values of width, the widths are relative to the size of the graphics device. The default value of widths is `rep.int(1, ncol(mat))`.

The heights argument is similar to widths, but gives the values for the heights of the cells rather than the widths. The default value of heights is `rep.int(1, nrow(mat))`.

The respect argument is used to restrict the scaling of the grid in the horizontal and vertical directions. The argument can either take a single-element logical vector or a matrix that is the same size as mat and that contains 0s and 1s.

If respect is set to FALSE, the units in the horizontal direction are not necessarily of the same scale as the units in the vertical direction. If set to TRUE, the units are scaled the same.

If respect is set to a matrix and a row is set to 0s, then the row is allowed to scale freely if the plot is scaled. If the row contains a 1, the relationship between the scale of the row and the scale of the columns is fixed. Setting all 0s in a column behaves in the same way as with rows, except that the column is allowed to scale freely. The default value of respect is FALSE.

The layout.show() function has one argument, n – for the number of cells in the layout to outline. The argument takes a single-element integer vector that can be any value between 1 and the number of plots, inclusive. The default value of n is 1, that is, show the outline of the cell(s) containing the first plot.

The lcm() function has one argument, x – for the values to be converted to centimeters. The argument takes a numeric vector of lengths in centimeters. The function returns a character vector containing the lengths and the letter "cm". For example, running lcm(c(1, 1.5, 0.5)) gives [1] "1 cm" "1.5 cm" "0.5 cm". There is no default value for x.

In Listing 6-4, code is given for the example in Figure 6-5 of using the functions layout()and layout.show().

Listing 6-4. The code for the example in Figure 6-5 of using the functions layout() and layout.show()

```
par( oma=c( 0, 0, 4, 0 ) )

layout(
  matrix(
    c(
      1, 3, 0,
      2, 3, 4
    ),
    2,
    3,
    byrow=TRUE
  ),
  width=c( 1, 1.5, 0.5 ),
  height=c( 1, 1 ),
  respect=FALSE
)

layout.show(
```

```
  4
)

mtext(
  "Example of calling layout.show()",
  cex=1.5,
  font=2,
  line=1.5,
  outer=TRUE
)

plot(
  0:1,
  main="Plot 1"
)
plot(
  0:2,
  main="Plot 2"
)
plot(
  0:3,
  main="Plot 3"
)
plot(
  0:4,
  main="Plot 4"
)
mtext(
  "Example of calling layout()",
  cex=1.5,
  font=2,
  line=0.8,
  outer=TRUE
)
```

In Figure 6-5, examples of calling layout() and layout.show() are given.

Note that four plots are plotted. The grid matrix has two rows and three columns.

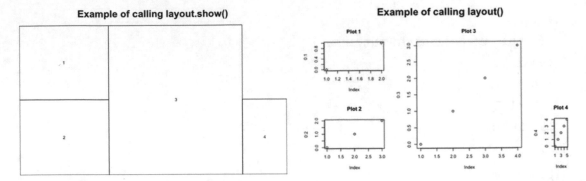

Figure 6-5. *Examples of calling layout() and then layout.show(). The arguments mat, widths, heights, and respect are set in layout()*

The numbers in the second column of mat are both 3, so the third plot spans both rows. The number in the first row and the third column is 0, so no plot is plotted in the cell associated with the first row and third column. The two rows are the same height, but the columns are of different widths.

6.2.3 The split.screen(), screen(), erase.screen(), and close.screen() Functions

The split.screen() function queries a graphics device or screen or splits a graphics device or screen into screens (regions and subregions). Each subsequent screen is treated separately with regard to plotting. If a graphics device has not been opened before split. screen() is run, split.screen() opens the default graphics device of R or RStudio.

The screen(), erase.screen(), and close.screen() functions work with the screens after split.screen() has set up the screens. The screen() function sets or returns the current screen, that is, the screen where plotting is done. The erase.screen() function erases the contents of a screen. The close.screen() function closes screens. After a screen is closed, no more changes can be made to the contents of the screen. When all of the screens have been closed, the split.screen() session ends.

According to the help page for split.screen(), the function cannot be used with mfcol or mfrow in par() or with layout(). However, most arguments of par() can be set. (When designing a graphic using values for par() that are different from the default values, running par() each time split.plot() is run helps reduce the frustration of the process.)

If run without arguments, the function split.screen() returns the numbers of all screens that are open or, if no screens are open, FALSE. If run with arguments, the function sets up and assigns number names to screens.

The function has three arguments. The arguments are figs, for the way to split up the screen; screen, for which screen to split; and erase, for whether to erase the screen selected by the argument screen.

The figs argument takes either a two-element numeric vector or a four-column numeric matrix. If figs is a vector, the two elements give the number of rows and columns for a plot grid. If figs is a matrix, then, for each row in the matrix, the four elements give the location of the left side and right side of a screen (on the x axis) and the bottom and top of the screen (on the y axis), in the order given. There is no default value for figs.

If figs is set to a matrix, the values of the matrix are in normalized device coordinate units (takes values between 0 and 1, inclusive.) The units are measured with respect to the selected screen. There is one row for each screen. The screens can overlap.

The number assigned by the screen argument is the number of the screen that is to be split. If no screens have been set up, then the graphics device is split.

The argument takes a one-element integer vector. For the first call to split.screen(), the screen argument is not set to a value (or screen can be set to 0). After the first call, the number must be within the numbers already assigned to screens, and the default value is the number of the current screen.

The erase argument takes a one-element logical vector. If set to TRUE, the content of a screen is erased if the screen is opened. If FALSE, the content is not erased. The default value of erase is TRUE.

(According to the help page for split.screen(), in split.screen(), screen(), and erase.screen()), erasing contents consists of setting the screen to the color given by the value of bg in par(), which is often "transparent" by default. In the case that the default value of bg is "transparent", the contents of the screen remain visible if bg has not been manually set to a color other than "transparent".)

The screen() function queries or sets the current screen (the screen where plotting functions create plots). If run without an argument, the function returns the number of the current screen. If a new screen is set as current, the number of the screen is returned. If no screens are open, screen() returns FALSE.

The function takes two arguments. The arguments are n, for the number of the screen to set as the current screen, and new – for whether to erase the contents of a screen when setting the screen to current.

The n argument takes a one-element positive integer vector. The value must be the number of an open screen; otherwise, an error is given. The default value of n is the number of the current screen.

The new argument takes a one-element logical vector. If set to TRUE, when a screen is set as the current screen, the contents of the screen are erased (see in the preceding text). If set to FALSE, the contents are overplotted. The default value of new is TRUE.

The erase.screen() function tells R to erase the contents of a screen (see in the preceding text). The function takes one argument, n – for the number of the screen to erase.

The n argument takes a one-element nonnegative integer vector. If n is set in erase. screen(), the value must be the number of an open screen or be 0. If there are open screens and if erase.screen() is run without an argument, the function erases the current screen. Running erase.screen() with n set to 0 erases all screens, if any screens are open. If there is no open screen, erase.screen() returns FALSE. The default value of n is the number of the current screen.

The close.screen() function closes screens. If the screens are all closed, individually or together, the split.screen() session ends. Calling close.screen() without arguments has no effect but returns the numbers of the screens that remain open. If no screens are open, close.screen() returns FALSE.

The function takes two arguments: n, for the numbers of the screens to close, and all. screens, for whether to close all of the screens.

The n argument takes a positive integer vector that can be of a reasonable arbitrary length. Numbers in the vector can be repeated, and numbers assigned to closed screens can be included. If a number assigned to an open screen is included, numbers larger than the largest screen number can be in the vector. There is no default value for n.

The all.screens argument takes a logical vector of length one. If set to TRUE, any screens that are open are closed and the split.screen() session ends. If FALSE, the value of n controls which screens are closed. The default value of all.screens is FALSE.

In Listing 6-5, code is given for the example in Figure 6-6 of using the matrix form of figs.

Listing 6-5. Code for the example in Figure 6-6 of using a matrix for the value of figs in split.screen()

```
# A function to do the actual plotting

plotter3 = function(
  id=1:3
){
    for ( i in id ) {

      par( oma=c( 0, 0, 3, 0 ) )

      screen( i )

      plot(
        0:i,
        main=paste( "Screen", i ),
        ylab=paste0( "0:", i )
      )

      mtext(
        "Example of split.screen()",
        outer=TRUE,
        cex=1.6,
        font=2,
        line=0.6
      )
    }
}

# Running par(), split.screen(), and plotter3()

par(
  ps=8,
  mar=c( 4, 4, 2, 1),
  oma=c( 0, 0, 3, 0 ),
  mex=0.9,
  bg="white"
)
```

```
split.screen(
  matrix(
    c(
      0.00, 0.70, 0.55, 1.00,
      0.00, 0.45, 0.00, 0.80,
      0.55, 1.00, 0.20, 0.80
    ),
    nr=3,
    nc=4,
    byrow=TRUE
  )
)

plotter3(
)

close.screen(
  all.screens=TRUE
)
```

In Figure 6-6, the code in Listing 6-5 is run.

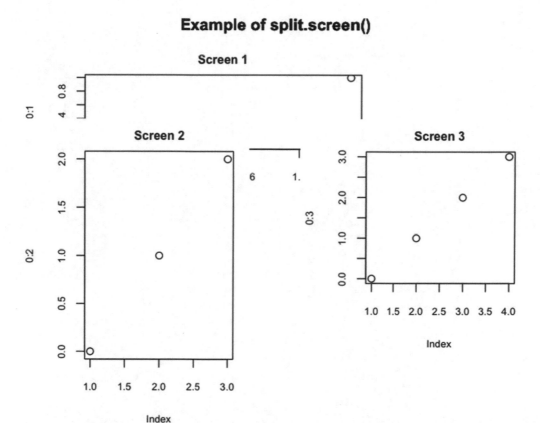

Figure 6-6. *An example of setting up three screens using split.screen() and plotting to the three screens*

Note that the screens are placed arbitrarily around the graphics device. In the figure, both screen 2 and screen 3 overlap screen 1. The function par() is used to decrease the point size, the margin widths, and the line width in the margins. Also, the color of the background is set to white in par(), and a three-line outer margin is added to the top of the plot. Note that the outer margin was, necessarily, set in every screen.

PART II

A Look at the ggplot2 Package

CHAPTER 7

Graphics with the ggplot2 Package: An Introduction

The ggplot2 package in R provides a simpler way to create graphics than generating graphics with plot() and the ancillary functions of plot(). The default plots generated by the functions in ggplot2 also have a more sophisticated appearance than those plotted by default when using plot(). Also, some tasks that in plot() require several steps are easily coded by the functions available in the ggplot2 package.

The two functions in ggplot2 that initiate plotting are qplot() and ggplot(). The function qplot() is the ggplot2 version of plot(). The function is a standalone function. The ggplot() function uses nontraditional R syntax to add *layers* to ggplot(). Functions that create and format layers are added to ggplot() by using the plus operator. The layers generate the contents of the plot.

The ggplot2 package is not a default package in R. The package must be installed before the package can be used. This is only done once – although the package should be updated when updates occur. Nor is ggplot2 a package that is loaded by default in R. To use the package during a session, the package must be loaded manually. Loading the package only need be done once in an R session.

To install the ggplot2 package in RStudio, select the Packages tab in the lower-right window. Select Install in the banner below the tabs. Install is to the left. Then enter ggplot2 in the form that opens. Also, make sure that the Install Dependencies box is checked. R will install the necessary packages.

In R, in the menu above the R window, select the Packages & Data tab. Then select Package Installer in the dropdown menu that opens below the Packages & Data tab. A window opens with options to install packages. Select the Get List button. Once the list is open, the search box on the right can be used to search for ggplot2. Select the ggplot2 name on the list and then find the Install Packages button below the list and to the right. Below the button, check the Install Dependencies box. Then select the Install Packages button (which is highlighted). The ggplot2 package and the dependencies of the ggplot2 package will install.

© Margot Tollefson 2021
M. Tollefson, *Visualizing Data in R 4*, https://doi.org/10.1007/978-1-4842-6831-5_7

This chapter is divided into three sections – a description of the language and syntax used with the ggplot2 package, a description of the function qplot(), and an overview of ggplot(). More detailed information about ggplot() can be found in Chapters 8, 9, and 10.

7.1 The Language and Syntax Used in the ggplot2 Package

The language and syntax used in the ggplot2 package are a little different from traditional R. The language of ggplot2 uses the concepts *aesthetics* and *geometries* or *statistics*. For ggplot(), plots are built-in layers. For qplot(), the call to qplot() is self-contained, but multiple layers can be plotted.

Aesthetics are the data that are to be plotted and the instructions for how to present the data. For example, x, y, the color of the points, and the width of the lines are all aesthetics and can be set. Data frames are often used to contain aesthetics.

Geometries and statistics give the functions that plot the data. The point geometry plots a scatterplot, for example.

Layers are combinations of functions and arguments that create a specific output on a plot. The points in a scatterplot are plotted by the point geometry. A new layer using the smooth geometry can plot a regression line over the scatterplot.

With regard to syntax, the call to ggplot() is followed by the operator +, which is followed by calls to one or more functions, with each two functions also separated by the operator +. Note that, according to the help page under +.gg, if the data frame in a layer is changed from a data frame set in ggplot(), instead of +, %+% must be used (due to precedence issues in R).

7.2 The qplot() Function

The qplot() (also called quickplot()) function is the ggplot2 version of the plot() function. Unlike ggplot(), qplot() does not use the plus operator to add layers. The plotting instructions are set within the call to the function.

The function takes 15 specified arguments, plus arguments that an aesthetic function would use and any arguments that the selected geometries use. The first three arguments in the function definition are x, y, and ..., for an x variable, a y variable, and any other aesthetic arguments – plus any geometry arguments that the geometry functions called by qplot() use.

Many of the arguments of par() can be used as aesthetic arguments in qplot().
However, when the values are assigned, the values must be enclosed in the function I(),
because aes() is a quoting function. (See the help page for qplot() for more information.)
For example, the 25 plotting character symbols can be plotted by setting pch=I(1:25)
in the call to qplot().

The third through sixth specified arguments are data, for the data frame in which
to find some of the aesthetic variables; facets, for the facet function to be used if one is
used; margins, for whether to plot marginal facets if faceting is done; and geom, for the
geometry to use to plot the aesthetics.

The seventh through thirteenth specified arguments are the familiar xlim, ylim, log,
main, xlab, ylab, and asp from Chapter 3. The 14th and 15th specified arguments are stat
and position, and both are deprecated – so not covered here.

The aesthetic arguments x, y, and any other aesthetic variables to be used – as well as
the variables used by the geometries and facets – are assigned values if needed. For the
aesthetics, usually x and y are numeric vectors of the same length. Sometimes, only x or y
is set to a value. Sometimes neither is assigned. Neither x nor y is given a default value in
qplot().

For aesthetics other than x and/or y, the values for the arguments must be vectors
of length one or of length equal to the length of x. For the geometries, the names and
formats of the arguments depend on the value of geom (the argument that sets the
geometries).

Since ... appears third in the order of the arguments to qplot(), the third through
fifteenth specified arguments must be assigned with the full argument name. The data
argument takes an object of the data.frame class and gives the data frame from which
some of the aesthetic arguments take values. According to the help page for qplot(), if no
data frame is supplied, then qplot() creates a data frame from the assigned variables. (The
assigned variables must be located within the environment in which qplot() is run or be
generated in the assignment to the argument. If the objects to be assigned do not exist in
the environment or the data frame, an error is given.) There is no default value for data.

The facets argument takes the value NULL or a character vector of length one. That
means that the object or expression that is used to do the faceting must be enclosed in
quotes, even though the object must be a multielement vector of length equal to the
length of x or two such vectors separated by a tilde. Examples are facets= "z", where z
is a variable in the data frame, or facets="rep(1:2, 12) ~ rep(1:3, each=8)",
where the length of x is 24.

The facets argument has some qualifications. If facets is assigned an object, the object must be in the data frame assigned to the argument data. If facets is assigned an expression rather than an object, the data argument must be assigned a data frame with the correct number of rows. Otherwise, all of the points are plotted for all of the facets. (The contents of the data frame can be arbitrary.) The default value of facets is NULL, that is, no faceting is done.

The margins argument takes a one-element logical vector. If set to TRUE and facets is set, plots of the marginal distributions of x are plotted below the facet plots. Otherwise, marginal plots are not plotted. The default value of margins is FALSE.

Geometries tell qplot() what to plot. The geom argument takes a character vector of arbitrary length. (More than one geometry can be included in the geom argument.) The vector contains the names of the geometries that qplot() is to use – in quotes. For arguments of a function called by a geometry, the arguments are set in qplot(). That is, the arguments are assigned a value in the call to qplot().

In Table 7-1, the names of the geometries are given, along with what the geometry plots. See Listing 7-1 and Figure 7-1 for an example of running qplot() with two geometries.

Table 7-1. *The geometries used by the qplot() function, with descriptions*

Geometry Name	Description
abline	Plot lines using vectors of slopes and intercepts – the arguments are named slope and intercept.
hline	Plot horizontal lines using a vector of y's.
vline	Plot vertical lines using a vector of x's.
area	Plot an area plot – x and y must be set.
ribbon	Plot a ribbon plot – x, ymin, and ymax or y, xmin, and xmax must be set.
bar	Plot a bar chart of the number of observations that have the same value for each value of x or each value of y – can set x or y but not both.
col	Plot a bar chart of the sum of the observations in y for each value of x – must set both x and y.

(*continued*)

Table 7-1. (*continued*)

Geometry Name	Description
bin2d	Create a heatmap of the number of observations with both x and y the same – both x and y must be set.
blank	Draw nothing – can be used to set a scale on the axes.
boxplot	Plot Tukey-style boxplots – can set x (for horizontal boxplots) or y (for vertical boxplots) but not both. The argument group can be used to create boxplots with one boxplot for each of the values present in group.
contour	Plot contours of the density z, where z is given for each observation and the x and y values for the observations are used for the axes – x, y, and z must be set.
contour_filled	Plot same contours as with contour but the area between contours is filled with graded colors.
count	Plot y vs. x, where the size of the plotting character depends on the number of observations that have the same values for x and y – both x and y must be set.
crossbar	For each value of x, a horizontal line is drawn at the levels of y for which data exists – with the width of the lines set by the argument width. Also, boxes are drawn around the lines – with the heights of the boxes given by the vectors ymin and ymax.
errorbar	For each value of x, a vertical line is drawn at the values of y for which data exists – the lengths are input with the vectors ymin and ymax. Also, horizontal lines are drawn at the top and bottom of the vertical lines – with the widths given by the argument width.
errorbarh	For each value of x, a horizontal line is drawn at the y's for which data exists – the widths are input with the vectors xmin and xmax. Also, vertical lines are drawn at the left and right ends of the horizontal lines – with the heights of the lines given by the argument height.
linerange	For each value of x, a vertical line is drawn at the y's for which data exists – with the length set by the vectors ymin and ymax.

(*continued*)

Table 7-1. (*continued*)

Geometry Name	Description
pointrange	For each value of x, a point and a vertical line are drawn at the y's for which data exists – where the lengths of the lines are set by the vectors ymin and ymax.
curve	Draw curves from the coordinates of the vectors assigned to the arguments x and y to the coordinates of the vectors assigned to the arguments xend and yend, with the curvature given by the argument curvature. Negative values give convex plots, positive values give concave - if the direction of the curve is from left to right - otherwise, vice versa. Larger absolute values give more curvature. The arguments x, y, xend, and yend must be set, and curvature can be set.
segment	Same as with curve, except line segments are drawn instead of curves.
density	Draw an estimated kernel density – can set x or y but not both.
density2d or density_2d	Plot two-dimensional estimated kernel density contours – must set both x and y.
dotplot	Plot a dot plot – x must be set and y must not be set.
freqpoly	Plot a line plot connecting the number of observations within equal-size bins – can set x or y but not both. The argument bins gives the number of bins in which to bin the data; the lines go to zero at the beginning and end of the plot.
histogram	Plot a histogram of the number of observations within equal-size bins – can set x or y but not both. The number of bins is set by the argument bins.
hex	Plot a hexagonal heatmap of the counts of observations within bins formed by making classes from x crossed with y – both x and y must be set, and the number of bins can be set by the argument bins.
jitter	Plot jittered points – must set both x and y.
label	Plot labels in boxes at the coordinates given by the x and y – both x and y must be set. Also, the argument label must be set and should contain the labels.
text	The same as label, except no boxes.
line	Plot a line connecting coordinates given by x and y; x is sorted before the plotting, and the order is used to reorder y – both x and y must be set.

(*continued*)

Table 7-1. (*continued*)

Geometry Name	Description
path	Same as line except that x is not sorted and y is not reordered.
step	Plot a step plot of x and y, where, as with line, x is sorted and y is ordered with order of x – the arguments x and y must be set.
map	Plot polygons based on a reference map – the argument map must be set.
point	Plot a scatterplot of y vs. x – both x and y must be set.
polygon	Plot the relationship between the vectors x and y by using polygons – both x and y must be set.
qq	Plot a quantile/quantile plot – the argument sample must be set (the value of sample is the data vector to be compared to the probability distribution), and the arguments x and y are not set.
qq_line	Plot the quantile/quantile line – the arguments are those of qq.
quantile	Plot the regression lines for specified quantiles using quantile regression – both x and y must be set. Also, the argument quantiles can be set.
raster	Plot equal-size rectangles at the coordinates given by x and y – the arguments x and y must be set. Also, the argument fill can be used to set the fill colors.
rect	Plot rectangles given the coordinates of the left side, the right side, the bottom, and the top of the rectangles – the arguments are xmin, xmax, ymin, and ymax. Also, fill can be set.
tile	Plot rectangles given the coordinates of the centers, the widths, and the heights – the arguments x, y, width, and height must be set. Also, fill can be set.
rug	Plot rugs in the margins of a plot – x and/or y must be set for a rug(s) to plot.
sf	Plot simple features objects – see https://cran.r-project.org/web/packages/sf/vignettes/sf1.html.
sf_label	Plot labels of simple features objects.

(*continued*)

Table 7-1. (*continued*)

Geometry Name	Description
sf_text	Plot text of simple features objects.
smooth	Plot a smoothed version of a scatterplot – both x and y must be set, and method can be set.
spoke	Plot line segments based on a location, angle, and radius – x, y, angle, and radius must be set.
violin	Plot a violin plot – both x and y must be set, and group can be set.

More information about the geometries can be found by looking at the contents of the ggplot2 package. The functions that begin with *geom_* are geometries. The second part of the function name gives the name of the geometry.

Listing 7-1. Code for the example in Figure 7-1 of using two geometries in qplot() and setting two arguments for the second geometry

```
qplot(
  x=pop75,
  y=pop15,
  data=LifeCycleSavings,
  geom=c( "point", "smooth" ),
  method="lm",
  se=FALSE,
  show.legend=FALSE,
  col=I(1),
  main="Example of Using Two Geometries in qplot() with Arguments"
)
```

In Figure 7-1, the code in Listing 7-1 is run.

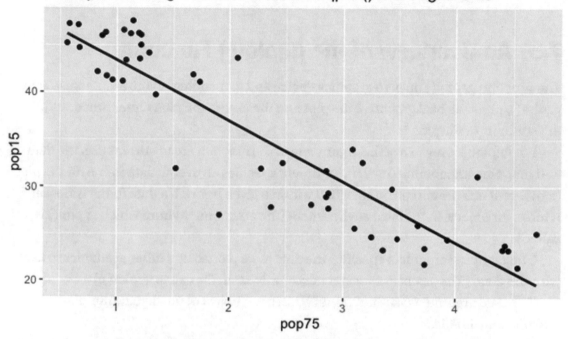

Figure 7-1. *Example of using two geometries with qplot(). For the "smooth" geometry, the smoothing method is set to simple linear regression, and the confidence bands are not plotted. The colors of the points and the line are set to black, and no color key is plotted*

Note that both the points and the regression line are plotted in one call to qplot(). The points are plotted because the value "point" is an element of the vector assigned to geom. The regression line is plotted because the value "smooth" is an element of the vector assigned to geom and because method is set to "lm" in the call. The confidence bands for the regression line, which are plotted by default, are suppressed by setting "se" to FALSE in the call.

The color of the points and line is set to black by setting col to I(1) (col is an argument of par()). The color key legend, which is plotted by default when col is set, is suppressed by setting show.legend to FALSE. The plot has the default background and grid used in the ggplot2 package – gray with white grid lines.

For the xlim, ylim, log, main, xlab, ylab, and asp arguments, the arguments xlim, ylim, main, xlab, and ylab are covered in Section 3.2.1. The argument log is covered in Section 3.4.6. The argument asp is covered in Section 3.2.2.

7.3 An Overview of the ggplot() Function

The function ggplot() opens a graphics device and, depending on the arguments set in ggplot(), plots the background of the plot and the axes of the plot. Other functions plot the contents of the plot.

For ggplot(), only two of the arguments of the function are in current use, the data and mapping arguments. The data argument specifies an overall data frame for the plot (a different data frame can be specified within a given layer). If a data frame is not set, R looks for objects in the local environment (the environment from which ggplot() is called).

The mapping argument specifies the data to be plotted and other aesthetics to use with the data. (The aesthetics are not necessarily set in the call to ggplot().)

The data argument takes the value NULL or an object of the data.frame class. The default value is NULL.

The argument mapping takes a call to the function aes(). The function aes() creates an aesthetic mapping. (Aesthetics can be set outside of the call to ggplot() by using the plus operator to add the aes() function.) The default value of mapping is aes(), that is, an empty aesthetic mapping.

If mapping is set and the values x and y are set in aes(), then a call to ggplot() opens a graphics device with the default background and with the x and y scales set. However, the aesthetics are not plotted.

In Listing 7-2, code is given on four ways to set essentially the same background. The difference between the first and third plots and the second and fourth plots is different axis labels.

Listing 7-2. Code for four ways to get essentially the same background

```
#1
ggplot(
  data=LifeCycleSavings,
  mapping=aes(
    pop75,
```

```
    pop15
  )
)

#2
ggplot(
  mapping=aes(
    LifeCycleSavings$pop75,
    LifeCycleSavings$pop15
  )
)

#3
ggplot(
  data=LifeCycleSavings
) +

aes(
  pop75,
  pop15
)

#4
ggplot(
) +

aes(
  LifeCycleSavings$pop75,
  LifeCycleSavings$pop15
)
```

The result from running the first code in Listing 7-2 is shown in Figure 7-2. The title was added by adding labs(title="Example of Just Calling ggplot()") to the first ggplot() function.

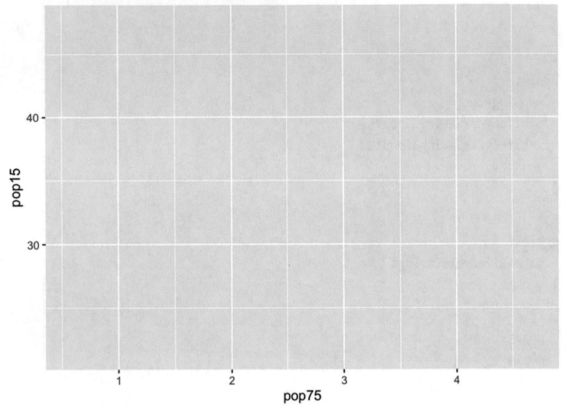

Figure 7-2. *An example of calling ggplot() without another layer*

Note that no data is plotted. The labels on the axes are the names of the variables that are plotted. The scales on the axes are based on the values in the x and y vectors.

After the call to ggplot(), the kinds of functions at the highest level are functions that generate *themes, aesthetics, geometries, statistics*, and *annotations* – also, the *borders()* function, which is used with maps.

The theme functions set the overall appearance of the plot. The aesthetic functions set any variables to be plotted or used in the plotting – also, arguments that affect the appearance of the plot contents.

The geometry and statistic functions give the plotting function that is to be applied to variables set by the aesthetic function (e.g., telling R to plot a scatterplot after x and y have been set by an aesthetic function). When a geometry or statistic function is called, a new layer is opened. (A new geometry or statistic layer can also be opened by calling the function layer() and specifying the geometry or statistic within the call.)

The annotation functions also create a layer and, according to the help page for annotate(), are a special kind of geometry. An annotation layer is used for adding a grid graphical object (object of the grob class – see the help page for the function grob() in the grid package) to a plot. The borders() function adds a map border layer to a plot from a shape file of map boundaries.

The preceding functions are added to ggplot() by using the plus operator. (Aesthetic functions can also be added within the call to ggplot(), as noted in the preceding text.) According to the help page under +.gg, there are three more kinds of functions that can be added to a call to ggplot() with a plus operator. The three kinds are the scale, coordinate, and facet functions. A few other functions can be added and are covered in Chapter 10.

The scale functions affect a layer in a plot created by ggplot() like the arguments of par() affect a plot created by plot(). For example, the cex argument in par() is a *scale_size_* function in aes(), and the pch argument in par() is a *scale_shape_* function in aes(). Other scale functions can reverse the scales on the axes or set a line type – among other changes that can be made to the appearance of what is plotted.

The coordinate functions affect the kind of coordinate system that ggplot() uses. For example, ggplot() can be switched from Cartesian to polar coordinates, or the units on the x and y axes can be made to have a fixed ratio with regard to the unit size on one axis and the unit size on the other.

The facet functions tell ggplot() to create a vector of plots or a grid of plots. The axes and backgrounds of the multiple plots are the same, but the points, lines, labels, and/or text plotted in each plot depend on one or two categorical variables. For example, given data on height and weight for boys and girls, along with an indicator variable giving the sex of the child, a facet function can be used to plot the data for girls and boys separately, but on the same scale.

In Chapters 8, 9, and 10, the functions that ggplot() uses to create and format plots are covered in more detail. In Chapter 8, the aesthetic and theme functions are described. In Chapter 9, the layering functions – geometry, statistic, annotation, and borders() – are covered. The scale, coordinate, and facet functions are described in Chapter 10, as well as functions not covered elsewhere.

CHAPTER 8

Working with the ggplot( ) Function: The Theme and the Aesthetics

This chapter covers the functions that control the appearance of the plot background and that which is plotted – the theme functions and the aesthetic functions. The theme functions set parameters for the appearance for the background of the plot, but not for the contents of the plot. The aesthetic functions set the parameters for the appearance of the contents. In Section 8.1, the theme functions are described. In Section 8.2, the aesthetic functions are described.

8.1 The Theme Functions

The theme functions fall into three kinds. The first kind is the function theme(), for setting up a theme. There are 94 specified arguments to theme(), plus some that are not specified. The second kind consists of preset themes, of which there are ten. The third kind of functions work with themes – to see the contents of a theme and to adapt preset themes. In this section, we look at each kind separately.

8.1.1 The theme( ) Function

The theme() function sets the properties of the background of the plot. That is, theme() sets the properties of the lines making up the background of the plot, the properties of the rectangles drawn in the background of the plot, the properties of the text plotted as part of the background of the plot (including the title), and the aspect ratio of the plot. The function theme() also sets the properties (not the contents) of legends.

© Margot Tollefson 2021
M. Tollefson, *Visualizing Data in R 4*, https://doi.org/10.1007/978-1-4842-6831-5_8

The 93rd argument is . . . and gives any arguments that can be used by theme() but that are not arguments of the functions in the ggplot2 package. (According to the help page for theme(), the arguments must be registered by setting the argument element_tree in the function register_theme_elements().) The 93rd and 94th specified arguments of theme() give R the information of whether the theme generated by theme() is a complete theme and whether to check if the theme is valid when theme() is run.

8.1.1.1 The First Five Arguments of theme( ) and the Theme Element Functions of ggplot2

The first five arguments of theme() are line, for setting the properties of the lines; rect, for setting the properties of the rectangles; text, for setting the properties of text; title, for setting the properties of the main title and the axis labels; and aspect.ratio, for setting the y to x ratio of the plot.

The line argument takes the value of a call to the element_line() function. The parameters that affect the appearance of lines are set in element_line().

The rect argument takes the value of a call to the element_rect() function. The arguments that affect the appearance of rectangles are set in element_rect().

The text argument takes the value of a call to the element_text() function. The title argument takes the value of a different call to the element_text() function. The arguments that affect the appearance of text in the legend and in the titles are set in the calls to the element_text() function.

The aspect.ratio argument takes a positive numeric vector of length one (and is the number of units on the x axis for one unit on the y axis). Any other type of value gives an error.

The element_line( ) Function

The element_line() function takes seven arguments. The arguments are color (or colour), for the color of the line; size, for the size of the line; linetype, for the type of line to plot; lineend, for the style of line ends to use; arrow, for specifications of the arrows if arrows are plotted; and inherit.blank, for whether to inherit from the function element_blank() if element_blank() is present in the line of inheritance (see the following note). Inheriting from element_blank(), which returns an empty named list, tells R to not plot the line argument.

The color (or colour) arguments takes a vector of color values (the possible color values are covered in Section 3.4.1 or in the `ggplot2-specs` vignette). The vector can be of arbitrary length and the values cycle (but are sorted in alphabetical order first). For grids, the order starts at the bottom of the grid and then – after the horizontal lines are plotted – at the left of the grid. The default value is usually "black".

The size argument takes a vector of nonnegative numeric values of arbitrary length. The elements of the vector cycle. The value of size gives the line widths in millimeters.

The linetype argument takes a vector of arbitrary length with the same values as used by lty in plot() (see Section 3.3.2 for the settings). The elements of the vector cycle. The default value of linetype is 1 or "solid".

The lineend argument takes a character vector of arbitrary length. The argument is similar to lend in par() (see Section 3.4.4). In the ggplot2 package, lineend can take the values "butt", "square", and "round". The default value is "butt".

The arrow argument takes the value of a call to the arrow() function. The arrow() function is in the grid package and takes four arguments. The arguments are angle for the angle of the arrowhead arms with respect to the arrow shaft, length for the length of the arrowhead arms, ends for the location of the arrowhead on the shaft, and type for an open or closed arrowhead. All of the arguments take a vector of arbitrary length and cycle – but how the elements cycle is not clear.

The angle argument of arrow() takes a numeric vector. The angle is measured in degrees. The default value is 30.

The length argument of arrow() takes the value of a call to the unit() function, where a nonnegative numeric vector is entered into unit(). The unit() function is in the grid package and sets the units used for the numeric vector. The default value of length is 0.25 inches.

The ends argument of arrow() takes a character vector with an element or elements that can take the value "open" or "closed". If set to "open", the arrowhead has two arms. If set to closed, the arrowhead is a triangle. The default value is "open".

The type argument of arrow() takes a character vector with an element or elements that can take the value "first", "last", or "both". If set to "first", the arrowhead is at the start of the line. If "last", the arrowhead is at the end of the line. If "both", arrowheads plot at both ends of the line. The default value is "last".

The inherit.blank argument of element_line() takes a logical vector of arbitrary length (see in the preceding text). The default value is FALSE.

The element_rect() Function

The element_rect() function takes six arguments: fill for the color with which to fill the rectangle, color (or colour), size, linetype, and inherit.blank. Note that, in element_rect(), the arguments color (or colour), size, and linetype affect the border of the rectangle and that only one color, size, and linetype can be set for a border. That is, each takes a vector of length one as a value. See the preceding description of element_line() for a description of the arguments color, colour, size, linetype, and inherit.blank.

In element_rect(), the argument fill takes a color vector (see Section 3.4.1 or the ggplot2-specs vignette) of arbitrary length. If the argument panel.border is set in theme(), the value is a call to element_rect(). In the call, the value of fill should be set to "transparent" or to a color value with the transparency set to a value that is less than 1. Otherwise, the grid, if a grid is set, and the contents of the plot are covered by the fill color and cannot be seen.

The element_text() and margin() Functions

The element_text() function takes 12 arguments. The arguments are family, for the font family to use; face, for the font weight to use; color (or colour), for the color of the text; size, for the size of the text; hjust and vjust, for the horizontal and vertical placement of the text away from the center; angle, for the angle of the text; lineheight, for the height of the text lines; margin, for the size of the margin around the text; debug, for whether to use specialized tools for visual debugging; and inherit.blank – see in the preceding text.

The family argument takes a character vector of arbitrary length that contains names of font families (see Section 3.4.2). For titles, only the first value is used, and a warning is given if the length is greater than one. For axis tick mark labels, the elements cycle, but a warning is still given if the length is longer than one. According to the ggplot2-specs vignette, only the font families "sans", "serif", and "mono" are consistently available across computing platforms.

The face argument takes a numeric vector of arbitrary length. For title, only the first value is used, and a warning is given if the length is greater than one. For axis tick mark labels, the elements cycle, but a warning is given if the length is greater than one. The legal values are the values that font can take in par() (see Section 3.4.2).

The color (or colour) argument takes a vector of color values (see Section 3.4.1 or the ggplot2-specs vignette) of arbitrary length. For a title, only the first value is used. A warning is given if the length is greater than one. For axis tick mark labels, the elements of the vector cycle through the labels, but a warning is given.

The size argument takes a nonnegative numeric vector of arbitrary length or a nonnegative vector on which the rel() function is run. If the vector is not an argument of rel(), the numeric values give the point size of the text, for example, 10 for a 10-point text. If operated on by rel(), the values are relative to the standard character size, that is, the value is relative to 1, where a value of 1 gives the standard character size.

The hjust and vjust arguments take numeric vectors of arbitrary length. The two arguments behave like hadj and padj in the function axis() (see Section 4.1.2.1).

The angle argument takes a numeric vector of length one. The value is in degrees from the horizontal for text on the x axes and from the vertical for text on the y axes.

The lineheight argument takes a numeric vector that should be of length one. Although a longer vector only gives a warning, just the first value is used.

The margin argument takes a call to the margin() function. The function margin() has five arguments, t, r, b, and l – for the size of the margin on the top, right, bottom, and left of the text – and unit, for the units of the values of t, r, b, and l.

The t, r, b, and l arguments take numeric vectors of arbitrary length. Only the first value is used. The default values of t, r, b, and l are 0.

The unit argument takes a character vector of arbitrary length. Only the first value is used. Some of the values for unit are "pt", "cm", and "inches" (see the help page for unit(), in the grid package, for more kinds of units). The default value for unit is "pt", that is, points.

The debug argument takes a logical vector of length one. If longer than one element, the function does not debug. This is a useful argument for seeing what your changes do. The default value of debug is FALSE.

The inherit.blank argument takes a logical vector of length one. See in the preceding text, under element_line(), for more information.

8.1.1.2 The Sixth Through Ninety-Fourth Specified Arguments of theme() and an Example

The next 87 arguments refine plotting instructions for the axes, the legend, the panel, the plotting region, and the strips around the outside of the plots when faceting is done. The 87 arguments contain 35 arguments that affect axes, 21 arguments that affect legends, 13 arguments that affect panels (the plotting region if no faceting is done and the spread between plots and the plotting regions if faceting is done), 9 arguments that affect the entire graphic, and 9 arguments that affect the strips around plots when faceting is used.

The names of the 87 arguments begin with the word axis, legend, panel, plot, or strip. The word is followed by a period, which is followed by another word and sometimes more words separated by periods. For example, the argument axis.ticks.y.right sets the properties of the y axis tick marks on the right side of the plot.

In the arguments of theme(), the periods delineate levels. At each level, the arguments that are not set take the values of the next higher level. That is, if axis.ticks.y.right is not set, then the argument is set to the value of axis.ticks.y. If axis.ticks.y is not set, then axis.ticks.y.right takes the value of axis.ticks. If axis.ticks is not set, then axis.ticks.y.right is set to the value of the argument line. This process is called inheritance – axis.ticks.y.right inherits from axis.ticks.y, which inherits from axis.ticks, which inherits from line.

Most of the 87 arguments take either element_line(), element_rect(), element_text(), or margin() for values. (The four functions and the function rel() share a help page.) Most of the other arguments take the function unit() from the grid() package for values. The help page for theme() gives more information about the values taken by the 87 arguments.

The last two arguments, complete and validate, take logical vectors of length one. The default value of complete is FALSE and of validate is TRUE.

In Listing 8-1, code for an example of setting a theme is given.

Listing 8-1. Code for the example in Figure 8-1 of setting arguments in theme()

```
ord = order(
  LifeCycleSavings$pop75
)

library(
  ggplot2
)

ggplot(
  LifeCycleSavings[ ord, ],
  aes(
```

```
      pop75,
      pop15
    )
  ) +

theme(

  panel.border=element_rect(
    color="grey40",
    fill="transparent",
    size=2
  ),

  panel.background=element_rect(
    fill="grey85"
  ),

  panel.grid.major=element_line(
    size=0.75,
    color="grey45"
  ),

  panel.grid.minor=element_line(
    size=0.5,
    color="grey60"
  ),

  title=element_text(
    color="grey45",
    face=4,
    family="serif",
    size=14,
    angle=3
  ),

  plot.title=element_text(
    hjust=0.5,
    vjust=0.5,
```

```
      lineheight=1.1,
      margin=margin(
      0,
      0,
      0.3,
      0,
      "cm"
      )
   ),

   axis.text=element_text(
      color="grey50",
      face=2,
      family="serif",
      size=rel( 1.1 ),
      hjust=1,
      vjust=1
   )
) +

labs(
   title="Example of \nSetting \nArguments in theme()"
)
```

In Figure 8-1, the code in Listing 8-1 is run.

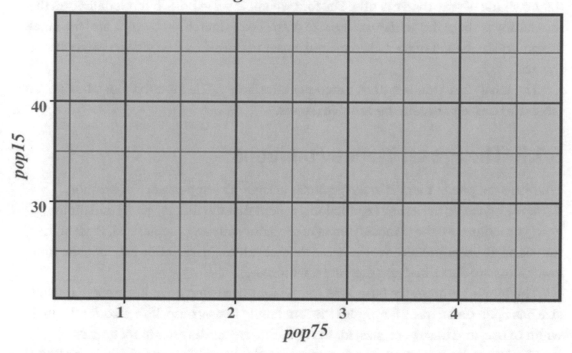

Figure 8-1. *Example of setting several arguments in theme(). No data is plotted*

Note that ggplot() is run with both a data frame and values set for x and y. In theme(), first, the plotting region border is set. The color is set to a mid-shade of gray and the width of the border to 2 millimeters. The area inside the border is set to be transparent.

Next, the background of the plotting region is set to a light shade of gray. Then the major gridlines are given a width of 0.75 millimeter and a gray that is slightly lighter than the border. Then, the minor gridlines are given a width of 0.75 millimeter and an even lighter gray color.

Then, the formatting for the title and axis labels is done. The color of the title and labels is set to the same color as the major gridlines. The font weight is set to bold and italic, and the font face is set to the serif font. The size of the text is set to 14 points, and the text is given a three-degree inclination away from the axes.

Then, specific formatting for the title is done. First, the title is centered in the vertical and horizontal directions. The line height is set to 1.1. Last, the margin between the text and the axis is increased by 0.3 centimeter.

The formatting of the axis tick mark labels is done last. The color is set to a slightly lighter shade of gray than the title. The font weight is set to bold, but not italic, and the font family is set to the serif font. The size of the text is increased by 10%, and the labels are plotted to the left of the tick mark and closer to the axis, when viewed with respect to the axis.

The labs() function is the last function in the listing. The function plots the title. The labels on the axes contain the variable names.

8.1.2 The Preset Theme Functions

There are ten preset themes in the ggplot2 package. The appearance of the plot background varies between the functions, except that the theme_grey() and theme_gray() functions are the same. All ten take the same four arguments; and, in all of the functions, the arguments have the same default values. In the following, first, the four arguments are described and then the ten themes().

The four arguments are base_size, for the font size when no adjustment to the font size has been done; base_family, for the font family to use; base_line_size, for the line width to use; and base_rect_size, for the width to use for the lines in rectangles.

The base_size argument takes a numeric vector of arbitrary length. Only the first element is used, and a warning is given if the length is greater than one. The base character size is measured in points. The default value for base_size is 11.

The base_family argument takes a character vector of arbitrary length. The values must be of a font family that the operating system recognizes. (See Section 3.4.2 for more information.) The default value of base_family is "".

Both of the base_line_size and base_rect_size arguments take nonnegative numeric vectors of arbitrary length. The line widths are measured in millimeters. The values cycle. The default value of both is base_size divided by 22.

The theme_grey() (or theme_gray()) function is the default background for ggplot() and qplot(). The plot background is a light gray; the gridlines are white. The font family is the default family for the operating system (which on my system is Arial Unicode). The full list of settings can be found either by entering theme_gray at the R prompt or by calling theme_grey() with no other functions (use the same method for any of the functions in this section).

The theme_bw() function gives text and a plot border that are black, a line width of 0.5 millimeter for the border, a white panel background, and light gray gridlines. The font family is the same as the font family in theme_grey().

The theme_linedraw() function plots strictly in black and white. The theme is the same as theme_bw() except that the gridlines are made lighter by making the widths of the lines smaller rather than by making the color of the lines gray. For theme_linedraw(), the major gridlines have a width of 0.1 millimeter and the minor gridlines a width of 0.05 millimeter.

The theme_light() function gives a white background and gray border and gridlines. The text is the same as with theme_grey().

The theme_dark() function gives a dark gray plot background and gridlines that are an even darker gray. No border is plotted. The text is the same as with theme_grey().

The theme_minimal() function gives a plot with the plot background and border not set. Light gray gridlines are plotted, and the text is the same as with theme_grey().

The theme_classic() function suppresses the border and gridlines. However, since the y and x axes are plotted, an L-shaped box is visible in the plot. The background is set to white, and the text is the same as with theme_grey().

The theme_void() function gives a plot with no border, no plot margins – except for margins for the title, subtitle, caption, and tags if labs() is called and only for the arguments that are set – and no gridlines. Calling xlab() and ylab() has no effect. The background color is white. However, the geometries plot if geometries are run.

The theme_test() function gives a plot that is the same as theme_linedraw(), except that no grid is drawn. According to the help page for theme_test(), the function is useful for testing new values for the arguments.

In Listing 8-2, code is given for Figure 8-2, an example of setting the four arguments in theme_light().

Listing 8-2. Code for the example in Figure 8-2 of setting base_size, base_family, base_line_size, and base_rect_size in theme_light()

```
ggplot(
  LifeCycleSavings[ ord, ],
  aes(
    pop75,
    pop15
  )
```

```
) +
theme_light(
  base_size=14,
  base_family="serif",
  base_line_size=1:3,
  base_rect_size=4
) +
labs(
  title="Example of Setting Arguments in theme_light()"
)
```

In Figure 8-2, the code in Listing 8-2 is run.

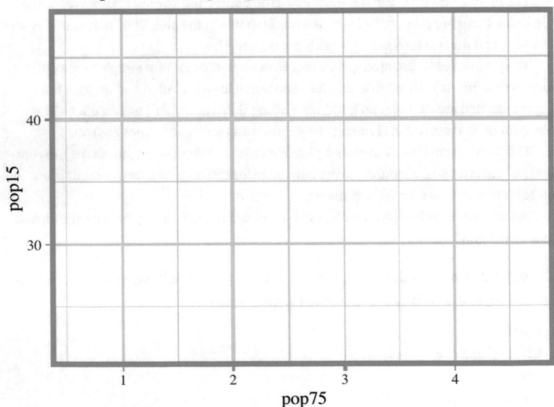

Figure 8-2. *Example of setting base_size, base_family, base_line_size, and base_ rect_size in theme_light()*

The text size is set to 14 points, and the text family is set to serif. The gridline widths are set to 1, 2, and 3 millimeters; and the widths cycle through the gridlines – starting with the minor gridlines and then cycling to the major gridlines (somewhat). The horizontal and vertical lines appear to cycle separately. The order of the lines starts at the furthest left or lowest minor line and ends at the furthest right or highest major line. The border line width is set to 4 millimeters.

8.1.3 Working with Themes

When the R session starts, the *current theme* – the theme that qplot() uses and that ggplot() uses if a theme is not set in the call to ggplot() – is theme_gray() (the default theme). Functions, run at the level of the R environment, can change the arguments of the current theme.

The current theme can be set to a new theme, updated, or replaced before ggplot() or qplot() is run. There is one function that returns the current theme and one function that sets the current theme. Changing some settings in the current theme or changing all of the settings in the current theme is done with two other functions.

When running ggplot(), sometimes most of the settings in a theme are appropriate for the plot, while a few of the settings should be changed. Changing a theme within a call to ggplot() is done with two operators. One operator updates the theme in the call, and the other operator replaces the theme in the call.

For developers, creating a new theme for a package under development can be done with four functions in the ggplot2 package. The first subsection in Section 8.1.3 covers setting and changing themes. The second subsection covers some functions used by developers.

8.1.3.1 The theme_get(), theme_set(), theme_update(), and theme_replace() Functions and the + and %+replace% Operators

The functions and operators that set and modify themes either work with the current theme or with a function added to a call to ggplot(). The functions theme_get() and theme_set() get and set the current theme. The functions theme_update() and theme replace() change or replace the current theme. The operators + and %+replace% update or replace a theme within a call.

The theme_get() function takes no arguments and returns the contents of the current theme(). The function returns a list with 93 elements, which are the 92 arguments that affect the appearance of the plot, listed on the help page for theme(), plus a 93rd element, `strip.text.y.left`. The arguments complete and validate are attributes of the list.

The theme_set() function sets the current theme to a new theme. The function takes one argument, new – for the new theme. The new argument takes a list containing the arguments that make up a theme and is usually a call to a theme function.

The theme_update() function updates the current theme using named calls to element functions. The element functions are assigned the names of the theme() arguments to be changed and contain the changes to be applied to the theme. Each two element functions are separated by a comma.

The theme_replace() function replaces the current theme. For the arguments that are present in the call to theme_replace(), the arguments are set to the values given. The other arguments of theme() are set to NULL by theme_replace(). The function theme_replace() takes the same kind of arguments as theme_update().

To update a preset theme when ggplot() is run, the + operator is used. The theme() function, with the changed arguments set, is added to the preset theme. The effect is the same as with theme_update().

To replace a preset theme when ggplot() is run, the %+replace% operator is used to add the theme() function. The effect is the same as with theme_replace().

In Listing 8-3, an example of using the preceding four functions and two operators is given.

Listing 8-3. Output from R of the various ways of changing all or part of a theme. The functions theme_get(), theme_set(), theme_update(), and theme_replace() are demonstrated, as well as the operators + and %+replace%

```
#   First, two objects are defined using the operators
#   %+% and %+replace%.

#   1
#   The object to.update.theme is given the value theme_bw()
#     plus an update to the theme using the operator +.

#     The change to the theme is printed out.
#     The argument color is "grey20" in theme_bw().
```

```
> to.update.theme <- theme_bw() +
theme( panel.border=element_rect( size=3, fill="transparent" ) )

> to.update.theme$panel.border
List of 5
 $ fill        : chr "transparent"
 $ colour      : chr "grey20"
 $ size        : num 3
 $ linetype    : NULL
 $ inherit.blank: logi FALSE
 - attr(*, "class")= chr [1:2] "element_rect" "element"

#     2
#    The object to.replace.theme is given the value theme_bw()
#    plus changes to the theme using the operator %+replace%.

#     The change to the theme is printed out.
#     The argument colour is now NULL.

> to.replace.theme <- theme_bw() %+replace%
theme( panel.border=element_rect( size=3, fill="transparent" ) )

> to.replace.theme$panel.border
List of 5
 $ fill        : chr "transparent"
 $ colour      : NULL
 $ size        : num 3
 $ linetype    : NULL
 $ inherit.blank: logi FALSE
 - attr(*, "class")= chr [1:2] "element_rect" "element"

#   The objects to.update.theme and to.replace.theme are now
#   used in theme_set(), theme_update() and theme_replace().

#   The functions theme_get() and theme_set() are run
#   a number of times.

#     3
#    The panel.border argument of the current theme is printed out.
```

```
#     The value is an empty list - that is, all values are NULL.

> theme_get()$panel.border
 list()
 - attr(*, "class")= chr [1:2] "element_blank" "element"

#     4
#     The current theme is set to the theme in to.update.theme
#     using theme_set().  The panel.border argument is printed out.

#     The current theme now has a transparent background,
#     a border colored "grey20", and a border 3 millimeters wide.

> theme_set( to.update.theme )

> theme_get()$panel.border
List of 5
 $ fill          : chr "transparent"
 $ colour        : chr "grey20"
 $ size          : num 3
 $ linetype      : NULL
 $ inherit.blank: logi FALSE
 - attr(*, "class")= chr [1:2] "element_rect" "element"

#     5
#     The current theme is set back to theme_grey() and
#     and panel.border is printed out.

> theme_set( theme_grey() )

> theme_get()$panel.border
 list()
 - attr(*, "class")= chr [1:2] "element_blank" "element"

#     6
#     The current theme is set to the value of to.replace.theme,
#     using theme_replace(), then printed out.

 #     Only the color and size are not NULL.
```

```
> theme_set( to.replace.theme )

> theme_get()$panel.border
List of 5
 $ fill        : chr "transparent"
 $ colour      : NULL
 $ size        : num 3
 $ linetype    : NULL
 $ inherit.blank: logi FALSE
 - attr(*, "class")= chr [1:2] "element_rect" "element"

#    7
#    The current theme is set to theme_bw() and
#    and panel.border is printed out.

> theme_set( theme_bw() )


> theme_get()$panel.border
List of 5
 $ fill        : logi NA
 $ colour      : chr "grey20"
 $ size        : NULL
 $ linetype    : NULL
 $ inherit.blank: logi TRUE
 - attr(*, "class")= chr [1:2] "element_rect" "element"

#    8
#    The function theme_update() sets the current theme to
#    the theme in #'s 1 & 4.

> theme_update( panel.border=element_rect( size=3,
fill="transparent" ) )

> theme_get()$panel.border
List of 5
 $ fill        : chr "transparent"
 $ colour      : chr "grey20"
 $ size        : num 3
```

```
 $ linetype    : NULL
 $ inherit.blank: logi FALSE
 - attr(*, "class")= chr [1:2] "element_rect" "element"

#    9
#    The current theme is set back to theme_bw()

> theme_set( theme_bw() )


> theme_get()$panel.border
List of 5
 $ fill         : logi NA
 $ colour       : chr "grey20"
 $ size         : NULL
 $ linetype     : NULL
 $ inherit.blank: logi TRUE
 - attr(*, "class")= chr [1:2] "element_rect" "element"

#    10
#    The function theme_replace() is run to replace the
#    current theme.  The theme is set to the theme of #'s 2 & 6

> theme_replace( panel.border=element_rect( size=3, fill="transparent" ) )

> theme_get()$panel.border
List of 5
 $ fill         : chr "transparent"
 $ colour       : NULL
 $ size         : num 3
 $ linetype     : NULL
 $ inherit.blank: logi FALSE
 - attr(*, "class")= chr [1:2] "element_rect" "element"

#    11
#    ggplot() is run with the current theme - given in #10.

> ggplot( data=LifeCycleSavings, aes( pop75, pop15 ) ) +
labs( title="Example of Using the Current Theme in #10" )
```

Figure 8-3 shows an example of running ggplot() with the current theme set in part #10 of Listing 8-3. The theme is set to theme_bw() in part #9 and the panel.border element of the theme is replaced in part #10.

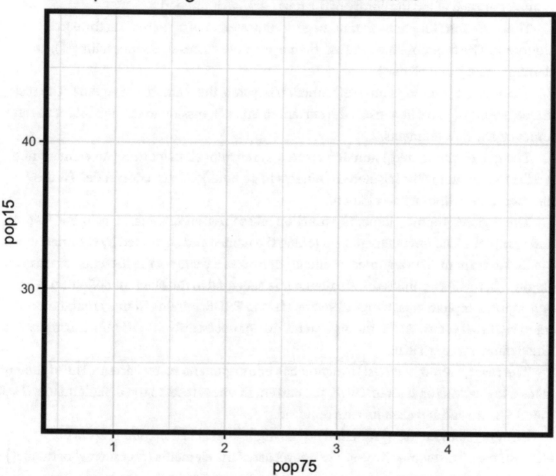

Figure 8-3. *Example of setting the current theme to theme_bw() and changing two arguments in the panel.border argument of the theme using theme_replace() – which sets the other arguments to NULL*

Note that the border of the plot is black instead of dark gray and that the width of the border is 3 millimeters. Since the fill is transparent, the grid lines show through.

8.1.3.2 Creating and Registering a New Theme

When developers develop a new package, sometimes the developer would like to put a new argument into theme(). The function theme() allows for new elements at the 93rd argument (which is …). To be used globally, the element must be registered in the ggplot2 package when the library of the new package is opened.

There are four functions that manage adding elements to theme() at the 93rd argument. The functions are register_theme_elements(), reset_theme_settings(), get_element_tree(), and el_def().

The register_theme_elements() function registers the elements in ggplot2. The reset_theme_settings() function resets the current theme of a session to the default theme and removes any new elements.

The get_element_tree() function returns the current element tree. (An element tree is a list that contains the registered elements in ggplot2.) The function el.def() is the function that defines a new element.

The register_theme_elements() function takes three arguments, …, element_tree, and complete. The new elements, including the names and separated by commas, are the first argument. The argument element_tree takes a vector of the list type, where each element of the list contains the element name set equal to the element definition. The argument complete takes a logical vector. If set to TRUE, missing theme arguments are set to NULL. If set to FALSE, the arguments do not necessarily inherit from an empty list. The default value is TRUE.

The reset_theme_settings() function has one argument, reset_current. The argument takes a logical vector. If set to TRUE, the current theme is reset to the default theme. If set to FALSE, only added elements are removed.

The get_element_tree() function has no arguments. The function returns the element tree. The element tree is a two-level list of the elements (arguments) of theme(). The names for the elements are at the top level. For each element, the class of the element, the inheritance path of the element, and a description of the element – which can be NULL – are at the second level. For my current session in RStudio, the length of the element tree is 98.

The el_def() function defines elements. The function takes three arguments, class, for the class of the element; inherit, for the inheritance path; and description, for a description of the element (usually NULL).

The class argument takes a character vector. Values in the current element list on my computer are "margin", "element_line", "element_rect", "element_text", "unit", "character", and "logical".

According to the help page for el_def(), the strings "character" and "margin" are reserved words. The meaning of "character" is a character or numeric vector. The meaning of "margin" is a four-element vector like those created by the function margin().

Similarly, "element_line", "element_rect", and "element_text" have the form of the result of running element_line(), element_rect(), and element_text(), respectively. The "unit" class takes the form of a call to the function unit() in the grid package.

The argument inherit takes the value NULL or a character vector giving the element from which the newly defined element inherits. The argument description takes the value NULL or a character vector containing a description of the newly defined element.

8.2 The Aesthetic Functions

The aesthetic functions affect the contents of the plot. There are four functions that set the aesthetics – aes(), aes_(), aes_q(), and aes_string(). The functions aes_(), aes_q(), and aes_string() share a help page and are described as quoting the aesthetic variables in order to make programming with the variables easier. We only cover aes() here. See the help page for the other functions for more information about the three functions.

Within ggplot() and the added functions, the variables to be plotted are entered as aesthetics. Descriptors (like point size and color) can also be entered as aesthetics. The function aes() can be called in three ways – in the call to ggplot(), added after the call to ggplot() with a + operator (at any layer), or set within a geometry or statistic function. When set within ggplot(), a geometry function, or a statistic function, the argument name to which aes() is assigned is mapping.

The aes() function takes two specified arguments, x and y, plus any other variables required by the specific function being plotted. Also, descriptive arguments can be included in a call to aes(), as noted in the preceding text.

While x and y are listed first in the aes() function call and are usually not assigned by name, the other arguments must be assigned the names that the function being plotted uses. The arguments must be of length one or of length equal to the length of the variable(s) to be plotted – usually the lengths of x and y. (Sometimes x and/or y is not set, depending on the function being plotted. If both x and y are not set, another variable, specified by the function being plotted, is plotted.)

According to the help page for aes(), the function aes() is a quoting function. Since the functions in ggplot2 usually work with data frames, the various variables in the data frame need not be of the same atomic class. By quoting the variables, all of the variables have the same type (character), which makes working with the variables easier.

From the help page for aes(), see the help page for nse-force in the rlang package, and the dplyr::programming vignette, for information about programming using quasiquotation – which must be used if variables have been created using a quoting function. Also, from the help page for aes(), the problem with quoted variables happens when ggplot() and the other associated functions are called from within another function. The other function is called a wrapper. See the help page for more discussion of wrappers and some examples.

R has four help pages describing groups of aesthetics. Also, R has a vignette describing possible values for many of the aesthetics. (For the vignette, enter `vignette("ggplot2-specs")` at the R prompt.)

The first help page is `aes_colour_fill_alpha` – for the color, fill, and alpha aesthetics. See the descriptions of col, fg, bg, and transparency in Section 3.4.1, the preceding help page, or the preceding vignette for the kinds of values that color, fill, and alpha take.

The second help page is `aes_linetype_size_shape`, for the linetype, size, and shape aesthetics. See the descriptions of lty, cex, and pch in Sections 3.3.2 and 3.4.3, the preceding help page, or the preceding vignette for the kinds of values that linetype, size, and shape take.

The third help page is `aes_position`, for arguments that give positions on the plot. The arguments are x, y, xend, yend, xmin, ymin, xmax, and ymax. The x and y arguments give the x and y positions of the points and are used (one or the other or both) in most plots. There are usually no default values for x and y.

The xend and yend arguments give the endpoints for curves and segments. The curves and segments start at the x and y locations and end at the xend and yend locations. The length of xend must be one or the length of x. The same holds for the lengths of y and yend. There are no default values for xend and yend.

The xmin, ymin, xmax, and ymax arguments give the corners of rectangles to be plotted on the plot or of images to be placed on the plot. The arguments take numeric vectors of length one or of length equal to the lengths of x and y. The two possible lengths can be mixed between the four arguments.

If one or more corners are outside the plot limits, setting the four arguments inside aes() causes the plot limits to expand. Setting the four arguments outside aes() does not expand the plot limits. Rather, the rectangle or image is cut off at the axes.

There are no default values for xmin, xmax, ymin, and ymax. See the help page or vignette for more information about the positioning arguments.

The fourth help page is `aes_group_order`, for creating plots or setting features of plots by groups. In plot(), the by argument tells plot() to plot by groups of a variable. For example, boxplots may be plotted in separate plots according to the value of a variable assigned to by. In the ggplot2 package, the similar variable is the aesthetic argument group.

Since group is an aesthetic argument, the length of group must be one or the length of the object to be plotted. According to the help page, the default value of group is the interaction of the discrete variables in the data frame assigned to data. See the help page or vignette for more information about the group argument.

For the other descriptive arguments, differing values of the aesthetic can be assigned based on groups. A descriptive argument can be set to a variable of length equal to the length of the object to be plotted. The variable would contain groups of values that are legal for the descriptive argument. The plotting function would then assign the characteristic of the argument by the groups in the vector (as is done in the function plot() for many of the arguments in par()). According to the help page for `aes_group_order`, the aesthetics that can be set to different values based on the values of a variable are x, y, color, fill, alpha, shape, size, and linetype.

The descriptors that, in par(), are called adj, str, col, fg, bg, lty, lwd, cex, and pch can be entered as aesthetics in ggplot2, with names specific to ggplot2. The respective names are hjust, angle, color (or colour), colour (or color), fill, linetype, size, size, and shape. (The function aes_all() shows the conversion from ggplot2 names to par() names if the par() name is entered within quotes.)

The col and fg arguments in par() are both named color (or colour) in the ggplot2 functions. Which of the plot properties is to be colored by the color argument depends on the type of the function in which color is set. Similarly, which of the properties, referred to by lwd and cex in par(), is resized depends on the type of function in which the size argument appears.

All of the aesthetics can be entered in the geometry functions outside of a call to aes() and without being in an assigned data frame. However, the arguments set outside of aes() must be assigned to objects in the environment in which R is run or to expressions. Arguments set outside an aes() function do not have access to the data frame assigned to data.

If a descriptive argument is entered within a call to aes(), a legend is created for the different groups in the variable assigned to the descriptive argument. If not set in a call to aes(), no legend is created. The choice of which aesthetics to use to create a legend can be done by putting some descriptive arguments within a call to aes() and the others outside the call. A legend is plotted for each argument within the call to aes(). Note that a descriptive argument set within aes() does not always behave the same as when the variable is set outside of aes().

In Listing 8-4, code is given for an example of using aesthetics in the geometry function geom_point(). The function geom_point() is covered in Chapter 9. The functions scale_size() and guide_legend() are used to change the legend and are covered in Chapter 10.

Listing 8-4. Code for the example of using aesthetic arguments in geom_point()

```
gray.scale=gray(
  c( 80, 70, 55, 35 )/100
)

cdpi = (21:24)[
  cut( LifeCycleSavings$dpi, 4 )
]

dpi.quantiles=floor(
  quantile(
    LifeCycleSavings$dpi,
    c(
      12.5, 37.5, 62.5, 87.5
    )/100
  )
)

ggplot(
  data=data.frame(
```

```r
    LifeCycleSavings,
    size=cdpi-18.5
  ),
  aes(
    pop75,
    pop15,
    size
  )
) +

theme(
  plot.margin=margin( 0.5, 0.5, 0.5, 0.5, "inches" )
) +

geom_point(
  aes(
    size=size
  ),
  fill=gray.scale[ cdpi-20 ],
  shape=cdpi
) +

scale_size(
  breaks=c( 2, 3, 4, 5 )+0.5,
  label=paste0( "$", dpi.quantiles ),
  guide=guide_legend(
    override.aes=list(
      shape=21:24,
      fill=gray.scale
    )
  ),
  name=
      "Disposable\nPersonal\nIncome\n\n(median of\nquartile)\n",
  range=c( 2.5, 5.5 )
) +

labs(
  title="Example of Aesthetics with a Legend"
```

```
) +

xlab(
  "% Population > 75 Years of Age"
) +

ylab(
  "% Population < 15 Years of Age"
)
```

In Figure 8-4, the code in Listing 8-4 is run. A plot is given using the pop75, pop15, and dpi variables from the LifeCycleSavings dataset (see Section 3.1).

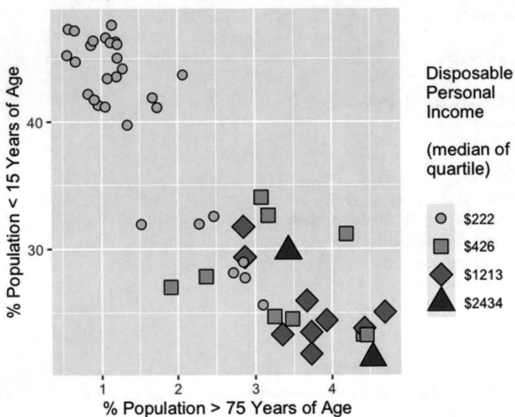

Figure 8-4. *An example of using the aesthetics size, shape, and fill in the geometry geom_point()*

Note that a one-half-inch margin is put around the plot. Also, that the argument size is set within a call to aes(), while shape and fill are outside of the call – so only one legend is plotted. The function scale_size() is used to change the shapes and fill colors of the legend keys as well as the labels on the keys and the title of the legend.

## CHAPTER 9

The Geometry, Statistic, Annotation, and borders() Functions

The geometry, statistic, annotation, and borders() functions create the contents of a plot. The functions open new layers on the figure and plot new information. The geometry functions, which all begin with *geom_*, create most of the many types of plots that can be created with the ggplot2 package. The statistic functions, which all begin with *stat_*, both create and add to plots. The functions statistically reduce the data before plotting. The annotation functions, which are the function annotate() or start with *annotation_*, provide a simple way to annotate plots created with ggplot(). The borders() function adds a border to a correctly formatted map object.

This chapter has four sections. The first section covers geometry functions, the second section covers statistic functions, the third section covers annotation functions, and the fourth section covers the borders() function.

9.1 The Geometry Functions

The geometry functions are the most basic plotting functions in the ggplot2 package. The geometry functions are formatted as geom_*extension*(), where *extension* is the name of the geometry (e.g., geom_abline() for the abline geometry). The name of the geometry function describes what the function plots. The name extensions of the 48 geometry functions are listed in Table 7-1, along with descriptions of what the functions do.

The geometry functions are added to the plotting functions with the + operator or, sometimes, the %+% operator (see Section 7.1.1). This section gives general information about geometry functions and about the help pages of the geometry functions.

© Margot Tollefson 2021
M. Tollefson, *Visualizing Data in R 4*, https://doi.org/10.1007/978-1-4842-6831-5_9

If the data and mapping arguments have been assigned in ggplot() and if the mapping in ggplot() includes all required arguments to the geometry function, the geometry function can use the data and mapping information from the ggplot() call. The geometry function can then be called with no arguments.

However, the first two arguments of all geometry functions are mapping and data, for the aesthetics and data frame to use. By default, both are NULL – except for the three simple feature geometry functions. For geom_sf(), geom_sf_label(), and geom_sf_text(), the value of mapping is aes().

Most geometry functions have an argument named stat, which is assigned the name of a statistic function – with the name in quotes. For example, the name `"identity"` is used for the stat_identity() function (see Section 9.2 for information about statistic functions). Since more than one geometry has the same value for stat, using the statistic function presumably reduces the effort involved in coding the geometry functions. Two geometry functions, geom_qq() and geom_qq_line(), have the argument geom – in which case geom takes the value "path", for the geom_path() geometry function.

Most of the geometry functions also have an argument named position. The position argument takes a character vector of length one. The vector contains the name of a position function, usually "identity". The position functions are named in the same way as the statistic and geometry functions – with the prefix being *position_* followed by the name. The position functions tell R how to place the information, generated by the geometric function, on the plot. The possible values for position are "dodge", "dodge2", "fill", "identity", "jitter", "jitterdodge", "nudge", and "stack".

Most of the geometry functions take the arguments na.rm, show.legend, and inherit.aes. The na.rm argument tells R whether to warn the user when the program removes missing values. The argument takes a logical vector of length one. If set to FALSE, a warning is given. If set to TRUE, no warning is given. The default value is FALSE if the argument is present in the argument list.

The show.legend argument tells R whether to include the layer opened by the geometry function in the legend of the plot. If set to NA, the layer is included if an aesthetic function is used in the geometry function. If set to FALSE, the layer is not included. If set to TRUE, the layer is always included. The logical vector can be of length greater than one if more than one aesthetic variable is included in the aes() function called within the geometry function. Each logical value must be named with the name of the argument to be included or not included. The default value for show.legend is NA when show.legend is included in the argument list.

The inherit.aes argument tells R whether to add to the list of aesthetic variables defined in the ggplot() call to aes() or to set up a new group of variables within the geometry function. If set to TRUE, the geometry function aesthetic is combined with the ggplot() aesthetic. If set to FALSE, a new aesthetic is set up. The default value of inherit. aes is TRUE when the argument is included in the list of arguments.

The other specified arguments vary with the geometric function. For example, in geom_abline(), the arguments slope and intercept are present and have no default values. The arguments must be assigned values for the function to run. Some of the specified arguments not listed in the preceding text are used across a number of functions, but there is no specified argument, other than the arguments listed in the preceding text, that is present in most functions.

The argument ... is used for the aesthetic arguments and any parameters for the geometry function not specifically listed. All of the geometry functions have the ... argument.

The aesthetics that can used with a geometry function are either listed on the help page for the function or given at a help page that is linked from the help page for the geometry function. For example, for geom_abline(), the possible aesthetic variables are alpha, color, linetype, size, slope, and intercept. Sometimes, only some of the possible aesthetics are listed.

For most of the help pages, the aesthetics are listed in a bulleted list, and the aesthetics that must be supplied are listed in the bold typeface. For many help pages, the page covers more than one function. Often, the list of aesthetics is nominally given for only one function. Presumably, in the case where only one function name is given, the aesthetics apply to all of the functions on the help page. Most help pages also give the kinds of values that are computed by the geometry functions.

9.2 The Statistic Functions

The statistic functions perform statistical reduction on datasets and plot the result. The statistic functions behave much like the geometry functions. There are 33 statistic functions listed in the ggplot2 package (a few are deprecated, removed, or duplicated).

As with the geometry functions, the first two arguments for the statistic functions are mapping and data. For all of the statistic functions, the default values of mapping and data are NULL – except for the value of mapping for the simple feature function stat_sf_coordinates(). For stat_sf_coordinates(), mapping takes the value aes() by default.

All of the statistic functions have an argument named geom, for the name of a geometry function. The value of geom is the quoted value of the name extension of a geometry function. For example, geom is set equal to "bar" for the geometric function geom_bar(). Different statistic functions can have the same value for geom.

Most of the statistic functions take the position, na.rm, show.legend, and inherit. aes arguments. The position argument has the same meaning as with the geometric functions and takes the same kinds of values. The na.rm, show.legend, and inherit.aes arguments take the same types and default values as in the geometric functions.

The help page descriptions for the statistic functions do not always give a list of the possible aesthetics that can be used by the functions. Often, both geometry functions and statistic functions share the same help page, and the aesthetic arguments are only listed for the geometry function. Presumably, the arguments can also be used by the corresponding statistic function. Aesthetic functions behave in the same way that the functions behave in geometry functions.

In Table 9-1, the statistic functions are listed along with a description of the functions. The original table was from the function list for the ggplot2 package.

Table 9-1. *The statistic functions in the ggplot2 package, with descriptions*

Statistic Function	Description
stat_bin()	Finds the number or standardized number of observations falling in bins constructed from the x or y variable. Only one of x and y can be set. The counts are plotted.
stat_bin2d()	An old name for stat_bin_2d.
stat_bin_2d()	Finds the number of observations falling in bins constructed from the crossed x and y variables. Both x and y must be set. Plots squares at the middle of the bins. The squares are colored based on the number of observations in the bin. Bins with no observations are not plotted.
stat_binhex()	An old name for stat_bin_hex().
stat_bin_hex()	Same as stat_bin_2d except that hexagrams are used as bins instead of squares.

(continued)

Table 9-1. (*continued*)

Statistic Function	Description
stat_boxplot()	Finds the values used by the boxplots and plots the boxplots. Either x or y can be boxed. Should set x or y, but not both. Uses the method used by Tukey.
stat_contour()	Plots contour lines on a two- dimensional plot. The aesthetics x, y, and z must be set. The value assigned to z must be given the name z when assigned. The variables x and y should be (at least approximately) equally spaced and increasing. Contour lines are plotted for the values of z.
stat_contour_filled()	The same as stat_contour() except that the area between the contour lines is filled with graded colors.
stat_count()	Finds and plots the number of observations in the variable x or y that share a value. Creates a bar plot. Only one of x and y is used.
stat_density()	Finds and plots a kernel density estimator for x or y – only one of which can be in aes() in ggplot(). If x is present, the density is on the x axis. For y, the density is on the y axis.
stat_density2d()	An old name for stat_density_2d().
stat_density2d_ filled()	An old name for stat_density_2d_filled().
stat_density_2d()	Plots a contour plot of the kernel density estimates based on the values of x and y, both of which must be set.
stat_density_2d_ filled()	Same as stat_density_2d() except the areas between the contours are filled with graded colors.
stat_ecdf()	Plots an empirical cumulative density function for the vector assigned to x. If y is set, the y axis is named the name of the variable assigned to y, but y has no other effect. The argument x must be set. The argument y can be set.
stat_ellipse()	Plots a confidence ellipse around two-dimensional data. Both x and y must be set.

(*continued*)

Table 9-1. (*continued*)

Statistic Function	Description
stat_function()	Plots an R function of one variable. The function must be a one-to-one mapping. The arguments x and y can be set in either stat_function() or ggplot(). If both are set, x is used as input to the function. The argument fun can be a function name or a function definition and must be given. The assignments fun=cos, fun="cos" and fun=function(x) cos(x) all give the same result. The function can be user defined.
stat_identity()	Plots a geometry function. By default, a scatterplot is plotted, and both x and y must be set. The arguments x and y are not transformed.
stat_qq()	Plots a quantile-quantile plot of a data vector against the quantiles of a distribution (the standard normal by default). The only argument that must be set is sample – for the data vector to be compared to a distribution.
stat_qq_line()	Plots the quantile-quantile line. The distribution function can be set, but defaults to qnorm() (in the stats package). The data vector sample must be set.
stat_quantile()	Plots the result of a quantile regression on x and y. Both x and y must be set.
stat_sf()	Opens a graphic with coordinates from an object of the sf (simple feature) class and with a uniform background. The aesthetic argument name for the sf object is geometry. Used by geom_sf() to plot objects of the sf (simple feature) class.
stat_sf_coordinates()	Plots the coordinates of the features of an object of the sf (simple feature) class. The aesthetic argument name of the sf object is geometry.
stat_smooth()	Plots a smoothed version of the points at the x and y coordinates. Both x and y must be set. The method used for smoothing is set by the method argument.
stat_spoke()	This function is deprecated. Use geom_spoke().

(*continued*)

Table 9-1. (*continued*)

Statistic Function	Description
stat_sum()	Plots points at x and y coordinates where a property of what is plotted depends on the number of observations at the specific points. Both x and y must be set. By default, black circles are plotted, and the circles vary in size. A legend is also plotted containing a key to the property.
stat_summary()	Plots, for each value of x, a function of the y value associated with the value of x. Both x and y must be set. The argument fun sets the function (which plots the mean plus and minus the standard error of the mean by default).
stat_summary_bin()	Same as stat_summary() except the x values are aggregated into bins. Both x and y must be set. The number of bins is set by the argument bins, and the default value is 30.
stat_summary2d()	An old name for stat_summary_2d(). R asks that the function stat_summary_2d be used instead.
stat_summary_2d()	Plots a square for each bin of x and y points, with the color of the square based on a function applied to the values of z in the bin. All of x, y, and z must be set. A legend is plotted for the values of the function applied to z. (The plotting region is split into bins based on horizontal and vertical coordinates using the argument bins or binwidth. The function is given by the argument fun.)
stat_summary_hex()	The same as stat_summary_2d() except that the bins are hexagons rather than squares.
stat_unique()	Plots a scatterplot of unique values in x and y. Both x and y must be set.
stat_ydensity()	Plots a violin plot. The arguments x and y must be set. The argument group can be set to plot by groups.

More information about the statistic functions can be found at the help pages for the functions. Note that there are arguments that are aesthetics and must be entered in an aesthetic function, there are arguments that are arguments of the function doing the plotting and that are not included in the aesthetic function, and there are arguments that can be both.

Only arguments that are defined on the help page in the argument or aesthetic lists (except that some aesthetic lists are not complete) can be set, but expressions using arguments in the environment from which ggplot() is run can be used on the right side of the assignments.

9.3 The Annotation Functions

The annotation functions, annotate(), annotation_custom(), annotation_logticks(), annotation_map(), and annotation_raster(), place annotation on a plot. The annotate() function uses a geometry function and takes data for the geometry function from the environment rather than an assigned data frame. The result of running the geometry function is placed on the plot at a location specified within annotate().

The annotation_custom() function takes a grid graphical object (grob – essentially a completely specified plot) and places the object on the existing plot at a specified location. The annotation_logticks() function puts a log scale on one or both axes. The annotation_map() function plots a map border on a plot that exists. The annotation_raster() function plots a raster image at a specified place on the plot.

This section is divided into four subsections. The subsections cover, first, the annotate() function; second, the annotation_custom() function; third, the annotation_logticks() function; and, fourth, the annotation_map() and annotation_raster() functions.

9.3.1 The annotate() Function

The annotate() function uses a geometry function to create a new plot on an existing plot. If the placement of the new plot is outside or partially outside the limits of the original plot, annotate() expands the axes of the original plot to include both plots. The aesthetic arguments that are used by the geometry function can be used in annotate(). Other than x and y, the aesthetic arguments only affect the new plot and do not affect any existing legend (according to the help page for annotate()).

The position units of the new plot are the units of the original plot. For example, if the x axis goes from 0 to 5 and the y axis from 20 to 50, then the x axis of the new plot is placed with respect to the 0 to 5 and the y axis of the new plot is placed with respect to 20 to 50.

The annotate() function takes ten specified arguments plus unspecified aesthetic arguments and any arguments used by the geometry function. The values assigned to the arguments can be taken from the environment in which R is run but not from an assigned data frame. The ten arguments are geom, for the geometry function; x and y, for the x and y coordinates used by the geometry function; xmin, xmax, ymin, and ymax, for the location at which to place the plot; xend and yend, for the endpoints of curves and segments if the geometry function is geom_curve() or geom_segment(); and na.r, for whether to give a warning if missing points are removed. The tenth argument is ..., for the unspecified aesthetic arguments and arguments used by the geometry function.

The geom argument takes a character vector of length one. The vector contains the name of the geometry in quotes. For example, set geom equal to "point" to use geom_point(), or set geom equal to gg and gg equal to "text" to use the geometry function geom_text(). There is no default value for geom.

The x, y, xmin, xmax, ymin, ymax, xend, and yend arguments are covered in Section 8.2. According to the help page for annotate(), at least one of the arguments must be set. The default values of the arguments are all NULL.

The other aesthetic arguments are also covered in Section 8.2. The arguments of the geometry functions used by annotate() are covered in Sections 7.2, 9.1, and 9.2.

The na.rm argument takes a logical vector of length one. If set to TRUE, no warning is given if an observation is removed due to missing data. If set to FALSE, a warning is given. The default value of na.rm is FALSE.

In Listing 9-1, the code used in an example of calling annotation() with the geom_text() function is given. A random method is used to select which observations in the dataset LifeCycleSavings to plot.

Listing 9-1. Code to annotate a plot with point labels using annotate() with geom_text()

```
sel = sample(
   1:50,
   15
)

ggplot(
  LifeCycleSavings[ sel, ],
  aes( pop75, pop15 )
) +

geom_point(
) +
```

```
annotate(
  "text",
  x=LifeCycleSavings$pop75[ sel ]+0.05,
  y=LifeCycleSavings$pop15[ sel ]-0.3,
  label=rownames(
    LifeCycleSavings
  )[ sel ],
  hjust=0,
  vjust=1,
  size=3.5
) +

labs(
  title="Example of Using annotate() with geom_text()"
)
```

In Figure 9-1, the code in Listing 9-1 is run. Note that the code was run several times until an acceptable data selection was produced.

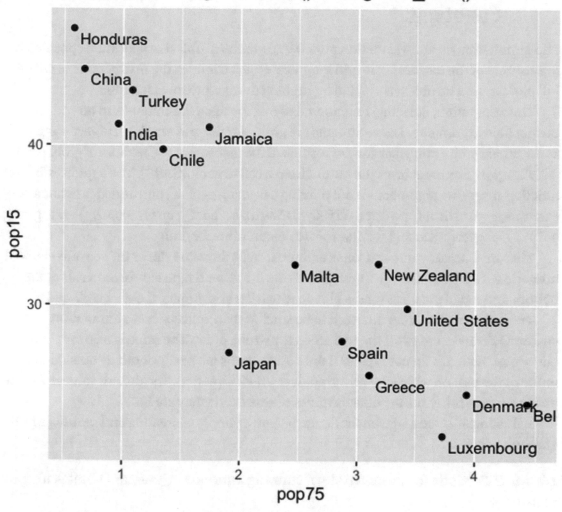

Figure 9-1. *An example of calling annotate() with the geometry function geom_text() to put labels on a random selection of 15 observations out of 50 observations*

Note that the labels are plotted a short distance to the right and below the points because hjust is set to 0, vjust is set to 1, an offset of 0.05 is added to the x locations, and an offset of 0.3 is subtracted from the y locations. Also note that the values of x and y include the data frame name since annotate does not use the aesthetics set inside any call to aes(). The size of the text is set to 3.5 – for a text size of 3.5 millimeters.

9.3.2 The annotation_custom() and ggplotGrob() Functions

The annotation_custom() function plots a grid graphical object at a location specified by the corners of the location. The grid graphical object contains the instructions to create a full plot figure. The object is created by running the ggplotGrob() function.

The annotation_custom() function takes five specified arguments and no unspecified arguments. The arguments are grob – for the grid graphical object – and xmin, xmax, ymin, and ymax for the corners of the placement of the value of grob.

The grob argument takes the output from a call to ggplotGrob(). The ggplotGrob() function takes one argument – a full plotting call using ggplot() and added functions, for example, ggplotGrob(ggplot(LifeCycleSavings, aes(pop75, pop15)) + geom_point() + geom_smooth()). There is no default value for grob.

The xmin, xmax, ymin, and ymax arguments take the value -Inf or Inf or a one-element numeric vector. The values -Inf and Inf indicate the left and right side of the x axis or the bottom and top of the y axis (of the plot on which the grid graphical object is plotted).

The value of xmin does not need to be smaller than xmax because annotation_custom() reverses the two if the two are in the wrong order. The same is true for ymin and ymax. The axes do not expand if the x and y limits fall partly or totally outside the limits of the plot on which the grid graphical object is plotted. The default values of xmin and ymin are -Inf, while the default values of xmax and ymax are Inf.

In Listing 9-2, code is given for Figure 9-2, an example of creating and plotting a grid graphical object.

Listing 9-2. Code for the example of running annotation_custom() that is in Figure 9-2

```
ggplot(
  data.frame(
    x=0:2,
    y=0:2
  ),
  aes(
    x=x,
    y=y
  )
) +
```

```
geom_point(
  color="transparent"
) +

labs(
  title="Example of Using annotation_custom with a grob"
) +

annotation_custom(

  grob=ggplotGrob(

    ggplot(
      LifeCycleSavings,
      aes(
        pop75,
        pop15
      )
    ) +

    geom_point(
    ) +

    geom_smooth(
    )
  ),
  xmin=0,
  xmax=1,
  ymin=0,
  ymax=1
)
```

In Figure 9-2, the code in Listing 9-2 is run. The annotation_custom() function is used with a grid graphical object consisting of a call to ggplot() and two geometric functions.

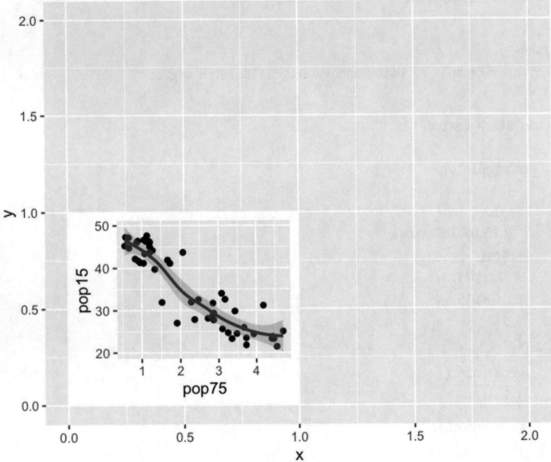

Figure 9-2. *An example of setting a grid graphical object in annotation_custom()*

Note that the units on the grid graphical object are different from the units of the background plot. In the background plot, color is set to "transparent", so the three points that set up the scale of the axes are not visible. Also note that the placement of the grid graphical object is set to between 0 and 1 on both the x and the y axes by xmin, xmax, ymin, and ymax. In both plots, the default theme is used. For the two geom's, the default values are also used.

9.3.3 The annotation_logticks() Function

The annotation_logticks() function puts tick marks for a log scale onto a plot. A log scale can be put on any or all of the four sides of a plot. Three different size tick marks, for three different interval levels, can be plotted on a side. The function can work with the functions scale_x_log10(), scale_y_log10(), and coord_trans().

The annotation_logticks() function takes 12 specified arguments plus some unspecified aesthetic arguments. The ... argument is the last argument in the order of the arguments. The first 12 arguments are base, for the base of the logarithm; sides, for which side(s) to annotate with a log scale; outside, for whether to plot the tick marks into the plot or away from the plot; scaled, for whether the data has been log scaled before the plot is created; short, mid, and long, for the length of the tick marks at the three interval levels; and the standard colour, size, linetype, alpha, and color aesthetic arguments.

The base argument takes a positive numeric vector of length one. The default value of base is 10.

The sides argument takes a character vector of length one. The value must be some combination of the letters b, l, t, and r – for bottom, left, top, and right sides of the plot. For example, use "bl" to put a log scale on the bottom and left sides. The default value of sides is "bl".

The outside argument takes a logical vector of length one. Any other length gives a warning. If set to TRUE, and clip is set to "off" in coord_cartesian(), the ticks are plotted away from the plot. If set to FALSE, the ticks are plotted into the plot. The default value of outside is FALSE.

The scaled argument takes a logical vector of length one. According to the help page for annotation_logticks(), if the variable that is to have a log scale is transformed before the plotting by running log10() on the variable or if scale_x_log10() and/or scale_y_log10() is called, then scaled is set to TRUE. If coord_trans() is called with x and/or y set equal to "log10", then scaled should be set to FALSE. The default value of scaled is TRUE.

The short, mid, and long arguments each take the output from a single call to the unit() function, which is in the grid package. (The shortest tick marks are associated with the smallest width division intervals on the scale; the midrange with the middle width division intervals; and the longest with the largest width division intervals.) The default values of short, mid, and long are unit(0.1, "cm"), unit(0.2, "cm"), and unit(0.3, "cm"), respectively.

The color (or colour) argument takes a color vector of length one (see Section 3.4.1 for kinds of color vectors). The default value of color is "black".

The size argument takes a nonnegative numeric vector of length one. The value gives the line width of the tick marks in millimeters. The default value of size is 0.5.

The linetype argument takes a vector of line types of length one (see Section 3.3.2 and the argument lty for line type values). The default value of linetype is 1 (for a solid line).

The alpha argument takes a numeric vector of length one which must be between 0 and 1, inclusive (see Section 3.4.1.2 for a description of how to use alpha). The default value of alpha is 1, that is, the tick marks are opaque.

In Listing 9-3, code is given for an example of using annotation_logticks() with scale_y_log10().

Listing 9-3. Code for the example in Figure 9-3 of using annotation_logticks() with scale_y_log10()

```
ggplot(
  LifeCycleSavings,
  aes(
    pop75,
    dpi
  )
) +

scale_y_log10(
) +

geom_point(
) +

geom_smooth(
) +

labs(
  title="Example of Using annotation_logticks()"
) +

annotation_logticks(
  side="l"
)
```

In Figure 9-3, the code in Listing 9-3 is run. Both geom_point() and geom_smooth() are run.

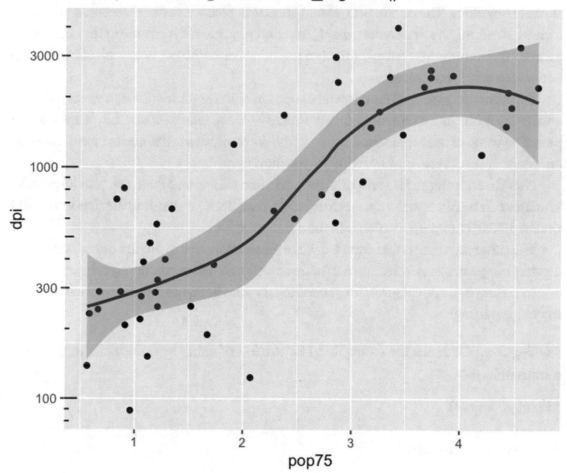

Figure 9-3. *An example of using annotation_logticks() with scale_y_log10(), geom_point(), and geom_smooth()*

Note that both geom_point() and geom_smooth() run. If the log scale is set by running coord_trans(y="log10") and setting scaled to TRUE in annotation_logticks(), then geom_smooth() gives an error.

According to the help page for coord_trans(), scale_y_log10() runs before the object to be plotted is transformed for plotting, while coord_trans() runs after the transformation. (See the example portion of the help page for the three ways of log transforming variables in ggplot2.)

9.3.4 The annotation_map() and annotation_raster() Functions

The annotation_map() function puts a map on a plot along with geometry and/or statistic functions. The annotation_raster() function places a raster object on a plot at a given location. The annotation_map() function requires a data frame in the correct format. The annotation_raster() function requires a raster object or an object with values between 0 and 1, inclusive.

The annotation_map() function takes one specified argument plus unspecified aesthetic arguments. The one argument is map – for the map with which to annotate the plot. The value of the argument must be in the correct format. The correct formatting for annotation_map() can be done with the function map_data().

Files that are shape files or spatial files, and in a computer folder, can also be plotted. The files can be put into the correct format for map_data() by reading the files into R with the readOGR() function – which is in the rgdal package.

The other arguments that can be used in annotation_map() are the descriptive aesthetic arguments. See Section 8.2 for descriptions of the aesthetic arguments.

In Listing 9-4, code is given for generating the plot in Figure 9-4. The world map is in the maps package.

Listing 9-4. Code for the example in Figure 9-4 of using annotation_map() to put a map on a plot

```
library( maps )

full_world = map_data(
  "world"
)

ggplot(
  data.frame(
    long=c(
      -180,
      179
    ),
```

```
    lat=c(
      -90,
      90
    )
  ),
  aes(
    x = long,
    y = lat
  )
) +

theme_classic(
) +

theme(
  panel.border=element_rect(
    color="black",
    fill="transparent",
    size=0.3
  ),
  axis.line=element_line(
    size=0
  )
) +

geom_point(
  color="transparent"
) +

labs(
  title="Example of Using annotation_map() with geom_point()"
) +

annotation_map(
  full_world,
  colour="grey30",
  fill="white"
)
```

In Figure 9-4, the code in Listing 9-4 is run. The maps package must be loaded to run the code.

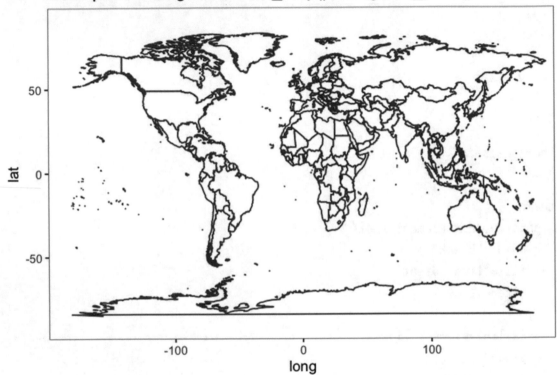

Figure 9-4. *An example of using annotation_map() with geom_point(), where the points are not plotted*

Note that the map is the world map from the maps package. In ggplot(), the ranges of the longitude and latitude to be plotted are set in a call to data.frame(). The aes() function in ggplot() sets x to the longitude variable and y to the latitude variable.

The theme is set to theme_classic(), which has no grid and a white background. A border is added, and axis lines are deleted, in the call to theme() that is added to the call to theme_classic().

Plotting with geom_point() creates the background on which annotation_map() is plotted. The axes are set to transparent, as are the points plotted by geom_point(). In the call to annotation_map(), the color of the plot lines is set to a dark gray, and the fill color for the map is set to white.

The annotation_raster() function takes six specified arguments and no unspecified arguments. The six arguments are raster, for the raster object; xmin, xmax, ymin, and ymax, for the corners of the raster image; and interpolate, for whether to interpolate when plotting the raster object.

The raster argument takes a vector, matrix, or array of the raster or nativeRaster class or a numeric vector, matrix, or array with values that are between 0 and 1, inclusive. There is no default value for raster. If raster is an array, but not a matrix, the array must have three dimensions and the third dimension must be of length 3 or 4. The first two dimensions contain the three or four matrices to be plotted.

Objects of the raster class contain values that are color character strings, for example, "#FFFFFF" or "black". The values of the objects of the nativeRaster class also contain a level of transparency, for example, "#FFFFFFAA", where "AA" gives the level of transparency. (See Section 3.4.1.1 for more information about color strings and transparency.)

The xmin, xmax, ymin, and ymax arguments behave like the same arguments in annotation_custom() (see Section 9.3.2). There are not default values for xmin, xmax, ymin, and ymax.

The interpolate argument takes a logical vector. If set to TRUE, interpolation is done when the cells of the matrix are plotted. If FALSE, the cells are treated as cells of constant color. The default value of interpolate is FALSE.

9.4 The borders() Function

The borders() function is the last of the functions that open a layer. After ggplot() opens a plot, borders() can be used to put a map on the plot. No accompanying geometry, statistic, or annotation function is necessary. The borders() function plots maps that are in the maps package, or similar objects. (To see the contents of the maps package, click the maps link under the Packages tab in the lower-right window of RStudio or enter help(package="maps") at the R prompt in the R console. The package must be installed first.)

The borders() function takes six specified arguments plus the arguments of geom_polygon() (see Sections 7.2 and 9.1). The six specified arguments are database, for the database to use; regions, for the region(s) of the database to plot; fill, for the color with which to fill the map; colour, for the color of the borders; and xlim and ylim, for the longitude and latitude ranges to be used by the plot.

The database argument takes a single-element character vector. The character string is usually the name of a database in the maps package, enclosed in quotes. However, there are map databases in other R packages. To access a database in another package, include the package name – with two colons between the package name and the database name – in the quoted string. The default value for database is "world", for a database of the countries of the world.

The regions argument takes a character vector containing the name or names of the region(s) to be plotted. To see the available regions, run the map() function with the database name and the arguments namesonly set to TRUE and plot set to FALSE. For subregions, include the region name as the second argument. For example, to see the subregions of the US state of Washington, run map("state", "washington", namesonly=TRUE, plot=FALSE). The default value of regions is "", that is, all regions in the database.

The fill and colour (do not use color) arguments take a one-element color value vector (see Section 3.4.1. for possible color values). The default value for fill is NA, and the default value of colour is "grey50".

The xlim and ylim arguments take two-element numeric vectors. The arguments need not be set. The default values of xlim and ylim are NULL, that is, the borders() function generates good limits.

In Listing 9-5, code is given for the example in Figure 9-5 of using borders() with ggplot().

Listing 9-5. Code for the example, in Figure 9-5, of using borders() with ggplot()

```
library( maps )

full_world = map_data(
  "world"
)

ggplot(
  full_world,
  aes(
    long,
    lat
  )
) +
```

```
theme_classic(
) +

theme(
  axis.line=element_line(
    size=0
  ),
  panel.border=element_rect(
    color="black",
    fill="transparent",
    size=0.25
  )
) +

borders(
  "world",
  ".",
  fill="white",
  colour="grey40"
) +

scale_x_continuous(
  breaks=c( -180, -90, 0, 90, 180 ),
  labels=c( "180", "90W", "0", "90E", "180")
) +

scale_y_continuous(
  breaks=c( -90, -45, 0, 45, 90 ),
  labels=c( "90S", "45S", "0", "45N", "90N")
) +

labs(
  title="Example of Using borders() with ggplot()"
)
```

In Figure 9-5, the code in Listing 9-5 is run. The world database is used, and all of the regions are selected.

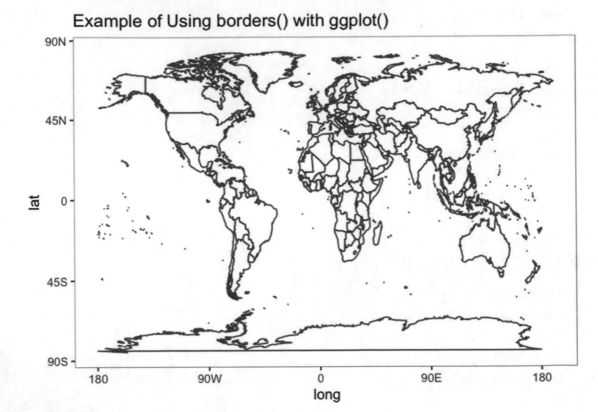

Figure 9-5. *An example of calling borders() after a call to ggplot() and selecting all regions of the world database in the maps package*

Note that the world database is converted to a data frame with the function map_data() and that the data frame is used as value for data in ggplot().

The variables for the aesthetic arguments x and y are long and lat (for longitude and latitude). The theme theme_classic() gives a simple background, but the axes are removed, and a border is added, with a call to theme() (used to update theme_classic()).

In the call to borders(), the world database is set, and all region borders are plotted (by setting database to "world" and region to ""). The fill color is set to white and the border color to a dark gray.

The scale_x_continuous() and scale_y_continuous() (see Chapter 10) are used to put nice breaks and labels on the axes. The default breaks include a longitude of 200, which is nonsensical.

CHAPTER 10

Formatting and Plot Management Tools

This chapter covers a number of ways to make choices about the appearance of a plot, some grouping and calculation tools, creating automatic functions for a specific class of objects, and creating object-oriented prototype functions. The chapter is split into three sections.

The first section gives an overview of the scale_, coord_, and guide_ functions along with related functions. The second section covers functions that cut data vectors into levels, summarize data vectors, and facet data vectors by faceting variables. The third section goes over functions to save, plot, print, and automate plots – as well as creating object-oriented prototypes.

10.1 Working with the scale_, coord_, and guide_ Functions

This section starts with, first, a subsection covering the scale_ functions, which affect the color, size, shape, and line type around and within a plot. The scale_ functions set up scales for properties that affect the appearance of the points and lines of a plot and, also, can set the properties of the legends associated with the scales.

The second subsection tells how to control the order of application for the functions that affect appearance. The third subsection is about formatting axes, with both scale_ and coord_ functions. The fourth subsection goes over the guide_ functions, which let the user set up a preset format that includes more than one formatting function.

© Margot Tollefson 2021
M. Tollefson, *Visualizing Data in R 4*, https://doi.org/10.1007/978-1-4842-6831-5_10

10.1.1 The Scale Functions That Affect Color, Size, Shape, and Line Type

The scale functions set up a scale of values that affect the transparency, color, fill color, size, shape, or line type of points and lines. The names of the scale functions take the form of *scale_* followed by the name of a characteristic (alpha, color, colour, fill, linetype, shape, radius, or size), usually followed by qualifiers.

Scales are usually applied to groups of points or lines but can be applied to ungrouped data. For numeric data, whether by groups or not, the types of scales available are plain scales or binned scales. For binned scales, the numeric data is binned, and the binned attributes are plotted. For categorical data – whether a factor object or a character object – only discrete scales are available. (Factor objects can be converted to numeric objects by the function as.numeric().)

For many of the functions in the ggplot2 package, the functions do not have a help page. Instead, the help page for the function is that of another function, which gives the arguments of the function. For example, scale_alpha_date() opens to the help page for scale_alpha() (and some other scale_alpha_ functions that do not include scale_alpha_date()). However, scale_alpha_date() is a function and can be called if the scale is for a vector of the Date class. Only functions with help pages are covered in this book.

Two qualifiers that most of the preceding characteristics use are identity and manual. The characteristics alpha, color, colour, fill, linetype, shape, and size have scale functions for the qualifiers identity and manual.

Note that, to use an aesthetic argument in a scale function, the group argument and/or a characteristic argument(s) must be set to a variable in an aesthetic function. The aesthetic function must be within the call to the preceding geometry or statistic function. The group argument and/or characteristic argument(s) should not be set in ggplot().

10.1.1.1 The Identity Qualifier

The identity qualifier tells the preceding geometry or statistic function to interpret the value of the characteristic argument without changes. For scale functions with the alpha, linetype, shape, and size characteristics, there are two arguments to the scale function with the identity qualifier, … and guide. For functions with the colour and fill characteristics, there are three arguments to the function, …, guide, and aesthetic.

The argument ... is for arguments to the function discrete_scale() or continuous_scale(). See the help pages for the two functions for lists of the arguments of the functions. The arguments are not covered here.

The argument guide gives the name of the guide to be used by the scale (see Section 10.1.4). The default value of guide is "none" for the scale functions with the preceding six characteristics.

The argument aesthetics gives the kind of aesthetic on which to apply the color, colour (or color), or fill. There are four possible values for aesthetics: "colour", "fill", c("colour", "fill"), and c("fill", "colour").

If both color and fill are set in the aesthetic function, both can be set in a color, colour, or fill scale function. For example, geom_point(aes(shape=shape, fill=shape-19, color=shape-17)) + scale_shape_identity() + scale_fill_identity(aesthetic=c("color", "fill")) sets both the color and fill for the shapes 21–24. Here, the variable shape is an integer vector containing values between 21 and 24, inclusive.

For the scale functions with the color (or colour) characteristic, the aesthetic argument takes the default value of "colour". For fill, aesthetic takes the default value of "fill".

10.1.1.2 The Manual Qualifier

The scale functions with the manual qualifier create scales manually. The scale functions with the alpha, linetype, shape, and size characteristics and the manual qualifier have three arguments. The arguments are ..., for arguments to the function discrete_scale(); values, for the values that make up the scale; and breaks, for the break points or levels of the scale.

On the help page for the functions with the manual qualifier (which the functions share and from which the information here is taken), the arguments of discrete_scale() are listed and described. The arguments are not covered here.

The values argument gives the values of the characteristic to be associated with each level or break class of the grouping variable. The argument takes a vector of the kind that the characteristic takes. The length of the vector is the number of classes in the grouping variable. There is no default value for values.

Formally, the elements of the values argument can be named, where the names are explicitly character strings. The character string must contain the character strings associated with the grouping classes. (Note that, in an aesthetic function, the grouping variable cannot be numeric.) For example, geom_line(aes(linetype=cut(dpi, 2))) +

`scale_linetype_manual( values=c( "(85,2.05e+03]"="dotted",` `"(2.05e+03,4.01e+03]"="dashed" ) )` assigns the names of the two cut classes to two different line types.

The breaks argument gives information as to whether to plot a legend and, if a legend is printed, which grouping classes to include in the legend. The argument takes the value NULL, waiver(), or a character vector containing all or a subset of the character strings associated with the grouping classes. The argument can, also, take a function that creates the character vector, but the match between the grouping class character strings and the results of the function must be exact.

If breaks is set equal to NULL, no legend is plotted. If breaks is set equal to waiver(), a legend is plotted, and all of the grouping classes are included. If breaks is set equal to a character vector (or a call to a function that creates a character vector) of grouping class character strings, only the grouping classes with strings present in the vector are included in the legend. The default value of breaks is waiver().

10.1.1.3 The Alpha Characteristic

The functions, other than those with the qualifier identity or manual, for the characteristic alpha are the function with no qualifier and the functions with the continuous, binned, discrete, and ordinal qualifiers. All of the functions, except scale_alpha_discrete(), take two arguments, ... and range. The discrete function takes one argument, ...

According to the help page for the preceding alpha scale functions, the ... argument takes the arguments to the continuous_scale(), binned_scale(), or discrete_scale() function, depending on which scale function is run. See the help pages for the three functions for a list and description of the arguments.

The range argument takes a numeric vector of length two. The values of the elements must be between 0 and 1, inclusive, and give the range of the transparencies of the color(s) used to plot the shapes or lines. The value of 0 gives total transparency and of 1 gives total opacity. The default value of range is `c(0.1, 1)` for the four functions that use range.

10.1.1.4 The Color, Colour, and Fill Characteristics: Introduction

The scale functions, other than those with the identity and manual qualifiers, with fill, color, or colour for a characteristic are the scale functions with the continuous, hue, gradient, gradient2, gradientn, steps, steps2, stepsn, brewer, distiller, fermenter, grey, viridis_c, viridis_b, and viridis_d qualifiers. The color scales come in three versions, un-binned continuous scales, binned continuous scales, and discrete scales. Un-binned continuous scales have a continuous color bar for a legend by default. Binned continuous scales have a continuous bar with steps of color by default. Discrete scales have a legend with separate keys by default.

10.1.1.5 The Color, Colour, and Fill Characteristics: The Continuous Qualifier

For scale_colour_continuous() and scale_fill_continuous(), the functions work with numeric (continuous) data. The functions have two arguments, ... and type. The argument ... takes arguments to the continuous_scale() function. (See the help page for continuous_scale() for more information.)

From the help page for scale_colour_continuous(), the type argument takes the value "gradient", "viridis", or any function that returns the name of a continuous color scale. The default value of type is getOption("ggplot2.continuous.colour", default="gradient") for the colour characteristic and getOption("ggplot2. continuous.fill", default="gradient") for the fill characteristic.

10.1.1.6 The Color, Colour, and Fill Characteristics: The Hue Qualifier

The scale_colour_hue() and scale_fill_hue() functions create discrete scales, rather than continuous scales, and work with factor or character vectors. The functions take eight arguments: ..., for arguments to discrete_scale(); h, for a hue range; c, for a chroma level; l, for a luminance level; h.start, for a beginning value for the hue; direction, for the direction to take around the color wheel; na.value, for the color value to use for missing values; and aesthetics, for the type of aesthetic to color. (See Section 3.4.1.3 for a description of hue, chroma, and luminance, under the functions hsv() and hcl().)

The h argument takes a two-element numeric vector. The first value is the smallest value of the range of hues, and the second value is the largest value. The values that R uses are between 0 and 360, inclusive; however, the values that are entered for the range limits are reduced modulus 360, that is, a range of 15–375 goes in a circle from 15 back to 15. (Note that the hue scale is circular rather than linear, that is, the scale comes back to the starting color over a range size of 360.) The default value of h is c(0, 360) + 15 for both functions with the hue qualifier.

The c argument takes a one-element nonnegative numeric vector. According to the help page for the hue functions, the possible values depend on the values for the hue and luminance. The default value for the two hue functions is 100.

The l argument takes a one-element numeric vector with a value that is between 0 and 100, inclusive. The default value for the two hue functions is 65.

The h.start argument takes a one-element numeric vector. The default value is 0 for both hue functions.

The direction argument takes a one-element numeric vector. The value must be either 1 or -1. If set to 1, the hues are chosen in the counterclockwise direction around the color wheel. If set to -1, the direction is clockwise. The default value for direction is 1 for both hue functions.

The na.value argument takes a one-element color value vector (see Section 3.4.1 for kinds of color values). The default value of na.value is "grey50" for both hue functions.

The aesthetic argument behaves the same as in the identity scale function for colour and fill (see Section 10.1.1.1). The default values are "colour" for the colour hue function and "fill" for the fill hue function.

10.1.1.7 The Color, Colour, and Fill Characteristics: The Gradient Qualifiers

The scale functions with the fill, color, and colour characteristics and the gradient, gradient2, and gradientn qualifiers are used with continuous variables. The functions have seven, nine, and eight arguments, depending on whether the qualifier is gradient, gradient2, or gradientn. The nine functions share five arguments. The five arguments are ..., for arguments of the function continuous_scale(); space, for the color space; na.value (see Section 10.1.1.5); guide, for the name of the guide to use; and aesthetics (see 10.1.1.1).

The space argument takes only one possible value. The value is "Lab". According to the help page for the nine functions, other color spaces are deprecated.

The guide argument takes a one-element character vector. Only two values are possible, "colourbar" for a continuous scale and "legend" for a discrete scale. The default value is "colourbar" for the nine functions.

The functions with the gradient qualifier also take the arguments low and high, for the colors at the ends of the scale. The arguments take a color value vector of length one. The default values for low and high are "#132B43" and "#56B1F7", respectively, that is the scale goes from a dark navy blue to a clear mid-blue.

The functions with the gradient2 qualifier take the arguments low and high, along with the argument mid, for the color of the middle of the scale. The default values of low, mid, and high are `muted("red")`, `"white"`, and `muted("blue")`, respectively.

The three gradient2 functions also take the midpoint argument, for the midpoint of the scale – measured in the units of the variable for which the scale is created. The default value of midpoint is 0.

The functions with the gradientn qualifier also take the colours (or equivalently colors) argument, for the colors to be used in the scale, and the values argument, for – according to the help page for the functions – the distance along a continuum from 0 to 1 of each color in colours.

The colours (or colors) argument takes a vector of color values of arbitrary length (see Section 3.4.1 for information about color values). The colors are used to generate a continuous scale. There is no default value for colours (or colors).

The values argument takes the value NULL or a numeric vector of unique values of the same length as colours (or colors). The values must be between 0 and 1, inclusive. The default value for values is NULL.

10.1.1.8 The Color, Colour, and Fill Characteristics: The Step Qualifiers

The scale functions that have the colour, color, and fill characteristics and that have the steps, steps2, and stepsn qualifiers create scales in binned steps. The functions are for continuous variables.

The arguments to the nine step functions are the same as the respective arguments to the nine gradient functions. The arguments also take the same default values as the nine gradient functions, except that the default value for guide is "coloursteps" in the nine step functions.

10.1.1.9 The Color, Colour, and Fill Characteristics: The Brewery Qualifiers

The scale functions that have the colour, color, and fill characteristics and that have the brewer, distiller, and fermenter qualifiers share a help page. The three functions that have the brewer qualifier are for discrete variables. The six functions that have the distiller and fermenter qualifiers are for un-binned continuous and binned continuous variables, respectively.

The brewer, distiller, and fermenter functions take five, nine, and seven arguments, respectively. The nine functions share five arguments. The arguments are ..., for the arguments to the discrete_scale(), continuous_scale(), and binned_scale() functions, respectively; type, for the style of the scale; palette, for the color palette of the scale; direction (see Section 10.1.1.6); and aesthetics (see Section 10.1.1.1).

The type argument takes a character vector of length one. From the help page for the nine functions, the value of type must be one of "seq", for sequential scales; "div", for diverging scales; and "qual", for qualitative scales (see the help page for a description of the three types). The default value of type is "seq" in the nine functions.

The palette argument takes either a one-element character vector or one-element numeric vector. For the character vectors, the character string is the name of the palette enclosed in quotes. The list of the names of the palettes is on the help page for the functions, under the section named "Palettes." The palettes that are available by the integers depend on the value of type.

For type set equal to "seq", 18 palettes are available, so the argument palette can take integer values from 1 to 18. For type set equal to "div", nine palettes are available, so the argument palette can take integer values from 1 to 9. For type set equal to "qual", there are eight palettes available, so palette can take integer values from 1 to 8. Any of the palettes can be accessed by setting the palette argument to the name of the palette enclosed in quotes. The choice does not depend on the value of type. The default value of palette for the nine functions is 1.

The direction argument has different default values for different qualifiers. For the brewer qualifier, direction is set to 1 by default. For the distiller and fermenter qualifiers, direction is set to -1 by default.

For the functions with the distiller qualifier, the four arguments not covered in the preceding text are values, space, na.value, and guide – which are covered in Sections 10.1.1.6 and 10.1.1.7. The arguments values, space, and na.value take the same defaults as in the gradient scale and hue scale functions. The argument guide takes the value "colourbar".

For the functions with the fermenter qualifier, the two arguments not covered under the brewer qualifier are na.value and guide – covered in Sections 10.1.1.6 and 10.1.1.7. The default value for na.value is the same as in the preceding value, and the default value for guide is "coloursteps".

10.1.1.10 The Color, Colour, and Fill Characteristics: The Grey Qualifier

The functions scale_colour_grey() and scale_fill_grey() work with discrete data (character or factor data) and create scales in shades of gray. The functions take five arguments. The arguments are ..., for arguments to discrete_scale(); start and end, for the start and end values of the gray scale; na.value (see Section 10.1.1.6); and aesthetics (see Section 10.1.1.1).

The start and end arguments take one-element numeric vectors. The values must be between 0 and 1, inclusive. The smaller the value is, the darker the shade of gray is. The default values of start and end are 0.2 and 0.8, respectively.

The na.value argument takes the default value of "red" in the two grey functions. The aesthetics variable behaves as the argument behaves in Section 10.1.1.1.

10.1.1.11 The Color, Colour, and Fill Characteristics: The Viridis Qualifiers

The functions with the characteristics colour, color, and fill and the qualifiers viridis_c, viridis_b, and viridis_d are used for continuous un-binned scales, continuous binned scales, and discrete scales, respectively. The color scales, of which there are five versions for each of the nine functions, are suitable for many persons who cannot see some colors (have color blindness) because the scales work as well as gray scales as the functions work as colored scales.

The viridis_c functions and viridis_b functions take the same 11 arguments. The viridis_d functions take seven arguments – which are shared with the viridis_c and viridis_b functions.

The first seven arguments are ..., for arguments to the continuous_scale(), binned_scale(), and discrete_scale() functions, depending on which viridis function is chosen; alpha, for the level of transparency; begin, for the beginning level of the scale; end, for the ending level of the scale; direction (see Section 10.1.1.6); option, for the color scheme; and aesthetics (see Section 10.1.1.1).

The alpha argument takes a numeric vector of length one. The value must be between 0 and 1, inclusive. The default value of alpha is 1.

The begin and end arguments take numeric vectors of length one. The values must be between 0 and 1, inclusive. The default values of begin and end are 0 and 1, respectively.

The direction argument is described in Section 10.1.1.6. The default value for the nine viridis functions is 1.

The option argument takes a character vector of length one. The character vector can either be a capital letter or a name. From the help page for the viridis functions, the possible values are "A" or "magma", "B" or "inferno", "C" or "plasma", "D" or "viridis", and "E" or "cividis". The default value of option is "D" for the nine viridis functions.

The last four arguments for the functions with the viridis_c and viridis_b qualities are values, space, na.value, and guide, which are covered in Sections 10.1.1.6 and 10.1.1.7. The default values for values, space, and na.value are NULL, "Lab", and "grey50", respectively. The default values for guide are "colourbar" for the viridis_c functions and "coloursteps" for the viridis_b functions.

10.1.1.12 The Line Type Characteristics

The line type scale functions, other than the line type function with the identity and manual qualifiers, are scale_linetype(), scale_linetype_continuous(), scale_linetype_binned(), and scale_linetype_discrete(). The functions scale_linetype_continuous() and scale_linetype_binned() require numeric data. The function scale_linetype_discrete() requires discrete data.

According to the error message returned when attempting to set linetype to a continuous object in geom_line(), geom_path(), geom_curve(), and geom_segment(), linetype cannot be set equal to numeric data in an aesthetic function. If geom_line() and geom_path() are run with the preceding scale functions, the functions return an error.

If geom_segment() and geom_curve() are run with scale_linetype() or scale_linetype_continuous(), an error is given. If run with scale_linetype_binned(), the functions run, but the line types cannot be set. (To set the line types, use scale_linetype_identity().)

The functions scale_linetype() and scale_linetype_discrete() give the same result for discrete data. The functions can be used to set up the legend format for discrete (character or factor) variables.

The functions scale_linetype(), scale_linetype_binned(), and scale_linetype_discrete() take the same arguments. The arguments are ..., for arguments to the discrete_scale() function, and na.value, for the value given to missing values. The default value of na.value is "blank" for the three functions.

10.1.1.13 The Shape Characteristics

The scale functions with the shape characteristic, other than the shape functions with the qualifier identity or manual, are scale_shape() and scale_shape_binned(). The functions are used to assign shapes (symbols) to points. The function scale_shape() works with discrete data. The function scale_shape_binned() works with numeric data.

There are 25 shapes available to the functions associated with plot() (the integers that can be assigned to pch). There are ways to use any of the 25 symbols in the ggplot2 functions. (For example, geom_point(aes(shape=(1:25)[cut(dpi, 25)])) + scale_shape_identity() can be used to plot 25 levels of dpi for the 50 points in the LifeCycleSavings dataset. Single letters can be used in the same way.) However, by default, the ggplot2 functions only use six shapes, with two versions for the first three shapes – solid and outlined. The shapes are circles, squares, triangles, crosses, squares with a diagonal cross inside, and asterisks.

Both functions take the same two arguments. The arguments are …, for arguments to the function discrete_scale(), and solid, for whether to plot the circles, triangles, and squares as a solid color or as an outline.

The argument solid takes a logical vector of length one. If set to TRUE, a solid symbol is plotted. If set to FALSE, the shape is outlined. The default value of solid is TRUE.

10.1.1.14 The Size and Radius Characteristics

The scales for the size and radius characteristics affect the sizes of points and lines. There are five scale functions with the size or radius characteristic: scale_radius(), scale_size_area(), scale_size(), scale_size_binned_area(), and scale_size_binned(). The scale function with the radius characteristic sizes linearly. The scale functions with the size characteristic scale by area (proportional to the square of the radius). The five functions work with numeric data (continuous data).

The difference between scale_size_area() and scale_size() is that scale_size_area() scales so that a value of 0 scales to zero area. The scale_size() function does not. The functions with the binned qualifier create bins for the data before plotting the points or lines. (The preceding information is from the help page for the five functions – which the functions share.)

The scale_radius() and scale_size() functions have the same seven arguments with the same default values. The scale_size_binned() function has two more arguments and has one different default value. The scale_size_area() and scale_size_binned_area()

functions have two arguments, both the same in both functions, including the same default value for the second argument.

The seven arguments for the first three functions are name, for the title of the legend if there is a legend; breaks, for the class levels in the legend; labels, for the class level labels in the legend; limits, for the lower and upper limits of the legend; range, for the range of point or line sizes in the plot and legend; trans, for the transformation to be applied to the data; and guide, for the style of the scale in the legend.

The name argument takes one of the values NULL, a character vector of arbitrary length, and a function that returns a valid object. If name is set to NULL, no title is plotted. If a character vector, only the first element is used. The default value of name in the preceding three scale functions is the waiver() function, that is, the value to which the argument size is set, if size is the first or only aesthetic set.

The breaks argument takes one of NULL, a numeric vector of arbitrary length, the waiver() function, and a function that takes the limits (see in the following) and returns break points. If the value is NULL, no legend is plotted. If the value is a numeric vector, the numbers are with respect to the values that size is set to in the aesthetic function. If some of the breaks are outside the range of the data, the keys or bin borders associated with the breaks do not plot – unless the limits argument (see in the following) is set and the breaks are within the limits set by the argument. The default value of breaks is waiver() in the first three scale functions, that is, R chooses breaks based on the value of the argument trans (see in the following).

The labels argument takes one of NULL, the waiver() function, a character vector of the same length as breaks, and a function that takes the value of breaks and returns a character vector of labels. For the first three scale functions, the default value of labels is waiver(), that is, R calculates good labels based on the value of trans.

The limits argument takes one of NULL, a two-element numeric vector, and a function that accesses the default limits and uses the default limits to create new limits. If set to NULL, the default limits are used. If set to a numeric vector, the two values give the lower and upper limits of the scale. The value NA can be assigned to a limit to use the current value of the limit, according to the help page. For the preceding three scale functions, the default value of limits is NULL.

The range argument takes a two-element numeric vector. The numbers give the smallest and largest sizes for the points or lines that are scaled. For the preceding three functions, the default value of range is c(1, 6).

The trans argument takes a one-element character vector or a transformation object for a value. According to the help page for the size and area functions, a transformation object is a function that uses a transformation, such as exponentiation, and the inverse of the transformation, to create a vector of breaks and labels.

If the trans argument is a character vector, the character vector must contain the name of a transformation, such as "log10" or "exp". A transformation object must exist for the transformation. (See the help page for the size and radius functions for a list of transformation names for which transformation objects exist, as well as the transformation object names. Transformation objects can also be found in the scales package.)

A new transformation object can be created with the function trans_new() in the scales package. The names of the transformation objects have the form *transformation_ trans*, where transformation is the name of the transformation and trans is an extension.

The default value of trans is "identity" for the preceding three scale functions. The identity transformation makes no transformation to the data.

The guide argument takes either a one-element character vector or the output from a guide function (see in the following). The default value of guide for scale_radius() and scale_size() is "legend".

The scale_size_binned() function takes two more arguments, n.breaks, for the number of bin breaks, and nice.breaks, for whether to create nice-looking break points (e.g., 1000 instead of 1002.06). The n.breaks argument is not always followed, unless the nice.breaks argument is set to FALSE.

The n.breaks argument takes either the value NULL or a one-element numeric vector. The default value of n.breaks is NULL, that is, the transformation object determines the number of break points.

The nice.breaks argument takes a one-element logical vector. If set to TRUE, nice-looking break points are found. If set to FALSE, break points are set by a simpler method – without concern for the look of the break points. The default value of nice. breaks is TRUE.

The scale_size_binned() function has a default value for guide that is different. The default value of guide is "bins".

For the scale_size_area() and scale_size_binned_area() functions, the arguments are ..., for the arguments of the continuous_scale() function, and max.size, for the maximum size of the points or lines. The default value of max.size is 6 for both of the scale functions.

10.1.2 Setting the Order of Evaluation

The after_stat(), after_scale(), and stage() functions can be used within geometric functions to set the order of the evaluation of aesthetic arguments. When one of the preceding functions is used, the aesthetic argument is set equal to the preceding function within the aesthetic function of the geometry function.

Most geometric functions make use of a statistic function. By using after_stat(), a variable created by the statistic function can be used in calculating the value of an aesthetic argument.

The after_scale() function can be used to calculate new values for aesthetic arguments based on aesthetic arguments that have already been set. An aesthetic argument can be used on both sides of the equation.

The stage() function allows for the scaling of an aesthetic in multiple ways, both (either) after the statistic function is done and (or) after the initial scaling is done.

According to the help page for the three functions, if after_stat() is used, only those arguments created by the statistic function or that are in the environment from which ggplot() is called can be used to create a value for the aesthetic argument. The variables in the data frame are not available. The after_scale() function can only use variables created by the application of the initial aesthetic or variables in the parent environment. For stage(), variables from the data frame can only be used in the first argument of the function.

The after_stat() and after_scale() functions both take one argument, x, for the formula creating the value for the aesthetic. Both functions can be applied more than once. An example of using after_scale() twice is given in Listing 10-1.

Listing 10-1. Code showing an example of using after_scale() twice in one geometry function. Since two aesthetics are used for the variable, a warning is given when the code is run

```
ggplot(
  data.frame(
    LifeCycleSavings[ ord, ][ 1:49, ],
    LifeCycleSavings[ ord, ][ 2:50, ]
  ),
  aes(
    pop75,
```

```
          pop15,
          xend=pop75.1,
          yend=pop15.1
      )
    ) +

geom_segment(
  aes(
    group=cut(
      dpi.1,
      6
    ),
    color=after_scale(
      grey(
        ( group+1 )/9
      )
    ),
    size=after_scale(
      group-0.5
    )
  )
)
```

Note that both the color and size of the line segments are based on the value of group. A warning is given that the two aesthetics are based on the equivalent scales.

The stage() function takes three arguments. The arguments are start, for a function of a variable in the ggplot() or geometry data frame, with which the statistic function or the scaling function operates; after_stat, for a function of the variables created by the statistic function; and after_scale, for a function of the aesthetic variables. The default value of the three arguments is NULL. In Listing 10-2, an example of using stage() is given.

Listing 10-2. An example of using stage() to set fill colors in a histogram is given

```
ggplot(
  LifeCycleSavings,
  aes(
    pop75
```

```
  )
) +

geom_histogram(
  aes(
    color=cut(
      dpi,
      10
    ),
    fill=stage(
      cut(
        dpi,
        10
      ),
      after_scale=alpha(
        fill,
        0.6
      )
    )
  ),
  bins=10
)
```

Note that the aesthetic to which stage is assigned is fill and that the fill color is lightened by using the alpha() function on fill. The aesthetic argument color is set to the same color at full strength. (The example is based on an example on the help page for the three functions.)

10.1.3 Formatting Axes with the Scale and Coordinate Functions, Plus Some

The scale functions for which the characteristic is x or y and the coordinate functions both operate on the axes of a plot. According to the help pages for the functions, the scale functions operate before the statistic function used by the geometry function is run. The coordinate functions operate after the statistic function is run. For a scatterplot, both give the same result except that the tick marks differ.

The x and y scale functions have the continuous, binned, discrete, reverse, log10, sqrt, date, time, and datetime qualifiers. The coordinate functions begin with *coord_* and have the cartesian, fixed, flip, map, quickmap, munch, polar, sf, and trans characteristics.

10.1.3.1 The Scale Functions

The scale function with the continuous qualifier gives the usual scale for x or y aesthetics that are continuous (numeric and un-binned). The binned qualifier creates bins for continuous x or y aesthetics and plots the points at the center of the bins. The scale functions with the continuous and binned qualifiers only run with x and y aesthetics that are continuous. The scale function with the discrete qualifier runs on both continuous and discrete x and y aesthetics but does not provide axis ticks or axis tick labels for continuous aesthetics.

The scale function with the reverse qualifier reverses the order of the axis. The scale function with the log10 qualifier transforms the scale of the axis to a base 10 log scale and changes the plotted geometry accordingly. All values of x or y must be positive for the log10 qualifier. The scale function with the sqrt qualifier transforms the axis to the square root of the values in x or y and changes the plotted values accordingly. All values of x or y must be nonnegative.

The scale function with the date qualifier creates a scale with values that are dates. The x or y aesthetic argument must be of the Date class for the date scale function. The scale function with the datetime qualifier creates a scale with values for both dates and times. The aesthetic argument x or y must be of the POSIXct class.

The scale function with the time qualifier creates a scale with values of time. The x or y aesthetic must be numeric and is converted to the format of the hms class (that is hh:mm:ss, where hh is the hours, mm is the minutes between 00 and 59, and ss is the seconds from 00 to 59). The hms() function can be used to format numeric data to the hms class. The numeric data is interpreted as in seconds if no formatting is done. There is not upper limit for hours. The values can be negative.

10.1.3.2 The Coordinate Functions

The coordinate functions all affect both axes, except that the function coord_trans() can also affect just one axis. The functions transform the coordinates of the axes.

The coord_cartesian() function creates Cartesian (linear) coordinates. The function coord_fixed() gives a plot for which the units on the x axis are in a fixed ratio to the units on the y axis, independently of the size of the graphics device. The ratio is given by the ratio argument and is set to 1 by default.

The coord_flip() function flips the axes. The coord_map() and coord_quickmap() functions create coordinates of longitudes and latitudes. Three of the six arguments for the map characteristic functions are projection, for the type of map projection; xlim, for the longitudinal limits; and ylim, for the latitudinal limits, assuming the usual orientation.

The coord_polar() function uses polar coordinates. Three of the four arguments to the function are theta, for which of x or y to use for the angle; start, for the starting angle in radians, with 0 at the top of the plot; and direction, for the direction to go around the plot – the value of 1 for clockwise and -1 for counterclockwise.

The transformation to polar coordinates plots the relative sizes of variable assigned to theta through 360 degrees and ignores the absolute sizes of the values, except for the numbers in the labels. The other variable gives the radius for each value in theta.

The coord_sf() function creates coordinates for simple feature data. Simple features are spatial data.

According the help page for coord_munch(), the function is used within geometry functions. The function breaks the coordinates on the axes into small pieces for cleaner vector plotting.

The coord_trans() function provides for manual transformation of one or both axes by a function. The argument(s) x and/or y are set equal to a function name(s) in quotes or a transformation object(s). The transformation can be user generated. See Section 10.1.1.14 for more information about transformation names and transformation objects.

10.1.3.3 Other Axis Functions

There are a few other functions that affect axes. The xlab() and ylab() functions can be used to manually set axis labels. The lims(), xlim(), and ylim() functions can be used to set limits for an aesthetic variable or axis. The expansion() and expand_scale() functions are used as values for the expand argument in scale functions. The functions calculate the axis limits needed to put an area of a given size between the axes and the plot.

The dup_axis() and sec_axis() functions are used as values for the sec.axis argument in x and y scale functions. The functions format a second axis opposite the original axis. The dup_axis() function duplicates the original axis. The sec_axis() function creates a new axis based on a one-to-one transformation of the scale of the original axis.

The xlab() and ylab() functions have one argument, label, for the character string containing the label. (The label can also be assigned in a scale function by setting the argument name.)

The lims() function takes named two-element vectors, where the name is of an aesthetic argument (e.g., x=c(5,20)). The vectors can be of the numeric, character, factor, Date, POSIXct, or hms class, depending on the class of the aesthetic argument. The vectors are separated by commas in the call to lims().

The functions xlim() and ylim() take two single numeric values giving the lower and upper limits of the x or y axis. The functions are for numeric (continuous) axes.

The expansion() and expand_scale() functions have the same arguments. The arguments are add, for the value to add to and subtract from the axes for the expansion area, and mult, for a multiplicative expansion factor.

The dup_axis() and sep_axis() functions have the same five arguments. The arguments are trans (see Section 10.1.1.14), name, breaks, labels, and guide. (See the help page for continuous_scale(), binned_scale(), or discrete_scale() for a description of the four arguments – which help page function depends on the type of scale.) The default value of trans is NULL in sec_axis() and ~. in dup_axis(). The default values of name, breaks, labels, and guide are waiver() in sec_axis() and derive() in dup_axis().

10.1.4 The Guide and Draw Key Functions

The guide functions are used to format properties of the axes or the key to the scaling variables (e.g., a legend or color bar). Most of the guide functions are used within scale functions. (The guide argument appears in the list of the arguments of continuous_scale(), binned_scale(), and discrete_scale().) The draw key functions give the style of the keys used in legends.

10.1.4.1 The Guide Functions

There are nine guide functions that are supported in the ggplot2 package and five that are not supported, but that exist. Of the nine functions, one function, guide_axis(), provides structuring for axes. Two are colour/color duplicates. Four structure the key to the scaling variables. The four are guide_legend(), guide_colorbar(), guide_colorsteps(), and guide_bins(). One function, guide_none(), gives no legend or no axis tick marks and tick mark labels. One function, guides(), combines more than one guide in one object.

The functions are set by setting the argument guide equal to either a name in quotes or the full function (e.g., guide="bins" or guide=guide_bins()), in a scale function. See the help pages for the guide functions for a list of the arguments to the functions.

The Guides That Affect Axes

The guide_axis() function has six arguments. The arguments set the axis label, what to do when axis tick labels overlap, the angle of the labels, the position of the axis by side, and the order in which the axis plotting is done.

The guide_none() can be used with the x and y scale functions. The function is used to assign an axis label without tick marks or tick mark labels. The axis label is assigned to the title argument. The position of the label can be specified with the position argument, by setting the argument to "bottom", "left", "top", or "right".

The Guides That Affect the Key to the Scaling Variables

The guide_none() function can be used to suppress the key to the scaling variable when used with the scale functions that are not axis scale functions. The guide_legend() function sets up a legend with keys for the scaling variable (which is usually a function of the aesthetic arguments). The guide_bins() function sets up a strip of distinct steps with levels shown at the intersections of the steps. The steps are keys within blocks. The function guide_colorsteps() is a version of guide_bins() with keys that are rectangles filled with the colors of the scale. The three functions can be used with un-binned continuous (numeric) data, binned continuous (numeric) data, and discrete (character or factor) data.

The guide_colorbar() function can only be used with continuous data (un-binned or binned). For un-binned continuous data, the function plots a continuous graded color scale. The scale is labeled with increasing or decreasing levels of the scaling variable. For binned scales, guide_colorbar() behaves like guide_colorsteps().

The guides() function is used to easily assign a set of guides to plots. There are no specified arguments to guides. Instead, each guide is assigned to the aesthetic argument to which the guide is applied, and each guide is separated from the others by commas. The result can be assigned a name. The name can then be used in the functions added to ggplot(). The name is added to the geometry or statistic function and does not include parentheses. No scale function is necessary. In Listing 10-3, an example is given of using guides().

Listing 10-3. An example of code for setting up a set of guides using the function guides()

```
gd=guides(
  size=guide_legend(
    title="dpi"
  ),
  color=guide_legend(
    title=NULL
  )
)

ggplot(
  LifeCycleSavings,
  aes( pop75, pop15 )
) +

geom_point(
  aes(
    size=as.numeric(
      as.factor(
        cut( dpi, 5 )
      )
    ),
    color=after_scale(
      grey( (size+1)/12 )
    )
  )
) + gd
```

In the listing, the guides are first assigned to an object named gd. After the plot is set, the guides are run by including the name gd after the geometry function. Note that the guides are not set within a scale function.

10.1.4.2 The Draw Key Functions

There are 16 draw key functions. The names of the functions start with *draw_key_*, which is followed by the name of a geometry. The geometry names available are point, abline, rect, polygon, blank, boxplot, crossbar, path, vpath, dotplot, pointrange, smooth, text, label, vline, and timeseries. (Note that vpath is not a listed geometry but is included in the list from the help page for draw_key, from where the information here comes.)

The key styles are automatically assigned by the geometry and statistic functions, but the default key style can be changed. The draw key functions are assigned to the key_glyph argument in the geometry and statistic functions. (The key_glyph argument is in the layer() function. The geometry and statistic functions all call the layer() function.)

The form of the assignation is either the geometry name in quotes or the total function name without the ending parentheses and not in quotes (e.g., key_ glyph="abline" or key_glyph=draw_key_abline).

10.2 Functions That Cut, Summarize, and Facet

The cut functions discretize continuous (numeric) vectors. The facet functions plot several plots, where each plot contains the data associated with a value of a grouping variable. The summary functions give summaries of numeric vectors and can be done by groups. Most of the summary functions can be plotted on grouped (or ungrouped) data.

There are three cut functions in the ggplot2 package, three facet functions, and five summary functions. (The summary functions are based on functions in the Hmisc package and the dependencies of the Hmisc package.) There is also a function named resolution(), which gives the resolution (the smallest difference between different numbers) of a numeric vector.

10.2.1 The Cut Functions

The three cut functions in the ggplot2 package are cut_interval(), cut_number(), and cut_width(). The functions are based on the cut() function in the base function and can use the arguments of cut() as well as the arguments listed on the help page for the three functions. The first argument of the three functions is x, for the numeric vector to be cut into discrete factor levels.

The cut_interval() function cuts the range of the data into intervals based on either n, for the number of equal-length intervals, or length, for the length of the equal-length intervals. If the n argument is chosen, the width of the intervals is the range of the numeric vector divided by n.

If the length argument is chosen, the argument length does not necessarily divide evenly into the range of the data vector. The function determines the starting value for the intervals. Both n and length take a one-element numeric vector.

The cut_number() function has one argument, n, for the number of intervals. The function behaves like cut_interval() with the choice of n.

The cut_width() function provides more flexibility. The specified arguments, other than x, are width, for the width of the intervals; center, for the center of the first interval; boundary, for the beginning of the first interval; and closed, for whether to close the intervals on the left or right (closing a boundary means that a data point on the closed boundary of the interval is included in the interval).

The width, center, and boundary arguments take one-element numeric vectors. There is no default value for width. The default values of center and boundary are NULL.

The closed argument takes a one-element character vector, and the value must be "left" or "right". The default value is "right", that is, the intervals are closed on the right.

10.2.2 The Summary Functions and the resolution() Function

The summary functions in the ggplot2 package are used with the stat summary functions, that is, the functions that begin with *stat_summary*. The stat summary functions take the argument fun, to which the summary functions can be assigned. Four of the summary functions are based on functions in the Hmisc package, which must be installed for the functions to run, but need not be loaded. The functions are mean_cl_boot(), mean_cl_normal(), median_hilow(), and mean_sdl(). The fifth function is mean_se(). At the end of the section, the function resolution() is covered.

The summary functions all take two arguments: x, for the numeric vector to be summarized, and ..., for the arguments to the function in the Hmisc package with the preceding names preceded by the letter s. The functions all return a data frame of length three. The names of the data.frame elements are y, ymin, and ymax.

The mean_cl_boot() and mean_cl_normal() functions give the mean of the data and confidence interval limits for the mean of the data based on bootstrapping the data or based on the normal distribution (using quantiles of the t distribution), respectively. The median_hilow() function gives the median of the data and the lower and upper empirical quantiles of the data based on the level of confidence. For the three functions, the level of the confidence interval is set by the argument conf.int and takes the value of 0.95 by default.

The mean_sdl() and mean_se() functions return the mean of the numeric vector, the mean minus a constant multiplier multiplied by the standard deviation of the vector or the standard error of the mean, and the mean plus a constant multiplier multiplied by the standard deviation of the vector or the standard error of the mean. For mean_sdl(), the standard deviation of the vector is used. For mean_se(), the standard error of the mean is used. The multiplier is set with the mult argument in both functions. By default, the value of mult is 2 for mean_sdl() and 1 for mean_se().

In Listing 10-4, code for the example in Figure 10-1 is given. The code and figure show the use of the function mean_cl_boot() with the default values of the function.

Listing 10-4. The code for the example in Figure 10-1 of using mean_cl_boot() in stat_summary()

```
ggplot(
  LifeCycleSavings,
  aes(
    pop75,
    pop15
  )
) +

geom_point(
) +

labs(
  title="Example of Using mean_cl_boot() with stat_summary()"
) +

scale_x_binned(
) +
```

```
stat_summary(
  fun.data = "mean_cl_boot",
  colour = "grey60",
  size = 0.5
)
```

In Figure 10-1, the code in Listing 10-4 is run. The summary statistics are in mid-gray.

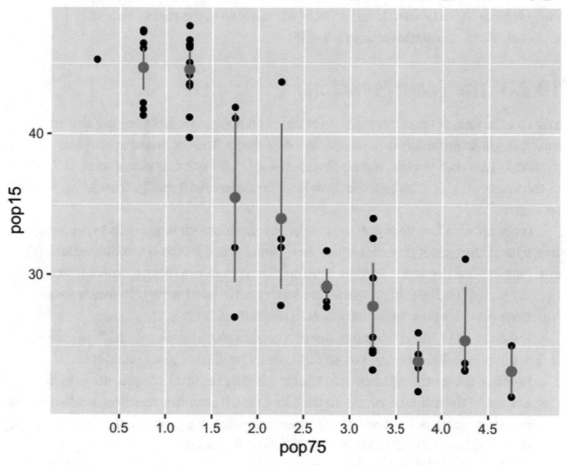

Figure 10-1. *An example of using mean_cl_boot() with stat_summary() and scale_x_binned() to plot summary statistics on a scatterplot within bins*

Note that scale_x_binned() is used to bin the pop75 values. The mean and confidence intervals are of the pop15 values within each bin. The means and confidence intervals are in mid-gray. The plotted data points are black.

The resolution() function finds the resolution of a numeric vector. The resolution is the smallest difference between adjacent values within the vector. If two adjacent values are the same, the resolution is set to 1. The function resolution() takes two arguments: x, for the numeric vector, and zero, for whether to automatically include the value 0 in the vector.

The x argument takes a numeric vector of arbitrary length. The zero argument takes a one-element logical vector. If set to TRUE, a 0 is added to the vector. If set to FALSE, no 0 is added. The default value of zero is TRUE.

10.2.3 The Facet Functions

The facet functions create multiple plots based on applying a grouping variable or multiple grouping variables to vectors in a data frame. The data used in the plots are from the given data vectors, but no plot shares data with another plot, and all of the data in the vectors is plotted. There are three facet functions, facet_null(), facet_wrap(), and facet_grid().

There are also functions that are used to create values for arguments in the facet_ wrap() and facet_grid() functions. The vars() function quotes the grouping variable(s) and behaves like the aes() function. The function is used with the argument facets in facet_wrap() and with the arguments row and col in facet_grid(). There are also functions used with the argument labeller (see in the following).

The facet_null() function is the function used to plot a single panel. The function is the function called by default when facet_wrap() and facet_grid() are not called. The function takes one argument, shrink, for whether to shrink the plot down to the dimensions of the output from the statistic function, if a statistic function is called, or the statistic function associated with the geometry function, if a geometry function is called. The default value of shrink is TRUE, that is, do the shrinkage.

The facet_wrap() function takes a vector of plots (the facets) and, by default, plots them from left to right. New lines are started as the function determines a new line is appropriate. The first argument is facets, for the one or more variables to be used for faceting the data. The value of the argument can take forms like vars(var1), "var1", ~ var1, vars(var1, var2, var3), var2 ~ var1, ~ var1 + var2, c("var1", var2"), and var3 ~ var1 +

var2, where var1, var2, and var3 are the names of the faceting variables and are variables in the data frame or are expressions based on variables in the data frame. If the function labeller() is used, the variables that are expressions should be assigned a name.

The number of rows and/or columns can be specified, but there must be enough places for the total number of facet plots. Otherwise, an error occurs. The direction of plotting can be changed from left-to-right to top-to-bottom. The position of the facet plot labels can be changed from the top of each plot to any of the other sides of each plot.

The facet_grid() function creates a matrix of plots. The first two arguments are rows and cols, for the variables to put in the rows and columns. One or the other or both can be specified. The argument rows can take the same kinds of values as the argument facets in facet_wrap(). The argument cols must be set equal to NULL or variable name(s) and/or expression(s) enclosed by the vars() function parentheses and separated by commas.

The levels of the value of rows go down the columns, and the levels of the value of cols go across the rows. By default, the facet labels for the rows go to the right side, and the facet labels for the columns go across the top.

A choice can be made about whether the plots should be the same size, whether to switch the row and/or column facet labels to the bottom and/or left, and whether to plot margin plots. Row margins, column margins, or both margins can be plotted.

The functions facet_wrap() and facet_grid() share five arguments. The first of the arguments tells the function whether the scales should be the same for the plots and, if not, what should be allowed to vary. By default, the plot scales are the same. The second is shrink, covered under facet_null().

The fourth tells the function whether to treat the layout with the rows starting at the top and the columns at the left or to have the rows start at the bottom and the columns at the left. The default is that rows start at the top.

The fifth tells the function whether to drop row and column combinations for which there is no data. By default, combinations with no data are dropped.

The argument switch in facet_wrap() is soft deprecated and should not be used. The argument facets in facet_grid() is deprecated and should not be used.

The third argument, labeller, takes a function of the labeller class. The value that labeller takes is either the name of a function of the labeller class (unquoted and with no parentheses), a call to the function as.labeller(), or a call to the function labeller(). In labeller() the names of the faceting variables are assigned a function of the labeller class or a call to as.labeller(). The function labeller() is used to assign different labeling functions to different faceting variables.

There are six preset labeling functions (which start with *label_*) for formatting and setting panel labels. The extensions of the labeling functions are value, for using the values of the variable for labels; both, for using both the variable name and the values of the variable for labels; context, for using the value if there is one faceting variable and both the variable name and the value if there are more than one faceting variable; parsed, for using names generated with plotmath() as labels; bquote(), for assigning names generated by plotmath() to labels for rows and columns; and wrap_gen, for using the strwrap() function to wrap the label text.

The function as_labeller() is used to create new labeling functions. To assign facet labels that are different from the default labels, as_labeller() must be used. If there are more than one faceting variable on which to change the labels, more than one labeling function is created (see Listing 10-5).

When using as_labeller(), the format must be correct. The first argument, x, can be a function with the correct form or a vector of values of the factor variable converted to names and set equal to the character strings containing the new facet labels. For example, if the values of a factor variable named process are "fn" and "1rw" and the labels for "fn" and "1rw" should be "Finished" and "Raw 1", then the expression c(fn="Finished", `1rw`="Raw 1") entered into as_labeller() as the value of x creates a function of the labeller class that gives the desired result. The labeller function created by as.labeller() is entered into labeller(). Note that, since "1rw" starts with a number, 1rw cannot be a legal name in R; however, `1rw` is a legal name. The backticks make the name legal.

In Listing 10-5, an example is given of using facet_wrap(), vars(), as_labeller(), and labeller(). The code is run in Figure 10-2.

Listing 10-5. Code for the example in Figure 10-2 of using facet_wrap(), vars(), as_labeller(), and labeller()

```
ggplot(
  LifeCycleSavings,
  aes(
    dpi
  )
) +

labs(
  title="Example of Using
```

```
facet_wrap(), vars(), labeller() and as_labeller()"
) +

geom_histogram(
  bins=7
) +

facet_wrap(
  facets=vars(
    cpop15=cut_number(
      pop15,
      n=2
    ),
    cpop75=cut_number(
      pop75,
      n=2
    )
  ),
  labeller=labeller(
    cpop15= as_labeller(
      x=c(
        `[21.4,32.6]`="% < age 15: 21.4% to 32.6%",
        `(32.6,47.6]`="% < age 15: 32.6% to 47.6%"
      )
    ),
    cpop75= as_labeller(
      x=c(
        `[0.56,2.17]`="% > age 75: 0.56% to 2.17%",
        `(2.17,4.7]`="% > age 75: 2.17% to 4.70%"
      )
    )
  )
)
```

In Figure 10-2, the code in Listing 10-5 is run.

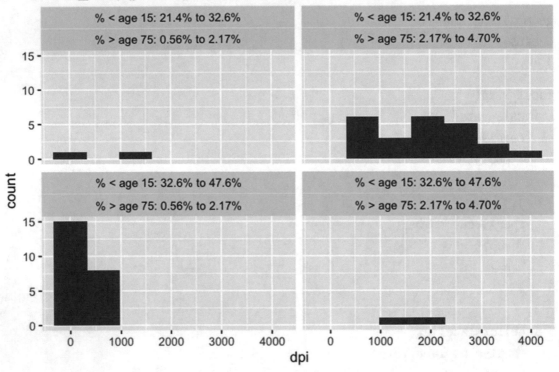

Figure 10-2. *An example of using facet_wrap() with vars(), as_labeller(), and labeller()*

Note that the labels are in the order that the faceting variables appear in the argument facets. Also, the first value of the first faceting variable stays the same as the values of the second faceting variable increase while the plots go from left to right. And the function creates a line break after the second plot, which creates a nice-looking figure. See the help pages for labeller() and as.labeller() for a list of arguments and more examples.

10.3 Working with Plots, Automatic Plots, and Prototypes

In this section, the functions that save, plot, and print plots are covered. Functions that create functions that automatically create a plot based on the class of the object(s) plotted are gone over. Last, the functions that create prototypes are described.

In Subsection 10.3.1, the functions ggsave(), plot() for ggplot objects, and print() for ggplot objects are covered. In Subsection 10.3.2, the functions auto_plot() and auto_layer() are presented. In Subsection 10.3.3, the functions used to create prototypes are given.

10.3.1 The ggsave() Function and the plot() and print() Functions Applied to ggplot Objects

The function ggsave() is a function that saves a plot to a file outside of R. The kind of graphics file created can be set by the extension given the file or by specifying the kind of device. The functions plot() and print(), when applied to ggplot objects, are useful when ggplot() is called within a function. Both functions, operating on an object of the ggplot class, create a plot.

The first argument of ggsave() is filename, for the file name to be assigned to the plot (enclosed in quotes). The file name does not include the path to where the file is to be saved, which is specified by the argument path (also enclosed in quotes) and which is the workspace by default.

The second argument of ggsave() is plot, for the plot to save. The argument plot, by default, saves the plot that is on the graphics device. Otherwise, plot can be assigned to the name of an object containing a plot generated by the ggplot() function or the code for the plot.

The third argument is device, for the kind of graphics format to use. The argument can be either the file extension in quotes or the name of the function that generates plots of the given extension, with the open and close parentheses (see Section 6.1 for a discussion of graphics devices and graphics formats). From the help page for ggsave(), the list of available extensions is "eps", "ps", "tex", "pdf", "jpeg", "tiff", "png", "bmp", "svg", and, on MS Windows devices, "wmf".

The fourth argument is path, described in the preceding text under the first argument. There are seven more arguments, including the last argument, ..., for the arguments to the graphics device function. The arguments give a scaling factor and the width, height, units, and resolution of the plot. By default, the scaling factor is 1, the width and height are given by the size of the graphics device, and the resolution is 300 dots per inch.

The tenth argument is limitsize, for whether to limit the size to 50 inches by 50 inches. According to the help page, the argument protects against the common mistake of using sizes in pixels rather than inches, centimeters, or millimeters. The default value of limitsize is TRUE.

The functions plot() and print() are used when ggplot() is run within a function (e.g., to create multiple plots by looping over datasets) If the usual aesthetic function is used, the functions give an error. See the introduction to Section 8.2 for the aesthetic functions that are used inside of functions calling ggplot().

If the correct aesthetic function is used and the ggplot() functions are run, but not within a plot() or print() function, then the functions run but the plots are not plotted. The plot() or print() function generates the plots externally.

10.3.2 The autoplot() and autolayer() Functions

The autoplot() and autolayer() functions are used to create a basic format for a class of objects. I think that once autoplot() (or autolayer()) is set for a class of objects within a workspace, when the class of objects is called in ggplot() (or layer()), the format in autoplot() (or autolayer()) is the starting format. So use with caution.

In Listing 10-6, an example is given of setting autoplot() for objects of the ggplot class. The assignation makes no sense, since an object of the ggplot class plots just by being entered at the R prompt, but the listing does demonstrate setting autoplot() for a class.

Listing 10-6. An example of setting autoplot() to plot objects of the ggplot class

```
> test.plot = ggplot( LifeCycleSavings, aes( pop75, pop15 ) ) + geom_
point() + geom_line()

> class( test.plot )
[1] "gg"      "ggplot"

> autoplot.ggplot = function(x) x

> autoplot( test.plot )
```

Note that one of the classes of the object test.plot is ggplot. Also, the function autoplot() automatically determines that a method exists for objects of the ggplot class, so the ggplot extension is not used in the call to autoplot().

10.3.3 Prototype Functions in the ggplot2 Package

The ggplot2 package has a number of functions for creating and working with ggplot2 prototype functions. There are five functions associated with prototypes in the ggplot2 package, ggproto(), for creating prototype functions; ggproto_parent(), for accessing a parent function of a prototype function; is.ggproto(), for testing whether a function is a prototype function; and format() and print(), for the format() and print() methods used with the prototype function.

According to the help page for ggproto(), the function implements an object-oriented styled approach to programming in R. The approach gives functions that run quicker than other approaches in R and that work across packages.

The function ggproto() has three arguments, `_class`, for the class name to give to the objects which the prototype function creates; `_inherit`, for the object of the ggproto class from which the prototype function inherits; and ..., for the named values that make up the prototype. The values can be any R object, including objects of the atomic types and functions.

The `_class` and `_inherit` arguments can be set to NULL and are set to NULL by default. The ... argument contains the objects – usually variables and function definitions – that make up the prototype function. The objects are separated by commas.

A function definition can refer to the prototype function by using the argument self in the argument list of the function definition. The objects in the prototype function can then be referred to with the notation self$*variable_name*, where variable_name is the name of the object in the prototype function.

The variables set in the prototype function can be updated at each call to the prototype function by setting the variable self$variable_name – with variable_name being the name of the variable that is to be set – equal to an expression. The expression can contain self$variable_name; self$variable_name_other, with variable_name_other being the name of another variable set in the prototype function; and arguments in the argument list of the function definition.

The function ggproto_parent() has two arguments, parent, for the names of the parent prototype function, and self, to refer to the prototype function being defined. Neither has a default value.

According to the help page for ggproto(), a function defined in the parent prototype function is referred to with the expression ggproto_parent(*parent_prototype_function_name*, self)$*defined_function_name*, where parent_prototype_function_name is the name of the prototype function and defined_function_name is the name of a function defined within the prototype function. The arguments to the function that is defined in the parent prototype function are set within parentheses after the expression `ggproto_parent( parent_prototype_function_name, self )$defined_function_name`.

The function is.ggproto() takes one argument, x, for the object to be tested. If the object is of the ggproto class, TRUE is returned. Otherwise, FALSE is returned. There is no default value for x.

The help page for ggproto(), which is shared with ggproto_parent() and is.ggproto(), contains simple examples of using ggproto() and ggproto_parent(). The help page for register_theme_elements() contains a practical example of using ggproto().

PART III

Appendixes

Plots for Contingency Tables and Discrete Data

In Table A-1, functions that create graphics for discrete data and contingency tables are given. Contingency tables are created by the function table(), where the variables to be included in the table are separated by commas in the call to table(), entered as a list object or entered as a data.frame object.

Table A-1. *Functions for plotting contingency tables and other forms of discrete data*

Function Name	Description
assocplot( )	For a two-dimensional contingency table or a numeric matrix (x). The first variable is plotted on the horizontal axis and the second on the vertical axis. The difference of the value in a cell and the estimated expected value for the cell is plotted, as a rectangle, against the horizontal and vertical classes. The width of a rectangle is proportional to the value in the cell. By default, negative differences are red and plotted down. Positive differences are black and plotted up.
barplot( )	For a numeric vector or matrix (x). For a vector, a bar is plotted for each element of the vector, where the height of the bar is given by the value of the element. For a matrix, the values in each row are plotted together, either stacked or side-by-side.
fourfoldplot( )	For a two-by-two-by-k contingency table or a two-by-two matrix (x). For each of the k classes, a plot is drawn showing a measure of the association between the classes. The plots are circular.

(continued)

© Margot Tollefson 2021
M. Tollefson, *Visualizing Data in R 4*, https://doi.org/10.1007/978-1-4842-6831-5_11

Table A-1. (*continued*)

Function Name	Description
heatmap()	For a numeric matrix (x). Draws a heatmap of the columns of the matrix.
mosaicplot()	For a contingency table based on multiple variables (x) or a formula connecting categorical variables (formula). Creates squares sized by the count in each cell and ordered by the classes in each variable. The first variable goes across the top, the second down the left side, the third across the top within the first, the fourth down the left side within the second, and so forth.
pie()	For a nonnegative numeric vector (x). Generates a pie chart – the areas of the slices in the pie are proportional to the values in the vector.
spineplot()	For a numeric or factor vector (x) and a factor vector (y). Can also be used with a two-dimensional contingency table (x) or with a formula connecting y to x with a tilde (formula). Creates a mosaic plot when both variables are categorical. Creates a spinogram when x is numeric. (For a spinogram, the classes in y are assigned different colors, and x is split into equal-length bins. The x bins are sized according to how many observations fall in the bin. Color blocks are plotted above each region giving the y classes of the observations within the region.

Plots for Continuous Variables

In Table B-1, functions that create graphics for continuous variables are given. Continuous variables are any kind of numeric variable.

Table B-1. *Functions for plotting continuous variables*

Function Name	Description
boxplot()	For a numeric vector (x), multiple numeric vectors separated by commas (…), a list of numeric vectors (x), or a formula with a numeric vector on the left and one or more categorical variables (can be numeric) on the right (formula). Plots boxplots for the variable(s) in the first three cases. Plots boxplots of the variable on the left by the variable(s) on the right for the formula case.
cdplot()	For a numeric vector (x) and a categorical vector of the same length (y) or a formula with a numeric vector on the left and a categorical variable on the right (formula). Plots conditional densities using the categorical variable for the conditioning. The densities are plotted in layers. In the vertical dimension, the conditional density for each class is normalized so that the densities sum to one.
dotchart()	For a numeric vector or matrix (x). Can group by using the groups argument. Plots a point at the value of x and a value of y equal to the index value (or row number) of x.

(continued)

© Margot Tollefson 2021
M. Tollefson, *Visualizing Data in R 4*, https://doi.org/10.1007/978-1-4842-6831-5_12

Table B-1 (*continued*)

Function Name	Description
hist()	For a single numeric vector (x). Plots a histogram of the vector.
matplot()	For two numeric objects, each of which can be a vector or a matrix (x and y). The lengths of vectors and the number of rows of matrices must be equal. The first column of y (or y, if y is a vector) plots against the first column of x (or x, if x is a vector). The second column of y plots against the second column of x and so forth. If the number of columns of y is not equal to the number of columns of x, the columns of the smaller matrix (or the vector) cycle(s). Points, lines, or points and lines can be plotted. The plots are all plotted in the same plotting region.
pairs()	For a matrix or data frame that can be converted to numeric with as.numeric() or data.matrix(), respectively (x). Or for a formula with variables that are vectors that can be converted to numeric (formula). Scatterplots are plotted for each column or vector against each other column or vector. All are plotted in a matrix of plots that are in one figure.
stem()	For a numeric object (vector, matrix, or array) (x). A stem-and-leaf plot is created using all of the numbers in the object.
stripchart()	For a single numeric vector (x), a list of numeric vectors (x), or a formula with a numeric vector on the left of the tilde and a grouping variable on the right side (x). The grouping variable can be of any atomic mode except raw. If x is a list, for each vector in the list, a horizontal line of plotting characters (squares by default) is plotted at the values in the vector. For a formula, a horizontal line of points is plotted for each group. Each vector or group has one line.

APPENDIX C

Functions That Plot Multiple Plots

In Table C-1, functions that plot multiple plots are listed.

Table C-1. *Functions for plotting multiple plots*

Function Name	Description
coplot()	For a formula with two numeric vectors along with one or two conditioning variables (formula). The conditioning variable(s) can be of any atomic mode except raw or complex. The argument formula takes values of the form x ~ y	g1 or x ~ y	g1 + g2, where x and y are the numeric vectors and g1 and g2 are conditioning variables. The function generates a separate plot for each condition level. The plots start at the bottom left and go to the right. By default, line breaks are set by coplot(), but can be set in the function call.
lag.plot()	For numeric vectors or matrices, usually time series (i.e., of class ts or mts) (x). Plots the original vector or matrix against lagged values of the vector or matrix. The number of lags is set by the argument lags, or a number of specific lags can be set by the argument set.lags. For matrices, the lags to the first column are plotted first, and then the lags to the second column, and so on. The plots start at the upper left and go right. The function sets line breaks by default, but the layout can be set.
pairs()	See Appendix B.

(continued)

© Margot Tollefson 2021
M. Tollefson, *Visualizing Data in R 4*, https://doi.org/10.1007/978-1-4842-6831-5_13

Table C-1. (*continued*)

Function Name	Description
stars()	For a matrix or data frame (x). The variables can be of any mode. Plots star plots, conic segment plots, or, if the locations argument is a two-element numeric vector, a spider plot. For matrices and data frames, a plot is generated for each row of the matrix or data frame. For spider plots, one plot is made out of the variables in the matrix or data frame. The plot is plotted at the point given by locations and looks somewhat like a spider web.

APPENDIX D

Smoothers

In Table D-1, functions that smooth data are given. Most of the smoothers do not automatically plot the smoothed data, which can be plotted with a call to plot() (or with lines() or points() after a call to plot()).

Table D-1. *Functions for smoothing data*

Function Name	Description
kernel()	For a one-element character vector or a numeric vector (coef). The possible character strings (preset kernels) for coef are "daniell", "dirichlet", "fejer", or "modified.daniell". The function gives the design of the kernel to use with smoothers that use a kernel. Returns an object of class tskernel. Can be plotted with plot().
kernapply()	For a numeric vector or matrix or an object of the ts, mts, or tskernel class (x) and a kernel (k). The argument k is set equal to a call to kernel(). Depending on the value of x, kernapply() smooths the vector, the columns of the matrix, the time series, or the individual time series in the time series matrix. Can be plotted with plot().
ksmooth()	For two numeric vectors of the same length (x and y) and a kernel (kernel) that must be set to "box" or "normal". Uses the Nadaraya-Watson kernel regression estimator. Can be plotted with plot().
loess.smooth()	For two numeric vectors of the same length (x and y). Smooths by the local polynomial regression (loess) method. Can be plotted with plot().
lowess()	For one numeric vector (x) or two numeric vectors of the same length (x and y). Smooths by locally weighted polynomial regression. Can be plotted with plot().

(continued)

© Margot Tollefson 2021
M. Tollefson, *Visualizing Data in R 4*, https://doi.org/10.1007/978-1-4842-6831-5_14

Table D-1. (continued)

Function Name	Description
runmed()	For a numeric vector (x) and a one-element numeric vector giving the width for the smoother (k). Smooths with a running median. Can be plotted with plot().
scatter.smooth()	For a numeric vector (x) or two numeric vectors of the same length (x and y). Plots the points and a line smoothed with loess().
smooth()	For a numeric vector or time series (x). Smooths with one of six running median smoothers developed by Tukey. Can be plotted with plot().
smoothScatter()	For one (x) numeric vector or two equal-length numeric vectors (x and y). Plots a version of a scatterplot with colored splotches. Smooths with a two-dimensional kernel density estimator.
smooth.spline()	For one numeric vector (x), two equal-length numeric vectors (x and y), or a time series (x). Smooths with a cubic smoothing spline. Can be plotted with plot().
supsmu()	For two numeric vectors of the same length (x and y). Smooths with Friedman's "super smoother". Can be plotted with plot().
tsSmooth(StructTS( ))	For a single time series (x). StructTS() fits a structural time series model. At the current time, tsSmooth only runs with an object of the StructTS class. If a call to tsSmooth() is plotted with plot(), two or three plots are plotted, depending on whether the frequency of the time series is 1 or greater than 1, respectively. The plots are of the level, trend, and seasonal components of the fitted model.

APPENDIX E

Plots for Time Series

In Table E-1, functions that are used for time series vectors and matrices are given.

Table E-1. *Functions for plotting contingency tables*

Function Name	Description
acf() and pacf()	For a time series vector or matrix (of class ts or mts) or a numeric vector or matrix (x). Plots the autocorrelation or autocovariance (acf) and the partial autocorrelation (pacf) against the lagged time series. (Only the univariate case works for pacf() – multiple time series and matrices give nonsense.) The number of lags to plot can be specified by the argument lag.max. An object that has been created by either function has class acf and can be plotted with plot().
ccf()	For two numeric vectors or two time series (objects of the ts class) (x and y). Plots the cross-correlations or cross-covariances between x and the lags of y – both forward and backward and starting at 0. The argument lag.max sets the maximum lag to plot. A call to ccf() returns an object of the acf class – which can be plotted with plot().
cpgram()	For a single time series (object of the ts class) (ts). Plots the cumulative periodogram.
lag.plot()	See Appendix C.

(continued)

© Margot Tollefson 2021
M. Tollefson, *Visualizing Data in R 4*, https://doi.org/10.1007/978-1-4842-6831-5_15

Table E-1. (*continued*)

Function Name	Description
monthplot(), monthplot(stl( )), monthplot(StructTS( ))	For a single time series, a call to stl() (for fitting a seasonal decomposition of a time series by loess), a call to StructTS() (for fitting a structural time series by maximum likelihood estimation), or a numeric vector (monthplot() assumes 12 periods per cycle for the numeric vector) (x). The function estimates and plots a graphic estimator for each period and plots the estimators by period across the plotting region.
ts.plot()	For single and multiple time series, separated by commas (...). Plots multiple time series with the same frequency on the same plot.
tsdiag()	For a call to arima() or StructTS() (object). Plots three diagnostic plots for the fitted time series model. The plots are the standardized residuals from the model, the autocorrelation function of the model, and the p-values of the Ljung-Box statistics for the model.
tsSmooth()	See Appendix D.

APPENDIX F

Miscellaneous Plotting Functions

In Table F-1, some miscellaneous functions for plotting not covered elsewhere are given.

Table F-1. *Miscellaneous functions for plotting*

Function Name	Description
biplot()	For two two-column numeric matrices, not usually with the same number of rows (x and y), or for a call to prcomp() or princomp() (x). Plots two sets of data, both on the same plotting region. By default, the second plot is in red and plots arrows, with the tick marks on the right and top sides and in red. The scale for the first plot is on the left and bottom, and the points and scale are in black. Both the points in the first plot and the points in the second plot are labeled, the first in black and the second in red. The red labels are Var1, Var2, … Varn by default, where n is the number of rows in the y matrix.
contour()	See Section 4.3.5.
curve()	See Section 4.3.2.
image()	See Section 4.2.4.
Interaction.plot()	For two factor vectors (can be any atomic mode except raw) and a numeric vector, all the same length (x.factor, trace.factor, and response). A function (by default mean and set by the fun argument) is applied to the third vector within the crossed factor levels (found by crossing the x.factor and trace.factor vectors). The result is plotted against x.factor. A line is plotted for each level of trace.factor.

(continued)

M. Tollefson, *Visualizing Data in R 4*, https://doi.org/10.1007/978-1-4842-6831-5_16

Table F-1. (*continued*)

Function Name	Description
grconvertX(), grconvertY()	Gives locations of points in nine different units. The units are related to the axis scales, absolute size, or graphics device, figure, or plot. For either the x or the y axis.
persp()	For a numeric matrix (z or, if x and y take the default values, can be the first argument listed and not named). If x and y are supplied, the two must be ascending numeric vectors. The number of columns in z gives the length of x, and the number rows in z gives the length of y. Plots a perspective plot. Creates a sense of three dimensions with x, y, and z axes shown.
qqline()	For a numeric vector (y). By default, plots a line through the 0.25 and 0.75 quantiles of y and those of a standard normal distribution (on the x axis). Can add a line to a plot generated by qqnorm() or qqplot() or plot a standalone plot.
qqnorm()	For a numeric vector (y). Plots the sorted y values against quantiles of the normal distribution.
qqplot()	For two numeric vectors (x and y) which are not necessarily the same length. Plots the shorter vector against quantiles of the longer vector.
screeplot()	For a list containing an element named sdev that contains nonnegative numeric values. Plots a bar chart of the square of the values in sdev. For principal component analysis, the result is a screeplot. (The output from both prcomp() and princomp() is a list with the sdev element.)
sunflowerplot()	For a numeric vector or two numeric vectors of the same length (x or x and y). Plots like plot(), except places on the plot with more than one observation are plotted as "sunflowers", having as many petals as there are coincident observations.
termplot()	For a call to a regression function (like lm() or glm()), which generates a list that contains an element named terms (model). For the independent variables in the model, termplot() plots a plot for each variable. The value of the regression coefficient is multiplied by the values of the variable and plotted against the variable. Each variable generates one page. The partial residuals for each variable are also plotted if the argument partial.resid is set to TRUE.
xspline()	For a numeric vector (x) or two numeric vectors of the same length (x and y). Connects the points with lines. Adds to an existing plot.

Index

A

abline() function, 115–117

absVal argument, 225

add.smooth argument, 215

adj argument, 90, 140, 143, 149

aes() function, 290, 315, 324

Aesthetic arguments, 282, 283, 317, 325, 326, 328, 330, 331, 337, 340, 349, 352, 360

Aesthetic functions, 282, 292, 315–318, 320

after_scale() function, 360

after_stat() and after_scale() functions, 360

aliases, 32

alpha() function, 362

Ancillary functions, 4, 10, 11, 61, 83, 88, 99

angle argument, 122, 125, 295, 297, 299

annotate() function, 323, 330

annotation_custom() function, 330, 334–336, 343

Annotation functions, 293

    annotate(), 330, 331, 333

    annotation_logticks(), 337, 338

    annotation_map()/annotation_raster(), 340–343

    definition, 330

    grob argument, 334–336

annotation_logticks() function, 330, 337

annotation_map() function, 330, 340, 342

annotation_raster() function, 330, 340, 343

argument pch and lty, 28

Arguments, plot()

    axes, 49–51, 53–55, 57, 58

    box type/aspect ratio/expand plotting, 19, 21–24

    character size, 42–45

    colors, 31

    dataset, 13–15

    label and axis limits, 16, 17

    log scales, 58–60

    lwd/lend/ljoin/lmitre, 46, 48, 49

    points/lines, 24, 25, 27–30

    scatterplot, 15, 16

arrows() function, 121

ask argument, 167, 217, 219, 269

aspect.ratio argument, 296

at argument, 68, 149

atpen argument, 152

auto_plot(), 377, 378

axis() function, 68–70, 74

axTicks() function, 75, 79

B

base_family argument, 304

base_size argument, 304

bg argument, 138

borders() function, 292, 323, 343, 344, 346

box() function, 79, 81

boxplots argument, 100

bty argument, 138

M. Tollefson, *Visualizing Data in R 4*, https://doi.org/10.1007/978-1-4842-6831-5

Printed in the United States
by Baker & Taylor Publisher Services